An Invitation to the Opera

An Invitation to the Opera

John Louis DiGaetani

ANCHOR BOOKS

DOUBLEDAY

NEW YORK LONDON TORONTO SYDNEY AUCKLAND

AN ANCHOR BOOK
PUBLISHED BY DOUBLEDAY
a division of Bantam Doubleday Dell Publishing Group, Inc.
1540 Broadway, New York, New York 10036

ANCHOR BOOKS, DOUBLEDAY, and the portrayal of an anchor
are trademarks of Doubleday, a division of Bantam Doubleday
Dell Publishing Group, Inc.

An Invitation to the Opera was originally published in hardcover by
Facts on File Publications in 1986. The Anchor Books edition is
published by arrangement with Facts on File, Inc.

Library of Congress Cataloging-in-Publication Data
DiGaetani, John Louis, 1943–
    An invitation to the opera / John Louis DiGaetani.
    —1st Anchor books ed.
        p. cm.
    Reprint. Originally published: New York, N.Y.:
    Facts on File Publications, c1986.
    Bibliography: p.
    Discography: p.
    Videography: p.
    Includes index.
    1. Opera. I. Title.
[ML1700.D53   1989]   89-33815
782.1—dc20   CIP
ISBN 0-385-26339-2   MN

Dedicated
to the
Memory of Nicholas Cavallo

Acknowledgments

I would like to record my gratitude
to the following people
for their generous help
with this project:

Christine Hofmann
Earl Harbert
Gary Harris
Norman Oakes
Marion Ponsford
Arthur Gewirtz

Contents

viii   *Contents*

An Invitation to the Opera

Introduction:

Why Opera?

No good opera plot can be sensible, for people do not sing when they are feeling sensible.

—W. H. Auden

She's suddenly attracted to a stranger she's barely met. She feels trapped in a loveless marriage arranged for her by the powerful men who surround her. Deciding to run off with the handsome stranger, she slips a drug into her husband's supper to make him sleep early and soundly that night. After the husband has been dispatched, she begins to talk with the mysterious stranger, falls in love with him with each word, and discovers that he is her long-lost brother. Ecstatic at this discovery, the couple immediately make love.

Does this sound like a scene from a soap opera or B movie? Actually, it's the plot of Act I in Wagner's *Die Walküre*. Throughout the ages, opera has enjoyed a large popularity, as it captured the imaginations of generations of common folk in Europe, just as James Bond and "Star Trek" have captured ours. Don't be deceived by opera's many debunkers.

"An exotic and irrational entertainment!"—that's how Dr. Samuel Johnson dismissed opera. Yet opera has survived and prospered since the eighteenth century—despite Dr. Johnson's powerful invective—to reach huge audiences around the world, on television and in person. Since the eighteenth century, opera has been a popular entertainment in most of Europe, particularly in Italy, Germany, and France. But in the United States, many people seem to have resisted opera's attractions until fairly recently. In fact, many

Americans once considered opera an exotic, irrational entertainment reserved for a snobbish and wealthy clientele who lived in world capitals like New York; but now, opera companies have sprung up in Boston, Chicago, New Orleans, Minneapolis, St. Louis, Manchester, and Tokyo, as well as many smaller and less well-known cities around the world. With the Metropolitan Opera's "Live from the Met" television series, the Chéreau-directed *Ring* cycle from Bayreuth, and frequent simulcasts from Vienna's Staatsoper or Milan's La Scala, opera can even be considered a staple of television, if not yet a competitor with the soaps for the top Nielsen ratings. Opera has truly become a popular international art form.

THE MOST ARTIFICIAL OF THE ARTS

Why does this ancient and most artificial of arts continue to attract growing audiences? Because opera entertains them in a special way. For example, in Donizetti's *Lucia di Lammermoor* a woman goes insane, yet she manages to sing a fiendishly difficult aria studded with several high C's. In Wagner's *Götterdämmerung* a man is stabbed in the back, but his death is delayed until he has sung a long farewell to life. In Puccini's *Tosca*, when a woman is being threatened with rape, the villain stops his pursuit of her while she sings a long prayer to her heavenly (and earthly) audience. What could be more contrived than these scenes? Yet they have worked for many years—and they still work—as grand entertainment because they reach the soul. With its special artifice, opera captures our imaginations and allays all protests, as sublime operatic music moves us to believe in its dramatic situations.

Of course, there are skeptics, those noninitiates who sneer about fat sopranos, preening tenors, and silly plots. The truth is greater than they know, for opera can touch the soul as few arts can—when the audience is receptive to its magic. One proof is found in history: Opera is an old art form. Its roots go back to ancient Greek culture, that wellspring of Western civilization that also cultivated architecture, philosophy, sculpture, drama, literature, and even democracy. Small wonder that, even though most opera was composed in Europe, an American audience feels comfortable with opera's artistic heritage. A second proof of opera's appeal is less in its lineage than in the experience it provides for the audience that wishes to understand and enjoy it.

THE COMBINATION ART FORM

Unlike musical concerts or drama, opera combines several arts in a unique way. When one attends a concert, the ears may be filled with sound and the mind fully engaged with unsuspected harmonies, but nothing much happens to satisfy the eyes. At a concert eyes tend to wander from the conductor to the soloists, orchestra players, and even to other members of the audience. Throughout the performance the ear and spirit may be fulfilled, but the eye is not. When one attends the theater, on the other hand, the eye may be riveted to the stage in fascination and the mind stimulated, but nothing much happens musically (except, of course, at a musical comedy). Some dramatists write their plays in verse, but the musical effects that language alone produces are pretty meager when contrasted to the sounds of an orchestra. Among the arts only opera combines the best musical possibilities of the orchestra and magnificent voices with the visual, dramatic, and intellectual excitement of the theater. All these elements melt into extraordinary entertainment, and the audience can be engaged totally. Richard Wagner called opera the *Gesamtkunstwerk*—the "combination art work" —and this fact of combination, more than any other, accounts for opera's uniqueness. Moreover, the scope of artistry is practically unlimited since opera combines all the arts—ballet (in many operas); painting and sculpture (in the sets and properties); theater; poetry; sometimes history; and, of course, music.

Yet outside of opera, theater and music have sometimes seemed to be natural enemies. The playwright scoffs, "Music slows down the action of a play, it's too abstract. Can the immediacy of an actor's haughty 'Drop dead!' transfer effectively into a progression of chords or a melody?" To these charges, the composer replies, "Can the concrete (words) possibly work with the most abstract and spiritual of arts (music)? Can a lovely melody be sung to words in a particular dramatic situation and still qualify as great music?" Opera answers yes to both. An operatic genius not only combines words and music but combines them in a uniquely effective way.

In truth, opera can create effects that are ravishingly beautiful, dramatically significant, and personally meaningful. No other art form does as much.

For example, in a famous dramatic monologue during the first act of Strauss's *Der Rosenkavalier*, the Marschallin tells her young lover, Octavian, about her fear of growing old. Sometimes, she says, she gets up in the middle of the night to stop the ticking of her bedroom clock, and at that moment the ticking sounds from the orchestra stop. We instantly perceive the meaning of her nocturnal wanderings as she seeks to stop time; we understand her fear of the relentlessness of time; and we realize that we, too, are growing old. Here, an apparently artificial combination of words and music gives the opera its unique power to entertain, fascinate, and drive its meaning home.

OPERA AND CHARACTERIZATION

Language and music together can do what neither could do alone. This unique combination creates both dramatic insight and musical beauty—an instant understanding of character or situation—that no other art form can achieve. Thus, in the first act of Wagner's *Tristan und Isolde*, Isolde hates Tristan, but even while she sings of her hatred the orchestra plays love music. Here the orchestra tells us that she really loves Tristan, at a moment when even Isolde herself does not recognize her love. Can one create such an immediate and paradoxical effect with words alone? No. But an interaction of words with music *can*, just as the human mind itself creates paradox in us. The simultaneous wedding of love and hatred in *Tristan und Isolde* suggests that hatred is a powerful, complex emotion, with which at least some love is often mixed. In *Tristan und Isolde* Wagner described this very human truth some fifty years before Sigmund Freud first wrote about it.

Verdi also uses music to characterize his people—often even before they speak—in the overtures to his works. His overture to *Aïda* uses musical themes to portray the character of Aïda, and the fragility of the music, orchestrated primarily with violins, suggests Aïda's fragility. For her, life is just too hard, too complicated, too conflicted, too dangerous. Such a weak person might welcome death, as Aïda herself does before the end of the opera. Although theater alone could create scenes to communicate this, it would take several scenes at least, while Verdi portrays Aïda's character instantly with the music of his overture. In his opera *Otello*, Verdi presents Otello as a direct, military man easily trapped by Iago's subtle civilian wiles. Martial brass music singles out Otello as the decisive general, a man who acts in terms of friends or foes, winning or losing; his personality is instantly portrayed by his music.

In *Turandot*, Puccini's Princess Turandot, an icy and neurotic woman, comes instantly and fully alive in the music of her first aria, "In questa reggia." A high-pitched, trumpetlike music accompanies her voice and helps to describe her experience with men, as it instantly communicates injury, fear, and vindictive hatred. Yet the aria is not only dramatically appropriate for the character; it is exciting and beautiful in its own right. So, too, Puccini's complicated Minnie in *La Fanciulla del West* comes alive through both rhythmically lively music and quiet, sad arias. Puccini everywhere creates human complexity with both text and music, thereby bringing his fascinating characters to life for the audience.

OPERA AND DRAMATIC SITUATION

Wagner's *Ring* cycle fully illustrates the uniqueness of opera, especially in its use of music and language to create foreshadowing and intensely dramatic situations. Wagner's music foreshadows the tragic end of the vast tetralogy in a uniquely operatic way. When Hagen welcomes Siegfried to the Hall of the Gibichungs, during the first act of *Götterdämmerung*, the composer employs the curse motif, telling us instantly that this happy welcome will result in Siegfried's murder by his seemingly hospitable hosts. The eventual horror of Siegfried's murder is communicated not only through the actual murder on stage, but also through the power and grief conveyed by the funeral music just after the murder. Could spoken theater do all this? Could music alone communicate so much? Together they can, at least when music and theater are combined by a genius.

This unique power we see again in the simple chords that accompany the opening of Otello's final monologue before he takes his life in Act IV in Verdi's opera. These sad chords tell us about a world of tragedy so rich that words or situations alone could not convey it. Or when Tristan and Isolde sing of their love, and the fateful union that results from that love, the music weaves from melody to melody and key to key in a way that is not only dramatically meaningful but also intoxicatingly beautiful. These dramatic situations are more than beautiful; they are dramatically effective because they are reinforced and supplemented by the power of the music.

But opera is not always intense drama and profound meaning. It can also be fun and gags. Opera is Verdi's Sir John in *Falstaff*, singing in Act III a comic parody of early Verdi opera's fondness for the word *mezzanotte* (midnight). Opera is also Rosina in Rossini's *The Barber of Seville*, who playfully boasts early in that opera that she will easily outsmart her possessive, half-witted old guardian—which she does. Opera is also Zerbinetta in Strauss's *Ariadne auf Naxos*, poking fun at serious opera itself, with its somber tone and fat sopranos. Again, opera is Leporello in Mozart's *Don Giovanni*, laughing about how easy it is for the Don to seduce thousands of silly, lecherous women. Opera is also Despina in Mozart's *Così Fan Tutte*, singing about how fickle men can be when in an amorous mood. So comedy as much as tragedy lends itself to opera's most compelling dramatic situations, and the results can be magical in both cases.

OPERA AND ITS TRADITION

Opera inherited its basic nature from the theater and has evolved from centuries of theatrical tradition. Yet opera remains enticingly human. For example, French court politics determined the failure of Wagner's *Tannhäuser* at its Paris premiere on March 13, 1861. Arturo Toscanini's affair with the opera's leading soprano, Rosina Storchio, provided the main cause for *Madama Butterfly*'s disastrous premiere at La Scala on February 17, 1904. On the other hand, Verdi's *Aïda* was commissioned by the Khedive Ismail Pasha of Egypt for Cairo's new opera house, and the opera provided an immediate triumph at its Egyptian premiere on Christmas Eve, 1871. Another fascinating chapter in the lore of opera as theater is the traditional superstition held by some singers that Verdi's *La Forza del Destino* is an unlucky opera—a superstition confirmed by Leonard Warren's death on stage during a performance of that opera at the Met on March 4, 1960.

In Italy, singers often will pick up a bent nail from backstage before they go on stage, a bent nail being a sign of good luck. In Germany, at Wagner's Bayreuth Festival, it is customary for the audience to eat sausages between acts. At the Baths of Caracalla in Rome, between acts of summer opera performances, vendors come down the aisles to sell ice cream, caramels, and beer and soda—just as at an American baseball game. It is customary not to applaud after the first act of Wagner's *Parsifal*, and it is also traditional for opera singers to take bows after each act for most operas. Some opera houses have traditions for formal dress in some parts of the house while other houses have audiences that traditionally dress informally. Opera's fascination includes its varying traditions and how they affect both audiences and performers.

VARIETIES OF OPERA FANS

Aside from its rich theatrical traditions, many other facets of opera attract an amazing variety of fans. For example, one kind of opera buff goes only for the production, and insists that opera be valid, workable musical theater. Another type is the CD or record fan, who hears opera only at home and explains that this is the only way to experience a perfect performance. Then there are the voice fans who attend live performances only to hear a particular soprano or tenor for the purpose of comparing and contrasting that voice with the great singers from the past, available on recordings. Also, there are the "standard repertory" people, those who want to see and hear only the opera classics, often by only one composer—only Wagner or Verdi or Puccini or Mozart—and nothing else, in person or on record.

But there are also the operatic experimenters, who want to hear only obscure operas from the past, the operatic rarities, or perhaps the newest operas only, but never *Il Trovatore* or *La Bohème*. And we surely shouldn't forget those "fans" who go to the opera to exploit its social status, to be seen, rather than to hear and see, and then to mention to friends a night spent in furs and jewels at the opera.

Clearly then, opera has many different audiences, as many as it has attractions for its fans. The following pages tell what opera can offer us, where those special attractions may be found, and how we can enjoy them. Since one part of our appreciation for opera depends on an awareness of its rich past, this book summarizes the lengthy operatic legacy in some detail.

BARRIERS TO ENJOYING OPERA

Of all the arts, opera most demands an introduction. As you have seen, there are many reasons for this. One can simply buy a ticket and go to a Broadway musical, but a ticket will not give you a real appreciation of opera. You have to do your homework if you want to understand what's happening on stage. First, there is the music. Operatic music is often complex and symphonic. Although the Broadway musical is often, though not always, composed of a few tunes cleverly orchestrated, operatic music is generally harmonically, melodically, and rhythmically much more demanding. This means that, in opera, the music may not be as immediately understandable and likable as popular music can be. Thus, the first time you hear *Lohengrin* or *La Forza del Destino* or *The Magic Flute*, you may like some of the music, but you will probably find some musical passages that just don't appeal to you. These passages seem boring at first because on just one hearing you are not familiar enough with the music to appreciate them.

Also, unless you are hearing opera in translation or subtitled, or one that was written in English, you will be listening to singing in a foreign language—certainly a barrier to appreciation. Again, the way to appreciate and enjoy opera is to do your homework beforehand.

How? Either buy a complete recording or tape of the opera, or borrow one from your library. Some record libraries permit you to use their collection only on their equipment; if that is the case, you could listen to the entire opera there. Most opera recordings come with a libretto, with the original language on one side of a page and an English translation on the other. You can listen to the whole opera, following the libretto, so you know exactly what is being sung at every moment. With this study technique, you not only get to know the libretto line-by-line (and this is something a simple reading of a plot summary in the program before the performance will not do for you), but you also become familiar with the music of the opera. By studying the entire opera in this way at least twice, if possible, before you attend a performance, you will be ready to appreciate the opera when you see it. Of course, once you have done this homework, you can see the opera over and over again, and always know what's going on, though you might want to follow the libretto with the recording occasionally, both to refresh your memory and just to enjoy the music itself more.

But why go through so much homework? Isn't opera supposed to be for pleasure? The answer is that our homework is well rewarded in the opera house. Serious opera fans testify to the fascination and the unique experience of operatic music and dramatic intensity on stage—a combination of rewards like no other, and one renewable with every new performance. Nevertheless, that reward usually comes in Italian, German, or French, and only seldom in English.

Opera in English

Here, we should consider the question of opera in translation: If it can be done (as surely it can), then why not translate all operas into English? First, it is very difficult to translate an opera well, primarily because of the nature of language. For example, it is difficult enough to come up with a good translation of a play, but an opera demands even more because in every word the syllables have to be made to fit the notes written for it. The accents on certain notes, which the composer often put there because they reflect the natural accents of the language he worked in, should be placed in the same spots in English (even though they might not fit the natural accents of English on a note-for-note basis).

Inevitably, then, translated opera is very, very difficult to do well; much will be lost no matter how well the job is done. Also, not many English-speaking singers are trained to sing in English. So even with a good translation, the audience often cannot understand the words because of the singers' poor diction. Again, at least in part, singing itself necessitates some alteration of language—which is true no matter what language is being sung. Given these difficulties, then, why bother with translations that can produce such horrible results? Regular opera-goers can tell many horror stories about dreadful English translations of their favorite operas, translations they have endured in pain for the pleasure of the beautiful music.

Well, one reason to go through the translation effort is that, every once in a while (and this happens only rarely), a translation into English really does work. Andrew Porter's translation of Wagner's *Ring* cycle, for example, is one of the very few English translations that works well in the theater, though its audience still benefits from reading the English text beforehand, as an aid to understanding what's going on.

Also, our own emotional reactions to English words are bound to be more intense and more immediate than our reactions to foreign words. For example, we can know that *mio figlio* means "my son," but the English words have a far more potent meaning for us than do the Italian.

Another reason for translating opera derives from the popularity of English versions. In fact, some opera companies perform opera only in English (most notably the English National Opera in London), and their audiences now do not cheerfully accept hearing opera in a foreign tongue.

I should add, as well, that for much of its history, translated opera has dominated the stage. When Wagner's *Tannhäuser* was staged in Paris, he had no objection to the work being performed in a French translation. Most nineteenth-century European audiences wanted opera in their own language (which is often still the case on the Continent). But since opera is a more foreign experience in English-speaking countries, many modern opera-goers there want opera only in its original tongue and not in translation—despite the occasional good English translation. Also, the international opera circuit, composed of major houses such as the Metropolitan Opera, Covent Garden, La Scala, the Paris Opéra, the Bavarian State Opera, and the Vienna Staatsoper, usually performs opera in the original tongue and only rarely in translation.

Another solution has been borrowed from opera on television. When opera is televised, it generally includes subtitles in English, as with foreign films. Some opera companies now project subtitles (actually "surtitles") over the proscenium during performances. As a result, the performance can be sung in the original language, to the immense pleasure of the opera fan who hates translations, but the English translation is projected just above the stage, to the immense pleasure of the less experienced opera fan who wants to know exactly what the characters are saying. Although this solution seems successful, and many fans like subtitled opera very much, others find it an unnecessary distraction during a performance.

Clearly, then, we have here a complicated issue. Some respectable translations do exist, but since opera recordings are generally made in the original language rather than in translation, your homework will probably have to be in the original tongue. After you have once prepared yourself, and gone to the opera house for a performance, you may be most comfortable with an opera in its original language. After all, you have prepared for it. Yet you should know that an English version may be available, even when the original opera was not English.

THE ROOTS OF OPERA

Opera, as we have seen, is a uniquely complex art form that appeals to a uniquely diversified audience. The basic reason for this complexity and diversity is the nature of the art itself—a nature that may be defined in terms of organic parts. Opera has six major roots: its history, singing language, theatrical dimension, conducting tradition, vocal tradition, and standard repertory. All six are important to an understanding of opera, and this book is designed to present and analyze each operatic element clearly so that you will understand how every root nourishes the whole. That is, you will discover how opera works, why it attracts people, and most important, how you can enjoy opera more.

To do this, the book has been organized around these major roots of opera and divided into eight chapters. In order, the chapters take up: (1 and 2) the history of opera (and the geniuses who changed opera's history); (3) opera's singing language; (4 and 5) opera production (with an emphasis on opera as a branch of theater); (6) opera's conducting tradition (with a history of how opera has been conducted by its most influential conductors); (7) opera's great vocal tradition (featuring short biographies of the greatest singers in the history of opera, such as Caruso, Callas, Nilsson, and Pavarotti, and how they influenced the art); and (8) the standard repertory (discussing the fifty operas that form the international body of "most popular" and "best" operatic works —the accepted classics of the art). Every opera in this standard repertory is analyzed for dramatic and thematic conflicts, rather than being dismissed with a mere plot summary.

Yet the musical dimension in opera, while receiving serious attention here, does not overshadow other operatic elements—thus, it will not be the major focus of this book. Elsewhere, all too often, introductions to opera have been written by eminent musicologists, usually to be read only by other eminent musicologists. Unlike such specialized studies, this book does not assume any prior knowledge of music or any ability to read music, so that the reader who lacks formal musical training but still likes opera will find this text accessible. On the other hand, this book does emphasize language and drama in opera since these elements are indispensable to its art and part of any comprehensive understanding. It is my hope that *An Invitation to the Opera* will satisfy a real need for an adequate introduction to that strangely fascinating and often complex art form—the opera.

Quite aside from this book and every such book, however, and whether in its original tongue or translated, opera is a truly remarkable phenomenon. It continues to grow in popularity as more and more people become fascinated by its unique mixture of several arts. Both complex and simple, posing barriers yet speaking of universal experiences, simultaneously musical and theatrical, opera remains for us today what it has always been—a joy for the minds and senses of those who know how to approach it.

One

A History of Opera: The Early Years

The custom of using music in connection with dramatic presentations is universal. It is found throughout the history of European culture and among primitive and civilized peoples alike. This is perhaps because the desire to add music to drama is really part of the dramatic instinct itself.

—Donald Jay Grout, *A Short History of Opera*

Opera's history begins with one of the most ancient sources of Western civilization, the culture of ancient Greece. One of the most enduring and impressive gifts of the ancient Greeks to our culture is drama in the form of tragedy. The plays of Aeschylus, Sophocles, and Euripides remain the foundations of theater in the West. From that rich field of early Greek tragedy grew the art form that we call opera.

THE ANCIENT GREEKS

From what present-day historians know of Greek tragedy, much of the play was chanted and sung, in particular the choral sections, when several or many voices were heard in unison. Although the music for Greek tragedies has not survived, Aristotle and other literary critics of the time report that music, especially chanting to the accompaniment of a lyre or flute, represented an important part of the spectacle that formed tragedy. The following is Aristotle's famous definition of tragedy:

> Tragedy, then, is the imitation of some action that is important, entire, and of a proper importance—by language, ornamented and rendered pleasurable, but by different ways in different parts . . .
> By *pleasurable language*, I mean language that has the ornaments of rhythm, melody, and meter. And I add, by *different ways in different parts*, because in some parts meter alone is employed, in others, melody.

In Greek tragedy, the reason for including music was probably acoustical, at least in part, since many of the amphitheaters where the tragedies were performed were very large, and lack of audibility and echoes sometimes caused problems. While reverberation does create a hearing problem for the audience when actors are speaking, it can add to the effect of music. So given the large size of typical Greek and Roman amphitheaters, music may have been acoustically necessary.

Another reason for the inclusion of music, according to Aristotle, was to add to the effect created by the play. Music, one of the most abstract arts, is perfect for emphasizing the moral lesson of a play, and morality could always be found at the core of Greek tragedy. The musical parts of Greek tragedy, however, served the moral drama; they were never allowed to stand on their own or overtake the primacy of the text. Clearly, Greek playwrights understood that the musical component of any spectacle had to be kept within strict bounds, or it would overwhelm the other dimensions of language and theater.

Other elements of Greek tragedy continued to recur in opera as the form evolved. Most Greek tragedies were structured around five conflicts, generally involving two characters in each of five dialogue confrontations. The concept of conflict forms the basis of all successful opera, as it does for all successful theater. The five-part form also would be used again and again in opera, especially in the customary five acts of French nineteenth-century opera, or in the five-part form of Strauss's *Elektra*, a modern version of the ancient Greek play.

Intense, fascinating characters motivated and propelled much of the action in Greek tragedy, and the desire for fascinating characterization remains in opera, although it has been achieved to a greater or lesser extent throughout its history. The moral and ideological issues in Greek tragedy continue to characterize much opera, as they do in all great theater. Moral issues are still one of the major concerns of Western theater, as they were on the Greek tragic stage.

Greek tragedy presented the myths of Greek history and culture—perhaps one of the reasons why characterization soon became primary on the Greek tragic stage. Since the audience knew the plot of the play already—everybody had heard the story of Oedipus or Electra or Antigone—the audience came to experience its other aspects. This mythic approach continued to characterize much of opera, especially the retelling of Greek myths such as Orpheus and Euridice or Electra. Later, this technique would be turned by opera composers to other myths, German, Italian, or French.

Other central features of Greek musical tragedies were their elegiac tone and elegance and restraint of presentation. Comic relief was not part of Greek tragedy, and the Greek tragic playwrights rarely employed comic devices in their tragedies. Also, the murders and other bloody scenes were not performed on stage; classical restraint dictated that they occur out of the audience's sight. A consistent, elegiac tone typified what the Greek tragic playwrights tried to achieve—a serious, fateful note throughout the work. An elegance of presentation and an elegiac tone, however, were reflected in the musical component provided by the instruments and chorus. Opera continued this tradition. Greek comedy, on the other hand, employed primarily speech, unlike tragedy, but the chorus in Greek comedies was often sung. These choruses were mostly in the form of animals—such as flies or frogs or sheep—and their singing undoubtedly generated much comedy because they parodied the chanting tragic choruses.

THE ANCIENT ROMANS

Roman drama also had a musical component. Descriptions of Roman theater given by writers of the period indicate that actors and actresses sometimes sang their lines, as did the choruses. The tragedies of Seneca—plays like *Medea*, *The Trojans*, and *Hercules on Oeta*—closely followed the Greek model and included a chorus meant to sing rather than speak. Characterization and musical poetry, borrowings from the fertile font of Greece, continued in Rome's tragedies.

Roman comedy also featured its own extensive musical dimension; in fact, some theater historians have treated Roman comedies as a forerunner of our Broadway musicals. The two most famous Roman comic playwrights, Plautus and Terence, generally included songs in their plays, and often about half of their lines included musical accompaniment. Titus Maccius Plautus's greatest comedies are *The Comedy of Asses*, *The Merchant*, *The Braggart Warrior*, and *The Pot of Gold*. Publius Terentius Afer's six plays include important musical numbers, especially in *Andria*, *The Mother-in-Law*, and *The Eunuch*. With the fall of Rome and the barbarian invasions, however, there wasn't much time for theater—musical or otherwise. In our time, Stephen Sondheim's *A Funny Thing Happened on the Way to the Forum* (1962) brilliantly re-creates the effects of Roman comedy, especially its musical dimension.

THE MIDDLE AGES

After the glory of Greece and Rome, the next period to have some form of operatic entertainment occurred from the eleventh to the fifteenth centuries, and much of this drama revolved around religion. During this time, priests and nuns staged plays in churches, especially in the cathedrals in large cities, and many of these plays illustrated the liturgical calendar. Clerics mounted Easter plays and Christmas plays in the churches to instruct the people about the meaning of religious celebrations, and also to attract them to the traditional religious services. These plays generally lacked specific titles since they were chanted or sung by church choirs and soloists during regular services. Once again for acoustical reasons, music held a major role in these liturgical plays: Most of the Gothic cathedrals of the period had echoes that made individual speech difficult to understand, but that same reverberation enhanced music and song since it helped to amplify these sounds, and it must have made them seem more authoritative and beautiful.

Medieval liturgical pageants were often operatic in nature, especially when they employed an organ along with the soloists. Much of this music has been lost, although some Gregorian chants survive and are still performed today. Those chants, connected as they are with liturgical festivals, typically became operatic when fused with an Easter or Christmas play. Easter, the most joyous season in the Christian calendar, encouraged the most elaborate productions of these operatic performances. One of the most ancient of these is performed every ten years in the German city of Oberammergau.

The most famous and the oldest surviving of these operatic liturgical dramas is the *Quem Queritis* play (*Quem Queritis* means "Whom do you seek?"). In these plays, generally put on at Eastertime, a group of women go to the tomb to anoint Christ's body after the crucifixion. At the door of the tomb they see an angel who asks them whom they seek. When the women say they seek Jesus Christ, the angel tells them that Christ has risen from the dead. This short and dramatic encounter was staged and sung with music generally supplied by vocal soloists, choir, and organ. Gradually, other characters were added, and the initial dialogue was expanded to present the whole story of Christ's death, crucifixion, and resurrection—all or mostly sung. These rudimentary liturgical plays eventually required elaborate sets in the church, along with fine soloists, large choirs, and the church's organ accompaniment.

As these plays evolved they became more theatrical and distinctly less religious, especially when they began to include such figures as bawdy devils, who became very popular with the audience. Finally, the bishops ordered all plays removed from the church itself, to be performed in churchyards or in village marketplaces. There, the individual speaking voice, no longer affected by the echo of the

churches, carried well, and just as music had dominated while religious plays were performed in the cathedrals, now out-of-doors
the spoken word assumed primacy. Aside from acoustics, another
reason for less music was financial. It costs more to train a singer
than an actor, and the Church no longer cared to pay for music
once the plays moved outside church buildings. As medieval theater
developed, it became more secular and less musical, but some music
generally remained. *The Second Shepherd's Play*, for example, perhaps the most famous English medieval play, includes six musical
numbers. Many of the other medieval plays also allowed an actor
with a good voice to sing a ballad or a bawdy tavern tune. Choirs
of angels were often used for enactments of the lives of the saints,
even in the secular plays. All in all, then, musical and liturgical
pageants of the medieval church tended to make the secular drama
of the period more operatic in nature.

Some of those liturgical plays, such as *The Play of Daniel* and
The Play of Noah, are still occasionally performed. These sung
liturgical plays, with music pieced together from fragmentary man-
uscripts of the period, usually are staged in churches or theaters
during Christmas and Easter, and the musical components create
an overall operatic effect. Much of the authentic musical parts of
the secular plays are lost, however, because that music often con-
sisted of popular folk songs from the period, and these were seldom
written down.

In our own time, the British composer Benjamin Britten has revived interest in these medieval musical plays by writing four "new"
ones: *Noyes Fludde* (1958), *Curlew River* (1964), *The Burning Fiery
Furnace* (1966), and *The Prodigal Son* (1968). Britten called his
operas "church parables," designed to be performed in churches,
employing soloists and boys' and men's choirs. These works have
been performed at churches in both Europe and America.

THE RENAISSANCE

Following the medieval period, in the fifteenth to the seventeenth
centuries, the time of the Renaissance, royal courts developed their
own pageants, which included ballet, rich costumes, spoken words
and poems (usually in praise of the king, a visiting prince, or other
dignitaries), and some mime. These court spectacles also had music

and theater sets, and they soon became what can be called "pre-operatic." The Italian *mascherata*, the French *masquerade*, and the English *masque* were all forms of royal entertainments not available to a popular audience. They were called "masques" because the performers often wore masks.

Poetry and dance developed into principal components of these courtly entertainments, but, of course, where there was dance there also had to be music; so such presentations became what can be called preoperatic. In England, Inigo Jones gained fame in the seventeenth century for designing elaborate sets to be used in English courtly masque productions, while Henry Purcell wrote much of the music for many Stuart masques at the English court. Works such as *The Hue and Cry After Cupid* (1608), *The Masque of Oberon* (1610), and *The Temple of Love* (1635) were designed by Jones to give spectacle, dance, and music full scope, although masques usually lacked drama. In France, Louis XIV himself sometimes participated because he liked to dance in public, and he was very proud of his elegant legs. Several portraits show the Sun King in high skirts, which showed off his long, thin legs that were perfect for courtly dancing.

One can easily understand why these operatic masques were reserved for royal and aristocratic audiences, since they were undoubtedly very expensive to stage. Thus began a long tradition in opera: mammoth expense. The operatic courtly masque demanded the marshaling of many forces: singers, set designers, ballet dancers, directors, orchestra players, stagehands, mimes, and other assorted stand-in roles—in short, a cast of thousands. Opera, even to this day, has generally been an elaborate and expensive form of entertainment to stage, demanding the coordinated efforts of many highly trained artists. Such an elaborate endeavor was bound to be expensive, and indeed for most of its history opera has required the financial support of kings, other wealthy patrons, or the state. In the eighteenth century, Milan's La Scala had a casino attached to it to support the opera, and Raoul Gunsbourg ran a wonderful opera company at Monte Carlo from 1890 to 1954, and there too the casino supported the opera.

The Italian Renaissance and Opera

During the Renaissance, when Italy claimed to be home to all the arts, opera developed under Italian influence. First, the Camerata Group, sponsored by Count Giovanni Bardi, was founded in Florence in 1580. The group, composed of scholars who met regularly to discuss Greek culture, included Count Bardi himself, Vincenzo Galilei (father of the astronomer), Jacopo Peri, Giulio Caccini, Emilio de' Cavalieri, and Ottavio Rinuccini. Aside from their specialties, these men were amateur poets, singers, and musicians; so at a time when Greek culture held sway in the Italian Renaissance, the ancient Greek music play, or tragedy, was bound to arouse their interest. Thus, the Bardi circle discussed the ancient Greek forms of musical drama, and before long the Camerata arrived at its own theory of musical theater, a theory based on Greek tragedy and which recognized that the Greek combination of serious drama with serious music had enhanced the overall effect of both. Finally, Count Giovanni Bardi commissioned some members of his circle to produce a modern version of this Greek art form. So Jacopo Peri, with a libretto by his friend Ottavio Rinuccini, wrote *Dafne* (based on the ancient Greek myth of Daphne). Peri's work was staged in the Bardi household during 1597, and today it is regarded as the first modern opera, or as it was then called *un opera in musica* (a work in music). A major milestone had been reached.

This new entertainment achieved instant success; so it was staged in Florence for the general public, where it succeeded again and was repeated often. Unfortunately, the music for *Dafne* has been lost, but the play remains. From all evidence it is clear that the music was secondary to the play, and this relationship remained characteristic throughout the early years. The drama was of foremost importance to the first Italian theoreticians of "opera," as the form came to be called. From what we know, the play must have been sung and chanted with the orchestral music performed by *basso continuo*—harpsichord, cello, lute, and viola da gamba. Clearly, then, such a combination of musical forces produced the effect of what came to be known as *arioso*, or a vaguely melodic music that added another dimension to the play. But there were few choruses or ensemble pieces, since they would have made the words of the soloists less intelligible.

The earliest opera that has survived intact was also composed and written by members of the Camerata Group: Peri's *Euridice* to a text by Rinuccini, composed in 1600. This opera, first staged at the Pitti Palace in Florence on October 6, 1600, was composed to celebrate the wedding of King Henry IV of France to his Italian queen, Marie de' Medici. (This marriage, by the way, exported Florentine cooking to France, and thus created a foundation of French cuisine. So the event deserves to be recalled for several reasons.)

One year later, Giulio Caccini wrote another version of *Dafne* to the old text, but his music lacked some of the drama of Peri's, and it has been regarded as similar but far less successful. Already, early in the seventeenth century, opera had begun to flourish. From Florence, the new musical entertainment spread quickly to other cities in Italy, most immediately to Rome, Mantua, and Venice.

SEVENTEENTH-CENTURY VENICE

Although the Florentine Camerata Group treated opera as an aristocratic revival of Greek tragedy, the art form changed rapidly once it moved on to Venice, where Monteverdi in particular helped to popularize opera. Claudio Monteverdi wrote his first opera, *Orfeo*, in 1607 while living in Mantua. The text was by Alessandro Striggio, and it was similar to the earlier texts of the Camerata Group in Florence. But Monteverdi, an authentic genius, wrote much better music, so his *La Favola d'Orfeo* became a much more interesting work than Peri's version. Already famous for his madrigals, Monteverdi used a madrigal style for the opera and included dances as well; though he still began with a Greek myth, he made opera more musically sophisticated and less aristocratic and academic. These changes in the art form proved to be very important.

In Venice, meanwhile, the first opera house, San Cassiano, opened in 1637. There, Monteverdi could work for a large public rather than the few scholars in the Camerata Group. The audience soon became bored with the arioso; they wanted more tunes, even if the words could not be understood or if the music delayed the action in an opera. Monteverdi did everything he could to please his audience, and in doing so, he shifted the emphasis from dramatic action to more purely musical opera. Unfortunately, only two of

Monteverdi's Venetian operas have survived: *Il Ritorno d'Ulisse in Patria* (1641) and *L'Incoronazione di Poppea* (1642), both with texts by Francesco Busenello. This second opera is occasionally staged today because of the beauty of its music, its dramatic intensity, and the variety of its characterizations. As a demonstration of complex artistry, the opera contains effective comic relief in an otherwise tragic and even cynical story of love and infidelity in ancient Rome. The mastery of Monteverdi stands forth in every scene.

One of Monteverdi's pupils was Pier Francesco Cavalli, who wrote over forty operas for the twenty Venetian opera houses that existed by the end of the seventeenth century. Cavalli's most famous work is *Giasone* (1649) to a libretto by Cicognini. In this work, arias play a more prominent part than in any of Monteverdi's Venetian operas. Certainly, musical and vocal display had become more important than the text. But Cavalli continued to use stories from ancient Greece and Rome, and he continued to create a unified and elegiac tone for many of his operas.

Another Italian composer who achieved success in the Venetian opera houses of the seventeenth century was Pietro Antonio Cesti. Of the more than 100 operas he wrote from 1649 to 1669, only 11 have survived, and the best are: *Orontea* (written for Venice in 1649), *La Dori* (written for Florence in 1661), and *Il Pomo d'Oro* (written for Vienna in 1667). Cesti emphasized the soloists' arias and minimized the recitatives, and this change became very popular with both singers and audience. During his career, in fact, Cesti spread opera beyond Italy, to Austria. He also composed much ballet music for his operas, and ballets became especially popular with royal and aristocratic audiences. By 1670 opera had achieved substantial popularity; there were public opera houses in Florence, Rome, Genoa, Bologna, and Modena, as well as twenty in Venice, which by then had become the operatic capital of Europe.

It was in Venice during the seventeenth century that the terms *aria* and *recitativo* began to replace the Camerata Group's favored operatic label, the arioso. An aria was a song, often full of elaborate vocal ornamentation, that was sung solo. The recitativo, on the other hand, told the story, often with only harpsichord or basso continuo accompaniment. Opera had become a series of musical numbers or arias interrupted by recitativo to tell the story, at times as quickly as possible. The final effect emphasized the musical dimension, but sometimes at the cost of the dramatic. As the story progressed during the recitativo, there was either *recitativo secco* (harpsichord only) or *recitativo accompagnato* (with the whole orchestra).

Thus opera now offered more vocal display and, sometimes, less serious drama, a change very popular with most members of its growing audience. Castrati first began to dominate the operatic stages in seventeenth-century Italy, and they moved beyond Italy to the rest of Europe. Some Italian city-states had laws forbidding women from appearing on stage, which explained the need for castrati. In addition, with vocal agility and power, their voices could easily fill even the larger public opera houses; so castrati quickly became the darlings of the audiences and the backbone of *opera seria*, the serious opera of the Baroque period. Most castrati began singing as choir boys. If their voices showed unusual beauty, their families, especially if they were poor, would have the boys castrated (so the voices would not change) in the hope that the children would become famous opera singers. A very small percentage of these boys ever became famous castrati, but this barbarous practice continued until early in the nineteenth century. The usual procedure (allegedly painless) was to soak the boy in a very warm bath, press on his jugular vein until he fainted, and then cut off his testicles.

The male voice that might result had the vocal range and agility of a soprano, plus the lung power and force of a tenor or bass. The eighteenth century was the greatest period for castrato singers, when special roles were written for their unusual and impressive vocal abilities. Castrati such as Farinelli, Caffarelli, and Guadagni became the most sought-after singers of their time because their vocal effects were both impressive and popular with audiences. Some were great actors as well. But, despite their popularity, castrati did far less to set the course of opera history than did composers of that period.

HANDEL AND ITALIAN OPERA

Although Handel was born in Germany, he became one of the most successful writers of Italian opera seria. He studied for a while in Italy, but most of his career was in London, where he settled in 1710. Both his *Rinaldo* (1711) with a text by Giacomo Rossi and his *Alcina* (1735) with a text by A. Marchi achieved great success with London audiences. Handel wrote thirty-five operas for London, containing the kind of coloratura arias that the castrati could perform very well, and the public applauded heartily.

But Handel did not want to write only works that would showcase his star singers. He also wrote operas that sustained dramatic interest and presented well-characterized roles that the audience could respect. The critic Donald Grout has said of Handel's characters:

> Handel's dramatic creations are universal, ideal types of humanity, moving and thinking on a vast scale, the analogue in opera of the great tragic personages of Corneille. . . . If his characters suffer, the music gives full, eloquent expression to their sorrows—but it never whines; there is not a note in it of self-pity. We are moved by the spectacle of suffering, but our compassion is mingled with admiration at suffering so nobly endured, with pride that we ourselves belong to a species capable of such heroism.

Handel's desire to create nobly suffering characters derived from the Greek tragic drama's similar goals.

The combination of Handel's dramaturgy and his music made opera a popular as well as an aristocratic entertainment in eighteenth-century London. Handel's use of the orchestra often proved impressive, coming as it did from the German liturgical musical tradition of Bach, and his arias for the castrati and dramatic use of stage spectacle also proved popular. Flying witches, disappearing cities, heroic battle scenes, and huge mythological beasts appeared in Handelian opera, much to the delight of English audiences. Only his plots and somewhat imprecise language now seem to us to be weak, and, while Handel's operas usually included a series of bravura arias for the soloists, later opera composers varied the musical numbers to include more duets, trios, quartets, and so on. Handel's most important contribution, then, was to make the dramaturgy of operas largely dependent on artifice (which is why many present-day opera-goers simply do not take opera seria very seriously as drama). With Handel, the music had achieved its primacy, a position it maintains today.

Handel's characterization, classical tone, and especially his elegant music continue to impress audiences. Yet for most of the nineteenth and early twentieth centuries, Handel's operas were rarely seen or heard. But since World War II, his operas have been staged with increasing frequency, often to popular and critical acclaim. These performances have provided employment for a growing group of singers who specialize in producing his spectacular vocal effects. While modern audiences are not hearing castrati, modern sopranos, mezzo-sopranos, and countertenors have done full and splendid justice to the musical and theatrical demands of Handel's works.

FRENCH OPERA IN THE SEVENTEENTH CENTURY

Following the historical pattern of the Italian Renaissance spreading throughout Western Europe, an Italian composer named Giovanni Battista Lulli (known as Jean-Baptiste Lully) arrived in Paris to stage French opera for Louis XIV. Initially, Lully's efforts to bring opera to France met with some resistance from French intellectuals of the time. For example, the literary critic Saint-Évremond dismissed opera as a "bizarre affair made up of poetry and music, in which the poet and the musician, each equally obstructed by the other, give themselves no end of trouble to produce a wretched work." But Lully persisted in his operatic efforts, and he had the royal patronage of the Sun King.

What seems most interesting about Jean-Baptiste Lully, as he shrewdly called himself in France, was his sensitivity to the French interest in spoken language. Lully studied his French audience, and to please them he wrote operas in which the language dominated. So we find much arioso in his operas, where music rarely overpowers the libretto. In fact, this remains true of French opera in general, which claims a long tradition of works with highly literary texts that should remain clearly audible in performance. Lully also incorporated ballets into his operas, knowing that his royal patron was very fond of ballet. Opera under Lully became a royal spectacle singing the praises of the monarch. Lully's best operas, still occasionally staged, include *Alceste* (1674), *Bellérophon* (1679), *Armide et Renaud* (1686), and *Acis et Galatée* (1686). Quinault wrote most of the librettos for Lully's operas.

Lully was followed by his student in France, Jean-Philippe Rameau, who also wrote opera in the French style. By his time, that style skillfully combined language with music and spectacle, rather like the English masque of the period, though with much more music and drama. Rameau also greatly expanded the use of the orchestra in his operas; he did not want the orchestra only to accompany the singers. Though rarely performed in our time, any of his operas can be interesting when staged sumptuously and sung with a flair for high style. Generally, Rameau's operas are somewhat less formal and less stylized than Lully's, and certainly more tuneful. His first success was *Hippolyte et Aricie* (1733), followed by *Les Indes Galantes* (1735), *Castor et Pollux* (1737), and *Zoroastre* (1749). Today Rameau remains important not so much because of innovation, but simply because he continued the French operatic tradition begun by Lully, his master.

NAPLES AND EIGHTEENTH-CENTURY OPERA

Although Venice was the operatic capital of Europe in the seventeenth century, Naples by the middle of the eighteenth century began to give Venice major competition for that title. Naples was the home of a group of musical schools and conservatories that produced some of the greatest singers of the period. The famous castrati Farinelli and Caffarelli, among many others, studied voice at the musical conservatories in Naples.

In addition, Naples nurtured a series of opera composers who were considered the greatest of their time. As the French music critic Lalane wrote in 1769:

> Music is the special triumph of the Neapolitans. It seems as if in that country the membranes of the eardrum are more taut, more harmonious, more sonorous than anywhere else in Europe. The whole nation sings: gesture, tone of voice, rhythm of syllables, the very conversation—all breathe music and harmony. Thus Naples is the principal source of Italian music, of great composers and excellent operas: it is there that Corelli, Vinci, Rinaldo, Jommelli, Durante (learned in harmony above all the rest), Leo, Pergolesi, Galuppi, Perez, Terradeglias, and so many other famous composers have brought forth their masterpieces.

Though the composers Lalane mentions are hardly famous now, one remains familiar, Pergolesi (1710–1736). Even though he only lived until his middle twenties, and is now famous primarily for his religious *Stabat Mater* composition, in opera he is remembered as the composer of *La Serva Padrona* (1733). This comic opera includes one of the earliest uses of a soubrette role, that is, a clever servant woman, who in this opera succeeds in outsmarting her master. *La Serva Padrona* is still staged occasionally, and is well worth it for its drama and music. Comic opera became one of the specialties of eighteenth-century Neapolitan opera. *La Serva Padrona* had far-reaching effects on French opera as well. When the opera was staged in Paris in 1752, it began the famous "War of the Bouffons," involving tense public arguments and numerous essays about the relative values of French versus Italian music. Jean-Jacques Rousseau's position was on the side of Italian comic operas like Pergolesi's, and in fact he used Pergolesi's comic style to write his own comic opera *Le Devin du Village* (1752), which became very popular in France and remained in the repertory for sixty years in Paris.

Through Pergolesi and other opera composers such as Galuppi and Jommelli, Neapolitan comic opera came to be staged first in the major Italian cities and then all over Europe. In 1737 Naples's famous San Carlo opera house opened its doors and soon became one of the major Italian opera houses, and from San Carlo the operas of Neapolitan composers soon spread throughout Europe.

GLUCK AND OPERA REFORMING IN VIENNA

From the middle of the seventeenth century, the people of Vienna became attracted to opera. One of the earliest indications of this was the Vienna staging of Cesti's *Il Pomo d'Oro* in 1667. The opera was commissioned to celebrate the marriage of Emperor Leopold I of Austria to the Infanta Margherita of Spain, and the production resulted in a lavish display of royal munificence and splendor. The opera included five long acts and sixty-six scenes, all of which were beautifully and elaborately staged. The opera also required much scenery and stage machinery, in addition to a large *corps de ballet*. This lavish and successful production helped to make Vienna mad for opera, especially Italian opera.

This enthusiasm of the Viennese public was encouraged by the early Hapsburg sponsorship of opera. Most of the Austrian Hapsburg emperors supported opera with their own court opera companies, employing court composers, librettists, singers, and musicians. These court operas, attended primarily by the king and the aristocracy but also by the common people, produced a constant stream of new operas and so employed many Italian and German composers, singers, designers, and orchestral players. One of the earliest of these was the famous reformer Gluck.

During the eighteenth century, Christoph Willibald Gluck wrote his operas in Vienna and Paris. More of an innovator than Rameau, Gluck was responsible for what are now called the Gluckian reforms. Reacting against the musical dominance of bravura singers and their excessive vocal ornamentations and displays, Gluck wanted the language, poetry, and drama of opera to reflect once again the simplicity and power of Greek tragedy. He wrote several operas, most notably *Orfeo ed Euridice* (1762) and *Alceste* (1767), in an effort to incorporate ancient Greek tragedy and the restrained, elegiac approach of Greek drama into the mainstream of contemporary Viennese opera. For Gluck, music also had to be restrained, always reflecting, rather than overwhelming, the drama. His reform operas reflect these theories; both also had striking librettos by the famous master Ranieri Calzabigi, who was court poet to the Hapsburgs in Vienna. His text, and especially the audibility of the words, formed the functional core of these operas, which demanded a restrained, elegant, and somber style of performance, one very different from the often ostentatious style of some of the opera serias of this period. Gluck's best works became very popular with the public in both Vienna and Paris.

Of course, Gluck represents only one of the many reformers of the day. For, while opera always remains a delicate balance of words, music, and theater, that balance can easily shift to favor one of the three. As a result, opera always has its revolutionaries who consider the art in need of reform. Like Gluck, some of the other reformers of this period (but only some) were able to produce great opera in the process of creating change.

WOLFGANG AMADEUS MOZART

Mozart (1756–1791) was the greatest composer of operas in the eighteenth century, yet he was cursed with bad luck and a very short life. The Austrian emperor Josef II had definite musical and operatic tastes. When it came to opera, Josef admired much of Mozart's work but preferred the operas of his court composer, Antonio Salieri (1750–1825). All of Salieri's operas, especially his masterpiece *Tarare* (1787), typically reflected the operatic tastes of the eighteenth century and used predictable harmonies and simple orchestration to accompany the singers. As a result, Salieri became rich and famous under Josef II's royal patronage.

The Salieri/Mozart rivalry has become one of opera's legends, and it includes the rumor that Salieri poisoned Mozart to eliminate him as a rival. The playwright Peter Shaffer's marvelous play *Amadeus* (1979) (also made into a movie) portrays his lively, philosophical version of the Mozart/Salieri conflict in Vienna at the end of the eighteenth century.

Mozart did have operatic successes in Vienna, but he had to go elsewhere, to places like Prague, for additional performances and commissions for his operas. Yet in his short life, Mozart managed to make major contributions to the history of opera. He enjoyed success in three separate operatic genres. One of these, called the *Singspiel*, or "singing play," is a native German form that attracted Mozart. Singspiel resembles our modern musical comedy since it uses a spoken text combined with musical numbers. Two of Mozart's greatest operas, *The Abduction from the Seraglio* (1782) and *The Magic Flute* (1791), are singspiels, and classics of the form. Mozart also wrote in, and in fact most of his operatic composing was in, the two traditional Italian opera forms popular during the period: *opera seria* and *opera buffa*. *Idomeneo* (1781) and *La Clemenza di Tito* (1791) are examples of opera serias by Mozart; these works seem artificial and dramatically unconvincing today, but they contain some great music and intriguing characters and situations. They were written for castrato singers of the time and brilliantly reflect Italian musical style.

But the greatest music Mozart ever wrote for the operatic stage is contained in his three great comic operas: *The Marriage of Figaro*

(1786), *Don Giovanni* (1787), and *Così Fan Tutte* (1790). Here, using the basic forms of aria and recitativo, the composer created superb comedies filled with sublime music and intense drama. These are comic masterpieces, and with them Mozart brought the Italian comic opera form of the eighteenth century to its highest level of achievement. Today, what remains most impressive about these works is their comic situations, comic and serious characters, and the overall high quality of the music in them. Less well appreciated is the fact that Lorenzo Da Ponte's clever librettos for these comic operas played a key role in Mozart's successes. Of course, Da Ponte's special genius for comedy, as well as his knowledge of theater, language, and the particular needs of the opera, was used at Mozart's direction, but in fairness we should judge Mozart and Da Ponte together; their collaboration on comic opera represents a near-perfect blending of the talents of librettist and composer.

Musically, Mozart—essentially a conservative composer—accepted the operatic forms of the eighteenth century, but he implemented them with his own great genius. He was one of few composers of the period who wanted the plot of the opera to advance not just during the recitatives but also during musical numbers. Among the best examples of this are the finale of the second act of *The Marriage of Figaro* and the vaudeville finale in the last act of *Don Giovanni*; both demonstrate Mozart's great musical and dramatic facility.

Mozart wrote operas that were not merely a string of lovely arias, because he often added duets, choruses, and convincing action to vary an opera's levels of musical interest. Generally, he designed each operatic role for a particular voice in the court opera that commissioned a new work from him. As a result, his roles often demand a particular kind of voice, and a particular combination of vocal qualities and abilities. Thus, Constanze in *The Abduction from the Seraglio* was written for a very high and agile soprano; Fiordiligi in *Così Fan Tutte* was written for a soprano with a bright top and well-supported bottom notes but not much middle voice; and the Queen of the Night in *The Magic Flute* demands fiendishly high and technically very accurate soprano singing.

Mozart was also one of the first composers to use pairs of contrasting characters to represent conflicts within the human heart. Thus, the noble and resolute Constanze in *Abduction* seems very different from the comic, flighty Blonde; *Don Giovanni*'s libertine title character contrasts with the faithful, honest, and loyal Don Ottavio; and although the two sisters of *Così Fan Tutte*, Fiordiligi and Dorabella, are both in love, while the first struggles to be faithful to her departed lover, the second is quite easily seduced. Again, in *The Marriage of Figaro*, Figaro is a poor man trying to save his fiancée's honor, while his master enjoys the life of a wealthy aristocrat determined to cuckold Figaro, his servant.

In *The Magic Flute*, Prince Tamino is a noble aristocrat, willing to submit to tests of fire and water to prove himself worthy of the woman he loves. Papageno, on the other hand, is merely a bird catcher and chicken plucker who yearns for a warm house, a full stomach, lots of wine, and an attractive wife. Here, the contrasts and conflicts between the idealistic and noble, on the one hand, and the human and realistic, on the other, elicit from Mozart some of his most intense drama and painful, yet beautiful, music. Of course, such conflicts exist in most people as well; so the audience becomes fascinated with the human contrast between what we would like to be and what we know we really are. Thus Mozart created his famous "gray" comedies—happy yet also sad, and full of questions.

In this response lies dramatic credibility. As Mozart continued to write operas, he moved toward this goal with certain steps. First, he eliminated most roles for the castrati, a move much resented by some conservative elements in his audience. Then, as Mozart's genius illuminated other forms, there were produced fewer and fewer opera serias which had formed the backbone of eighteenth-century operatic repertory. As the group of conservative composers dwindled, the remaining voices asked out of fear for the future of opera: "Where are the great castrati singers of the present?" "Do opera and great singing have a future?" "Is opera dying?" What those pessimists did not and could not know was that the greatest period of operatic composition was about to begin.

Two

A History of Opera: The Modern Period

Whereas the Greek work of art expressed the spirit of a splendid nation, the work of art of the future is intended to express the spirit of free people irrespective of all national boundaries. The national element in it must be no more than an ornament, an added individual charm, and not a confining boundary.

—Richard Wagner, *Art and Revolution*

The nineteenth century can truly be called the Golden Age of opera, for most of the operas presently found in the standard repertory come from this period. In fact, opera has been called an essentially nineteenth-century art form, though the many successful works from the twentieth century strongly argue that such is not the case. But the nineteenth century does have an impressive claim to greatness, for it was blessed with the two most famous and outstanding composers in the entire history of the art—Giuseppe Verdi and

Richard Wagner. Both these men revolutionized opera and wrote works that have become staples of current opera performance.

THE AGE OF BEL CANTO

In opera, the early nineteenth century is often called the age of *bel canto*, for that Italian style came to dominate many of the European and American operatic stages during the period. The three great bel canto composers were Gioacchino Rossini (1792–1868), Vincenzo Bellini (1801–1835), and Gaetano Donizetti (1797–1848); together they developed the particular style and vocabulary of this art. The art of bel canto uses a special method of singing (*bel canto* means "beautiful singing"), at least as these composers interpreted it. And, in fact, much of the vocal training favored in our own time is still based on this technique.

As a group, bel canto composers excel at melody, and they continue the Italian tradition of the primacy of the voice and melody in opera. More specifically, they also changed opera by eliminating much recitativo secco, or recitative accompanied only by harpsichord. Bellini and Donizetti, especially, composed for full orchestra in recitatives, and worked to make them melodically and dramatically interesting.

Of the three bel canto composers, Rossini was certainly the greatest comic genius. Yet he also wrote successful serious opera—*Tancredi* (1813), *Mosè in Egitto* (1818), *Semiramide* (1823), and *William Tell* (1829)—although today his comic operas are staged more frequently. Here, part of the reason for the popularity of comedy lies in our lack of sympathy with a favorite eighteenth-century form, opera seria with its castrati roles, often static drama, and general artificiality. Most modern audiences find opera serias, including these serious operas of Rossini's, dramatically unconvincing even when musically interesting. But modern audiences clamor for Rossini's four great comedies: *L'Italiana in Algeri* (1813), *Il Turco in Italia* (1814), *The Barber of Seville* (1816), and *La Cenerentola* (1817). Rossini's melodic genius and wit abound; in these works their librettos (by Sterbini, Romani, and others) supplied Rossini with funny situations and plenty of clever dialogue. Even in his day, Rossini's orchestration was considered quite advanced, and his unusual choice of instruments often adds a comic element to an aria or a dramatic situation. In the nineteenth century, musicians liked to call Rossini "the little Mozart" because of his brilliant use of the orchestra.

When Rossini retired from opera composition to live in Paris, he acquired a reputation as the greatest wit and gourmet in that cosmopolitan city. It was Rossini who declared that Wagner's operas contained "great moments but horrible quarters of an hour." He claimed that he had wept only twice in his adult life, "once when my mother died, once when I was on a boating party having lunch and a roasted chicken filled with truffles fell overboard." Overall, Rossini's aphorisms were as witty as his use of the orchestra was skillful and imaginative. In his last years in Paris he wrote clever short pieces for solo piano and piano and voice called *Péchés de Vieillesse* (Sins of My Old Age).

Donizetti, on the other hand, did not use the orchestra in such subtle ways, but he did incorporate serious drama into opera with greater theatrical realism. While Rossini used eighteenth-century plots about heroes and heroines descended from epic poetry, Donizetti used the realistic theater of the early nineteenth century. As a result, many of his serious operas have held their places on the operatic boards, especially his masterpiece, *Lucia di Lammermoor* (1835), with a text by Cammarano. Donizetti's three Tudor operas, *Anna Bolena* (1830), *Maria Stuarda* (1834), and *Roberto Devereux* (1837), present musical and dramatic perspectives on English history; the chief parts are vocally challenging and dramatically demanding, especially for the leading soprano. Of all three bel canto composers, Donizetti demands the most acting talent, but he is not remembered for tragedy alone. Three of Donizetti's comedies have been revived by modern opera companies: *The Elixir of Love* (1832), with a text by Romani; *La Fille du Régiment* (1840), written for Paris's Opéra Comique with a text by Vernoy de Saint-Georges; and *Don Pasquale* (1843), with a text by Ruffini. All three, although not as witty and clever as Rossini's comedies, remain stageworthy, in part because they provide challenging music for bel canto singers and many smiles for the audience.

The third bel canto composer, Vincenzo Bellini, in many ways the most sublime and poetic of the three, wrote the fewest operas —only ten. He died the youngest, at the age of thirty-four. Yet his

Norma, to a text by Felice Romani, became wildly popular when it was first staged in Milan in 1831, and it has often been staged in our time. One important reason is the wonderful title role, which attracts dramatic sopranos, spintos, and even coloraturas because it is an awesome challenge, one of the most difficult roles ever written for the soprano voice. Its vocal demands are matched by its theatrical demands, and a truly great Norma is a rarity—usually just one per generation. *Norma* demands tremendous breath control because of Bellini's long melodic vocal line. The music also contains his characteristic melancholy elegance of tone and expression. In addition to the role of Norma, the mezzo-soprano role of Adalgisa and the tenor part of Pollione both require first-class singers who should also be able to act well. *Norma's* plot resembles Euripides' *Medea*, involving infidelity and children caught between feuding parents.

Bellini's other operas, especially *La Sonnambula* (1831) and *I Puritani* (1835), are still occasionally staged when the right voices are available. In general, what haunts audiences about Bellini's operas is the often sad, melancholy quality of his melodies, an effect much enhanced by the key preferences in his harmonies and his melodic style. Often called the Chopin of opera, Bellini added a dramatically elegiac voice to the operatic stage, primarily with his masterpiece, *Norma*.

GIUSEPPE VERDI

Drawing on the tradition of bel canto, but melding it also with his own unique genius, Giuseppe Verdi, one of the most prolific of opera composers, who wrote over twenty-five operas during his long life, was born in the same year as Wagner, 1813. Verdi lived on until 1901 and contributed to the opera over fifty years. His earliest works—*Nabucco* (1842), *I Lombardi alla Prima Crociata* (1843), and *Ernani* (1844)—combine the rollicking energy and rhythms of Rossini with the intense drama of Donizetti and the melodic genius of Bellini. With Verdi, however, new realms of possibility were realized.

After the early works, Verdi's middle operas combined the dramatic intensity of his early period with more subtle orchestration, as well as with variations of the standard forms of the bel canto period. Gradually, he became impatient with what he felt to be limitations on his talents, and as a result began to write expansively in both dramatic and musical ways. The great masterpieces of Verdi's middle period include: *Macbeth* (1847), *Rigoletto* (1851), *Il Trovatore* (1853), and *La Traviata* (1853). His primary librettist was Francesco Piave, who complemented Verdi's music with clever lyrics. Yet Verdi, in both his early and middle periods, did not restrain an unfortunate overfondness for the lurid theater of his time. To us, nineteenth-century drama seems mostly melodramatic, highly contrived, and filled with incredible coincidences. For these theatrical tendencies in his operas, modern critics have blamed Verdi's librettists rather than the composer; but Verdi chose his own librettists. Perhaps his real fault was his devotion to Romantic melodrama, that staple of nineteenth-century taste, which ensured the popularity of that style of operatic theater.

The reasons for Verdi's Italian audiences' wild applause included not only the beauty and excitement of his scores. In addition, Verdi's own commitment to the *Risorgimento*, Italy's political movement for unification and freedom from foreign domination, colored many of his early operas. *Nabucco* includes the famous chorus "Va, pensiero," which represents the yearning and homesickness of Israelites lamenting that they must live under Babylonian rule. Verdi used such subterfuge to get around the strict Austrian censorship in the theater, but his audience realized what he was trying to say about Italy's unhappy condition under foreign rule.

Another early Verdi opera, *Attila* (1846), also presents the theme of the glorious Italian past and the need for unification. Using the story of Attila the Hun and his attempt to destroy imperial Rome, Verdi reminded his audience of Italy's great past and her current lack of unity and political independence. Verdi's own name, in fact, became a code word in Italy at the time—Vittorio Emanuele, *Re d'*Italia, Vittorio Emanuele, King of Italy—and a message of Italian resistance to foreign domination of the fatherland. Between the excitement of Verdi's operatic theater and the expression of his political subtext, his operas became wildly popular in the middle of the nineteenth century in Italy and elsewhere.

But not all Verdi's operas are nationalistic or melodramatic. *Rigoletto* and *La Traviata*, while containing some melodramatic elements, present us with so many interesting characters that they create effective theater, and, in addition, the high quality of the melodies and ensembles makes them outstanding operas in any case. *Rigoletto* portrays the corrupt court of Renaissance Mantua, with its all-powerful Duke and his court jester, the hunchback Rigoletto. Rigoletto's enjoyment of the misery of other victims of the Duke's lechery ultimately results in the Duke's seduction of Rigoletto's own daughter, Gilda. The intensity of the love of father and daughter, a recurrent theme in Verdi's operas, and the powerless rage and grief of the hapless Rigoletto, caught in an unjust society that denies him protection, create truly moving music theater. *La Traviata*, based on the famous play *La Dame aux Camélias* of Alexandre Dumas, portrays the short life and tragic death of a famous courtesan of the Second Empire in France. This greedy, cynical woman's sudden love for the naive Alfredo, and the equally sudden destruction of that love, generate some of Verdi's most gorgeous melodies.

The two final operas of Verdi's middle period are *Don Carlo* (1867), to a text by Méry and du Locle, and *Aïda* (1871), with a text by Ghislanzoni. The former, perhaps his most ambitious and complex opera, dramatizes the political, social, and religious conflicts in sixteenth-century Spain, and relates the stories of people trapped and victimized by those larger conflicts. Don Carlo loves Elisabetta, the woman who was promised to him; because of reasons of state, however, she must marry his father, King Philip II. This state of affairs creates the tragedy of three loveless lives—Don Carlo yearning for Elisabetta, who must remain true to her husband even though she does not love him, and the King, realizing that his wife has never loved him and never will. In addition to these complex characters, Verdi adds the power of the Spanish Inquisition and its determination to control Spanish national and foreign policy. The famous confrontation between the blind Grand Inquisitor and the angry King Philip creates one of the greatest scenes in all opera. *Aïda* also involves the theme of frustrated love; Aïda's love for Radames is doomed because she is an Ethiopian slave and he is an Egyptian general. If tragedy involves people facing impossible situations, *Don Carlo* and *Aïda* are both great tragic operas.

Near the end of his career, when he was a very old man, Verdi wrote two astonishingly wonderful operas: *Otello* (1887) and *Falstaff* (1893). Here the composer chose his librettist very well— Arrigo Boito, a major librettist and a minor composer of the period, who provided Verdi with the theatrical and operatic theories that helped the composer to create these two final masterpieces, both based on plays by Shakespeare. *Otello* has often been called opera's greatest tragedy because of its dramatic and musical intensity and the way its characters never fail to engage an audience. *Falstaff*, Verdi's triumphant final work, is a comedy and an ensemble opera, both unusual for this composer. *Falstaff*, often called the greatest Italian comic opera, is based on Shakespeare's *The Merry Wives of Windsor*, and presents us with the central character of the rascally old knight, Sir John Falstaff. In his overweening pride and senile lechery, Falstaff pursues two of the merry wives in Windsor, and in the process learns much about himself and these clever women. The audience learns much about the characters, their situation, and Renaissance England—in addition to being treated to many wonderful jokes and some of the greatest and most sparkling music Verdi ever wrote.

It has been said that some opera companies could survive by staging nothing except three Verdi operas, *Rigoletto*, *Il Trovatore*, and *La Traviata*—a statement of only slight exaggeration. In all, Verdi's work marks him as a true giant, the greatest Italian opera composer during the Golden Age of Italian opera.

GERMAN OPERA BEFORE WAGNER

The nineteenth century can claim a second Golden Age, that of German opera. Originally under the influence of Italian opera, so much so that even Mozart used Italian operatic forms (except for the singspiel) for his masterworks, German opera emerged during the early nineteenth century with a native identity of its own. Perhaps the first original German opera of this Romantic period is Beethoven's *Fidelio* (1805), with a text by Josef Sonnleithner. Beethoven, while using the singspiel's customary spoken dialogue, also employed the new Romantic form of the rescue play; and he wrote sublime music for many of the dramatic moments in the work. *Fidelio* combines the rescue play form with elements of comic opera and even includes a cantata at the end—a peculiar and not entirely successful combination, but Beethoven's music saves much of the drama. Another countryman, however, is usually regarded as the father of German opera: Carl Maria von Weber, whose best-known works, *Der Freischütz* (1821) and *Oberon* (1826), actually set new directions for German opera. Basically, Weber altered the form by making it more Romantic and Germanic, using native fairy tales rather than history or realistic stories as the basis for opera.

His two chief works are singspiels, and both employ fairy tales (often from German sources). An interest in the nonrealistic fairy tale and in myths rather than the realistic characterizes much German Romantic art, especially opera. Weber's operas used the chorus extensively, and with it, folk music that provided a genuinely native quality to the operas. Dance rhythms and a symphonic use of the orchestra help to keep these operas musically alive. Again, unlike many Italian operas of the early nineteenth century, which were often orchestrated simply with *basso ostinato* (march rhythms), Weber orchestrated his operas with greater subtlety.

RICHARD WAGNER

The greatest genius of nineteenth-century German opera was Richard Wagner (1813–1883); in fact, he may well be the most influential opera composer who ever lived. Since the end of the nineteenth century, Wagner's major works have remained in the standard repertory, and, as performed today, are generally regarded as uniquely dramatic and beautiful. Wagner holds a key position in opera history as composer, librettist, and theoretician; he wrote important books of opera theory, especially *The Artwork of the Future* (1849), *Opera and Drama* (1851), and *A Communication to My Friends* (1851). Wagner hoped to create "music drama," a work of art that would combine the special qualities of language, theater, and music. The result would be a drama greater than any possible with action, language, or music alone. In effect, the composer wanted to combine Beethoven with Shakespeare, and thus to fashion what he called the *Gesamtkunstwerk*, the "combination art work." Opera, he argued, was the most exalted art form—the only one that could join music with poetry, theater, painting, dance, and sculpture. Finally, Wagner believed that such an exceptional and powerful art form could redeem the world from its superficial values and chronic unhappiness.

Yet Wagner did not set out to be the operatic revolutionary that he eventually became. In the beginning, he simply wanted success, like any other young opera composer. He began by imitating the nineteenth-century Italian forms he had inherited, filtered through the work of an old friend of his family, Carl Maria von Weber. Wagner's first works, *Die Feen* (1834) and *Das Liebesverbot* (1836), were Italianate in sound; and his third work, his first real success, *Rienzi* (1842), was written in the style of French grand opera. This work, Wagner hoped, would be staged at the center of the operatic world at that time, the Opéra in Paris. The Opéra never did stage *Rienzi*, but the work succeeded in Germany. Since Wagner wrote all his own librettos (one of very few composers capable of doing this), the success of each great opera became doubly his.

With his fourth opera, *The Flying Dutchman* (1843), the revolutionary aspects of Wagner's work became apparent. Although the opera does include standard forms of the period—aria, cavatina, duet, finale—it is based on a northern European myth, the story of the Flying Dutchman. Vanderdecken has been damned to wander at sea, yet he hopes for the love of a faithful woman to end his curse. Here, Weber's influence is apparent, both in subject matter and in the quality and nature of the orchestration. As one conductor has commented, all of the North Sea seems to be on stage during *The Flying Dutchman*. Even today, the effect of the music can be impressive.

Wagner created another revolution with his fine texts. Here, the clarity of narration plus the complexity and subtlety of each characterization proves that Wagner took drama very seriously; he did not use it merely as a hook on which to hang bravura musical pieces by the soloists. Especially interesting in *The Flying Dutchman* are the characters on stage. While most nineteenth-century theater presented people as heroes or villains—good guys versus bad guys—Wagner's characters emerge as far more complex and fascinating. Is Vanderdecken a hero? He seems a lonely, suffering soul, but he is also responsible for the death of Senta at the end of the opera. Then is Senta the heroine? She proves faithful to the Dutchman until death, and thereby lifts the curse, but she is neurotically attached to him and cruel to Erik, her other suitor. Is her father a kind man who wants to help the Dutchman, or is he a greedy merchant willing to sell his daughter to this cursed man for a sack of gold? Throughout his career, Wagner's characters become more human and fascinating, especially in *Tristan und Isolde* and the *Ring* cycle.

During his middle period, Wagner continued to experiment, and he became recognized as *the* German Romantic composer. *Tannhäuser* (1845) and *Lohengrin* (1850) are the great operas of this middle period, and both were written with an eye to Paris and the grand opera style. These works contain highly original characters and ideas, and clever uses of melody and harmony. Both works also include stage spectacle, something much applauded in the very fashionable Paris opera of the nineteenth century. The final product of this period, which also points toward Wagner's late period, is *Die Meistersinger von Nürnberg* (1868). This complex comedy presents the world of the German Renaissance as seen through Romantic lenses. It is a comedy of situation and character, which also analyzes the relationship between art and its audience, showing us how art can change in response to its reception. The opera also questions the relationship of the artist to his audience, and the place of the artist in society.

As a revolutionary, however, Wagner was most important in his final period, when he joined words and music together in a largely dramatic way to produce an entirely new kind of opera. Begun in 1848, the *Ring* cycle of four operas (*Das Rheingold*, *Die Walküre*, *Siegfried*, and *Götterdämmerung*), which premiered in Bayreuth in 1876 and has fascinated many people ever since, was the triumph of his final period. Simply, the *Ring* cycle is the greatest achievement in the history of opera. It uses music brilliantly to illustrate the drama on stage in a uniquely effective way. Involving gods, men, giants, and dwarves, the cycle portrays a whole universe convulsed in mortal conflict.

The more intimate *Tristan und Isolde* (1865), musically Wagner's most revolutionary work, completely ignores the key system of traditional Western music; instead, *Tristan* uses chromaticism to create an undulating, modern sound, a perfect complement to the drama on stage. This opera has been hailed as both the start of modern harmonics and the high point of German Romantic music. Overall, it avoids every traditional operatic form in music while it achieves a new operatic synthesis.

Wagner called his final opera, *Parsifal* (1882), "a sacred dedication festival play," and it is a uniquely unoperatic opera. A static work involving the problems of the Grail knights, it hardly employs a typical operatic situation. Still, there are mythic, religious, and erotic elements in the work, especially created by subtle orchestration and fresh harmonics, which point toward Debussy and the French Impressionist composers. Modern musicians such as Mahler, Bruckner, Webern, and Schoenberg regarded Wagner as the genius who led the way.

Altogether, Wagner changed opera in many important ways, both theatrical and musical. He wrote the most sensual of music, especially in his most sexual work, *Tristan und Isolde*. He also revived the old Italian method of using a melody to present a character or idea, and of repeating the melody to remind the audience about a character or idea, but he employed the old techniques with amazing subtlety and new dramatic intensity, in a symphonic way. The *leit-motiv*, as the technique came to be called (that term, however, was never used by Wagner), makes the orchestra a central force in the drama, which often acts, especially in the later works, like the chorus in ancient Greek tragedy, commenting on the action and suggesting interpretations and meanings where the characters can find none. Wagner actually used leitmotiv with both voice and orchestra to reveal the complexity of human motivation.

In other ways, as well, Wagner changed operatic style, production, and practice. For example, in an effort to gain as complete artistic control as possible, he built his own theater to house the production of only his operas. That building was placed in Bayreuth, a small Bavarian town near Nuremberg. There Wagner practiced innovations such as dimming the house lights during an operatic performance. (Earlier, the house lights had been kept on so the audience could chat, and of course notice each other's clothing and jewels.) Today, we take this practice for granted without realizing that it was introduced by Wagner and then imitated all over Europe and America. With this practical change, Wagner emphasized the primacy of the opera, and concentrated attention on the stage. Again, since he felt the orchestra distracted visually from what was happening on stage, in his theater at Bayreuth he placed the orchestra below stage level. This created a "mystic gulf," the invisible space between stage and audience, which allowed the orchestral sound to enter the theater from under the stage. Finally, a hood was used to shield the conductor so that singers and orchestra players could see him, while the audience saw only the stage. Since the orchestra was under the stage, the singers were easier to hear. This whole arrangement allowed the singers to be heard more easily and clearly through the often thick Wagnerian orchestration, and the balanced sound entered almost magically into the auditorium.

Wagner justified his changes—"reforms," as he called them—by harkening back to Greek tragedy, when audience and art were religiously connected. Many of Wagner's theories also recall the Camerata Group, who argued for the primacy of drama over music, and about the value of arioso. Certainly Wagner's late operas, especially the *Ring*, *Tristan*, and *Parsifal*, contain much of what the Camerata theoreticians would label arioso, while another source of Wagner's reforms was Gluck's theories, as well as his frequent use of an atmosphere of elegiac classicism. From all these sources Wagner learned, and with his own genius he went on to produce a fascinating and impressive body of operatic works, one that every major opera company must be ready to perform today.

THE PARIS OPERA

From early in the nineteenth century, Paris developed an audience mad for opera, an audience that included both royalty and the general populace. As a result, Paris quickly established itself as the operatic capital of Europe and managed to attract all the greatest composers to her theaters, primarily the Opéra, Opéra Comique, and the Théâtre Italien. Gluck was the first of the great opera composers who found success in Paris, especially with his reform opera *Orfeo ed Euridice*. After him, many Italian composers flocked to Paris to try their luck, and many of them enjoyed much success there. All three of the bel canto composers had successful premieres and subsequent performances of their operas in Paris, and in fact Rossini found the musical atmosphere of the city so congenial and the restaurants so appetizing that he retired there.

At the very end of the eighteenth century, Luigi Cherubini (1760–1842), a Florentine composer, journeyed to Paris and experienced most of his greatest operatic successes there. His *Médée* (1797) remains his most popular opera, occasionally staged if the right singer is available for the role of Medea. Using the Gluckian reforms, Cherubini created a striking dramatic vehicle for a great singing actress, and Paris rewarded his work with success. Another Italian composer to achieve eminence in Paris, Gasparo Spontini (1774–1851) became Napoleon's favorite composer. His position as the emperor's favorite was strengthened with *La Vestale* (1807), to a libretto by Étienne de Jouy, which triumphed at its premiere in Paris. Two years after, Spontini's *Fernand Cortez* received a successful premiere in Paris as well; it also uses the restrained, classical style that the French preferred. In his last twenty years, Spontini moved to Berlin and became one of the great early Romantic conductors.

In the nineteenth century, however, the operatic capital of Europe was clearly Paris, and every opera composer yearned for success there. Yet it seems significant that the two greatest opera composers of the period, Verdi and Wagner, experienced nothing but failure there. Paris and its opera came to stand for something special—a uniquely French operatic style, often called "grand opera." More than anything else, the requirements for French grand opera were spectacle and ballet. Dazzling scenic effects, large crowd scenes, and elaborate ballets defined the major aspects of this style and determined an opera's success in Paris. That this high style produced much second-rate opera, such as the then-popular *Les Huguenots* and *Le Prophète* of Meyerbeer, should not surprise us today, just as it did not diminish the attraction of Paris to major composers of the nineteenth century. Also in the style of French grand opera (as well as popular French operas during the period) are Auber's *La Muette de Portici* (1828) and *Fra Diavolo* (1830). Of greater significance today are the operas of Hector Berlioz, whose *Les Troyens* was composed from 1856 to 1858, although the work never had success at the Paris Opéra during his lifetime. The popular style of French grand opera also influenced Verdi's *Don Carlo* and Wagner's *Rienzi* and *Tannhäuser*.

Gradually, French grand opera came to represent all those superficial vocal displays and artificial stage effects that Wagner and Verdi hated most about the operas of their own time. Verdi, for example, called the Paris Opéra "La Boutique," to indicate his disgust with the materialism of the institution. But still the French opera did encourage minor composers during the period, and some of them produced successful operas. Perhaps the most famous of these now is Massenet, whose *Hérodiade* (1881), *Manon* (1884), *Werther* (1892), and *Thaïs* (1894) remain well known. Massenet rarely employed the grand opera style, yet his works were very popular in Paris at the end of the nineteenth century.

NATURALISM AND VERISMO

From French literary naturalism, especially writers such as Zola and Mérimée, came an operatic school of naturalism. Concerned with the harsh and often victimized lives of very poor people, naturalistic operas often use opéra comique form—that is, with spoken dialogue and musical numbers. But their stories are generally brutal, ending with murder and revenge. The most famous opera of this type, Bizet's *Carmen* (1875), uses a text by Meilhac and Halévy. Musically, *Carmen* was not revolutionary, but it did revolutionize operatic theater. The sordid story tells of a gypsy who falls in love with a soldier, falls out of love with him, and is murdered by him. *Carmen* is undoubtedly the most famous French opera. Because of its dramatic possibilities and strikingly realistic language (if not its music), this opera creates great realistic theater that seems to tempt every mezzo-soprano who can act. (Of course, it has also tempted mezzo-sopranos who cannot act—and some sopranos as well—but great singing can go far to please an opera audience.)

In Italy, naturalism came to be called *verismo*, and it also occurred in opera. There, the most famous verismo operas, *Cavalleria Rusticana* (1890) by Mascagni and *Pagliacci* (1892) by Leoncavallo, are both short; so most modern directors stage them together. Both remain musically traditional for the period, and certainly melodic, but in terms of Italian theater they were revolutionary—first establishing in Italy that notable French interest in the lives of poor people, and in the characters' obsessions with love, hatred, and revenge. Both works involve jilted lovers who seek and get revenge on their faithless lovers before the opera ends. Implied in both operas as well is a social criticism of capitalism, and of what extreme poverty can do to destroy human relationships.

Each of these works also uses language in a new way. *Cavalleria Rusticana*, based on a short story by Giovanni Verga, was written primarily in the Sicilian dialect by its librettists, G. Menasci and G. Targioni-Tozzetti. The main characters have the names of Sicilian peasants, Turiddu and Santuzza, and their elemental passions flame in their words. Leoncavallo set *Pagliacci* in Calabria and wrote his own libretto for the work. This opera centers on the lives of a touring group of commedia dell'arte players. The ugly relationships among the members of the troupe and the actions of the leading actress of the company, who is having an affair with one of the men in the town, start the drama and eventually lead to its vengeful ending during a play within the opera. The speeches create feelings and ideas at several linguistic levels, one being the realities of life as opposed to the demands of the theater.

More modern examples of verismo operas include Puccini's *Il Tabarro* (1918), Giordano's *Andrea Chénier* (1896), and Zandonai's *Francesca da Rimini* (1914). Verismo operas, often staged in Italy and regularly staged elsewhere, have many fans around the world. For colorful theater and intensity of emotions, and for great acting by sopranos, tenors, and baritones, verismo is hard to surpass and has produced an impressive body of successful operas.

RUSSIAN AND SLAVIC OPERA

In the eighteenth century Russian and Slavic opera began to develop. With the imperial blessing of the czar, Russian composers went to study in Italy, while Italian opera composers traveled to Russia to compose and teach—again, the classic pattern of the Italian Renaissance. Among the Italians, Galuppi, Paisiello, Cimarosa, Salieri, Cavos, and even Verdi all journeyed to Russia to stage or compose opera. One of these, Catterino Cavos (1776–1840), alone composed over forty operas in Russia, many with Russian texts. From all this musical activity eventually developed a school of Russian composers who wrote operas in Russian. In this early group were Glinka, Rimsky-Korsakov, Borodin, and Moussorgsky. Eventually even Tchaikovsky, the best known of the Russian composers, wrote operas in his native tongue, although he resisted at first. It was not until the end of the nineteenth century, however, that the works of this group became known in the West. Since then, Moussorgsky's *Boris Godunov* (1874) has captivated many audiences in the West, as have Tchaikovsky's *Eugene Onegin* (1879) and *The Queen of Spades* (1890).

In general, the contributions of the Russians to operatic history are easy to enumerate. Russian opera characteristically uses large choral forces, unusual orchestration, and repeated rhythmic patterns for large dance sequences. The realities and personalities of Russia's bloody history have provided many memorable roles for the operatic stage, Boris Godunov in particular. The Russian operatic style, while in some ways distinctive, shares many basic characteristics with all great opera.

OPERETTA

In a lighter vein, at the middle of the nineteenth century and early into the twentieth century, simpler forms of comic opera developed in several countries. While these works are not so complicated or sophisticated as Opera, with a capital O, they please us as musical theater, and thus they have earned an enormous popularity over time. In these various types of musical theater, the text, or book, is often much more important than the music.

The Englishmen Gilbert and Sullivan made the operetta a brilliant vehicle for Victorian satire, parody, and social comedy. Their most famous operettas—*H.M.S. Pinafore* (1878), *The Pirates of Penzance* (1880), and *The Mikado* (1885)—are often staged today, largely because of the cleverness of their lyrics, the comedy of their theater, and the liveliness of their music. It is significant to note that the librettist, W. S. Gilbert, is always listed first; his priority discloses the dominance of words over music, and his use of language is both comic and satirical, while Sir Arthur Sullivan's tunes cleverly fit these words. While neither musically complicated nor dramatically profound, Gilbert and Sullivan operettas paved the way for many later forms of comic entertainment on the musical stage.

Meanwhile, in Vienna another type of operetta became very popular, this one brought to success primarily by the music—the waltzes of the Strauss family. Johann Strauss's *Die Fledermaus* (1874), Franz Lehár's *The Merry Widow* (1905), and Oscar Straus's *The Chocolate Soldier* (1908) exemplify this kind of operetta, where the dialogue is spoken rather than sung and musical numbers are interspersed, especially the popular Viennese waltzes, which still have a secure place in the musical life of that Austrian city. Vocally, these operettas are considered somewhat more difficult than Gilbert and Sullivan roles, since they demand more trained operatic voices. Romantic love, gorgeous waltzes, and silly stories characterize this popular variation of opera.

In France, Jacques Offenbach made the operetta a form of popular entertainment, and his works became enormously successful. The best of these are: *Orphée aux Enfers* (1858), *La Belle Hélène* (1864), *La Vie Parisienne* (1866), *La Périchole* (1868), and his most ambitious work, *The Tales of Hoffmann* (1881). Although he did not live to complete this final work—his only serious attempt at opera—it was staged in Paris in 1881 and has become his most enduring work. Here, a sad, frustrated hero very different from the comic, frivolous people in Offenbach's operettas searches for, but never finds, the perfect woman. The music in this final work is not as effective as the drama, but, overall, Offenbach did find a satisfactory vehicle for his special brand of musical theater. This last work requires four sets in four divergent locations, which makes the opera popular with set designers in addition to audiences. And its theme of eternal frustration has certainly become popular in the twentieth century.

Yet another form of operetta blossomed in America—the Broadway musical. Out of this rich American tradition have come some real operas, such as Gershwin's *Porgy and Bess* (1935) or, more recently, Leonard Bernstein's *Candide* (1956) and Stephen Sondheim's *Sweeney Todd* (1979). Long before Sondheim, however, Cole Porter, Rodgers and Hammerstein, and Lerner and Loewe wrote Broadway musicals in the less ambitious operetta tradition, and uniquely American ones at that. The texts, not the music, are often the best parts of these works, though some of the show tunes are sublime and memorable. Using elaborate productions in the best Broadway tradition, these natively American shows attract large audiences everywhere they play—in both America and abroad. Among the best and most popular of Broadway musicals are Kurt Weill's *Knickerbocker Holiday* (1938), Rodgers and Hart's *Pal Joey* (1940), Rodgers and Hammerstein's *Carousel* (1945) and *South Pacific* (1949), Lerner and Loewe's *My Fair Lady* (1956), and Leonard Bernstein's *West Side Story* (1957). Written in a popular rather than original style, and only rarely requiring operatic voices, the Broadway musical has established the operetta tradition in the New World and gone on to add a uniquely American dimension to musical theater.

OPERA IN THE TWENTIETH CENTURY

Two twentieth-century composers have dominated the others: Richard Strauss and Giacomo Puccini. These two have given the most works to the standard repertory, and they also have strengthened its two major components, the German wing and the Italian wing.

Giacomo Puccini's operas by and large have remained very popular with opera-goers ever since their first appearances in the early part of this century. The three greatest Puccini operas are *La Bohème* (1896), *Tosca* (1900), and *Madama Butterfly* (1904); and despite their sometimes rough treatment by scholars and music critics, all three have enjoyed great popularity with the public. Since World War II, some of Puccini's lesser-known works have also become almost as famous, especially *La Fanciulla del West* (1910), *Il Trittico* (1918), and *Turandot* (1926). As a result, Puccini's reputation stands high, and most scholars and historians of opera now concede that the public has responded to high-quality works by a master.

More generally, Puccini combined the Italian heritage of Rossini and Verdi with many of the reforms of Richard Wagner. Though people sometimes label him the heir of Verdi, Puccini considered himself the hopeful heir of Wagner. Certainly his works contain many of the operatic reforms associated with Wagner, such as the use of a leitmotiv structure, complex characterization, an emphasis on drama, and subtle and harmonically interesting uses of the orchestra. From Verdi comes the use of such operatic forms as arias, love duets, and wonderful melodies—and undoubtedly the haunting and memorable quality of Puccini's melodies has helped to attract audiences to his works. He also employs two divergent theatrical directions: on the one hand, some works are realistic, such as *La Bohème, Madama Butterfly*, and *Tosca*, in the tradition of verismo, but with Puccini's distinctive brand on it; on the other hand, there are mythic, fairy-tale works, such as *La Fanciulla del West, Le Villi*, and *Turandot*.

Puccini, then, was interested in both mythic opera and realistic opera, and he produced impressive works in both genres. What he demanded from his librettists, among whom were Illica, Giacosa, and Forzano, remains substantial. Puccini drove them to anger and frustration with his repeated insistence on scene changes and dialogue revisions until their words seemed to him absolutely perfect for the music and drama he envisioned. The result was some wonderful librettos, despite all the aggravation and conflicts that ensued at the time. Puccini often envied Wagner's ability to write his own librettos, and he admired Wagner in other ways as well, especially in subtle characterization, for Puccini's characters are often as human and complex as Wagner's. Puccini even makes his villains sympathetic—for example, Jack Rance in *Fanciulla* and Turandot in the opera of the same name. His best operas provide a mother lode for most of the world's opera companies since they are staged so frequently.

The work of Richard Strauss shows similarities; his operas fall into two general categories: mythic, dissonant, expressionistic works (*Salome*, 1905; *Elektra*, 1909; and *Die Frau ohne Schatten*, 1919) and realistic, harmonically more conservative works (*Der Rosenkavalier*, 1911; *Ariadne auf Naxos*, 1912; *Arabella*, 1933). In fact, Strauss began as a youthful revolutionary, and produced two dissonant, strikingly modern, expressionistic works, *Salome* and *Elektra*. But he mellowed with the years, and his next work, *Der Rosenkavalier*, was Mozartian in its dramatic situations, comedy, and melodic style, though certainly without Mozart's standard eighteenth-century structure of set musical numbers and recitatives. With *Elektra*, though, Strauss began a long collaboration with his most successful and gifted librettist, Hugo von Hofmannsthal, an important Austrian poet and playwright. The Hofmannsthal/ Strauss collaboration produced some of the greatest and most popular works on modern operatic stages: *Der Rosenkavalier*, *Ariadne auf Naxos*, *Arabella*, and *Die Frau ohne Schatten*.

It was a difficult collaboration; the librettist was shy, introverted, and neurasthenic, while the composer was healthy, noisy, and extroverted. That they rarely saw each other, and worked primarily through the mail, probably saved the collaboration. From a distance their individual talents could balance and interact to produce classics of the modern operatic stage.

Yet, both men were fascinated with the heroic, noble dimensions in life, especially when that which was noble came into conflict with the more grossly human and realistic. The heroic, of course, is often connected with the spiritual and divine, and is pitted against the less-than-noble human elements of life. We see this conflict between Elektra and her sister Chrysothemis in *Elektra*, between the Empress and the Dyer's Wife in *Die Frau ohne Schatten*, and between Ariadne and Zerbinetta in *Ariadne auf Naxos*.

In Freudian terms, this is the battle between the super-ego and the id—what the parent in us wants versus what the child in us demands. Both sides have advantages, and both find it difficult to compromise their positions. In these timeless conflicts, Strauss and Hofmannsthal found room for unique expression.

Hofmannsthal himself was adept at both comedy and tragedy; he wrote the librettos for both the Greek tragedy *Elektra* and the comedy *Der Rosenkavalier*, whose libretto is written in the Viennese dialect, and yet creates comedy of situation in addition to the comedy of the language. Recently, the very late Strauss operas have been resurrected by several opera companies, even though they had not been very successful when premiered. Works like *Die Schweigsame Frau* (1935), *Daphne* (1938), *Die Liebe der Danae* (1940), and *Capriccio* (1942) are being revived and applauded. Especially interesting in Strauss's late period is his return to the conservative musical tradition that he had initially rebelled against and discarded, as well as his continuing fascination with Greek mythology, the original source of opera. Perhaps these late works would have been better had Hofmannsthal lived to write the librettos. But, when in July 1929, Hofmannsthal's son committed suicide, the poet died of a heart attack on his way to the funeral.

By the 1920s, other composers were more modernistic and atonal than the aging Richard Strauss. Opera itself had experienced a fertile period of radical change, especially in Germany and Austria. Vienna's Alban Berg wrote dissonant, angry music, and used his own texts, for two striking modern operas: *Wozzeck* (1925) and *Lulu* (1937). Both works reflect an expressionistic and cynical view of humans and their treatment of other humans, and both operas present memorable central characters—the pathetic, victimized Wozzeck and especially the complex and predatory Lulu.

In Berlin in the 1920s, Kurt Weill and Bertolt Brecht collaborated on the very popular *Threepenny Opera* (1928) and *The Rise and*

Fall of the City of Mahagonny (1927), both experimental, didactic works, written in the American jazz rhythms so popular in Berlin during the Weimar period of the 1920s. Another composer who used the jazz idiom in a classical way was Ernst Krenek, whose Jonny Spielt Auf (1927) has been staged often since its premiere. Starting with a libretto of his own, Krenek employed jazz and blues rhythms to create a shocking reflection of the political, economic, and social upheavals in Weimar Germany.

In Czechoslovakia, Leoš Janáček composed several operas that have since been staged with success and increasing frequency. Among these are Jenufa (1903), The Cunning Little Vixen (1924), The Makropoulos Affair (1926), and From the House of the Dead (1930). Janáček's mastery of theater and the musical demands of opera makes these works music dramas in the Wagnerian sense— profound theater pieces with impressive music, including the use of leitmotivs fitted to the dramatic situation and central ideas. His Cunning Little Vixen is especially impressive; using animals for most of the characters, the opera presents a completely unsentimental yet still joyful view of nature and man's connections with nature. The Makropoulos Affair examines the life of an ageless woman, and in the process probes the perennial themes of male, female, time, death, and eternity.

Since World War II, several composers have succeeded in creating their own versions of modern opera, using a variety of methods. Gian Carlo Menotti's approach has been traditionally melodic, in the fruitful tradition of Giacomo Puccini, especially in The Medium (1946), The Consul (1950), Amahl and the Night Visitors (1951), and The Saint of Bleecker Street (1954). An Italian composer who has spent many years in America, Menotti has composed successful and impressive operas in English that have been staged around the world. Benjamin Britten, also using English librettos, seems far more restrained in his use of melody and is more experimental, developing a British method of musical drama in the Wagnerian sense, complete with leitmotiv and a comparative absence of arias. Among his major successes have been Peter Grimes (1945), Billy Budd (1951), and A Midsummer Night's Dream (1960). Peter Grimes portrays the life and suicide of a gloomy, isolated figure who still elicits our sympathy, while Billy Budd masterfully adapts the Herman Melville novella for the operatic stage. Britten has managed to develop an operatic style that is melodic without being sentimental, and dramatic without being melodramatic. In Germany, Hans Werner Henze has used an atonal musical idiom, primarily in works such as *Boulevard Solitude* (1952), *König Hirsch* (1956), and *Der Junge Lord* (1965); his work provides a very modernistic and political brand of musical theater. Igor Stravinsky's *The Rake's Progress* (1951), on the other hand, uses traditional operatic forms from the eighteenth century, along with a cleverly literary libretto by W. H. Auden, to tell the familiar story of the gradual destruction of a rich and foolish young man. Reviving forms from the eighteenth century, Stravinsky cleverly reflects the eighteenth-century setting of the work.

Opera in the past hundred years has offered a running experiment featuring those old rivals, words and music, and each composer seems to be searching for a workable perfect balance. In fact, Strauss's *Capriccio* reflects this tense rivalry at the center of opera, and the rivalry remains unresolved at the end of that work. Of course, this conflict has evolved from opera's beginnings in ancient Greece. For opera reveals, as we have seen, a long and complex history filled with a complicated set of artistic variables. To understand opera, then, one must begin with an awareness of this history. Here, we have reviewed only the central events and concerns of that history, but enough has been said to develop a main theme: Over the years, composers and librettists have varied their methods in a search for a perfect combination of words, theater, and music. The result has been an impressive history of great operas.

Three

The
Operatic Voice

Una voce poco fa
Qui nel cor mi resuono.

A voice I've just heard
resonates here in my heart.

—Rosina in *The Barber of Seville*,
by Rossini and Sterbini

The trained operatic singing voice is a wondrous instrument that can create impressive, beautiful, and dramatic musical effects. Generally, the two categories of voice that attract the greatest number of fans and the highest decibels of cheering are the tenor and the soprano. Part of the reason, no doubt, is that these two voice ranges are the most clearly audible, and, as a result, the most impressive. They are, to use the circus term (which is not completely inappropriate), the high-wire acts, and they inspire the greatest praise from opera audiences.

THE VOICE IN SONG

There is something mysterious about the human voice; professional opera singers call it "the voice" rather than "my voice."

How is the singing voice produced? Where does it come from? There are many theories, but other than the basic fact of air moving from the lungs, through the vocal cords, and out the mouth, not much is definite. We can all sing. But to sing well, especially for opera, usually requires years of training.

For one thing, opera remains one of the few places where you can hear "honest" singing, without any amplification. Broadway musicals, television, cabarets, even some churches, all use some form of amplification—but, so far at least, not the opera house. Except for some outdoor performances, opera avoids amplification. That one person's vocal cords can fill with musical sound a theater the size of the 4,000-seat Metropolitan Opera House, over an entire orchestra, indicates what such a highly trained voice can accomplish.

Such a feat demands innate ability, long training, and intense concentration. No wonder those who do it well generate hysteria in their fans. There is something angelic about a gorgeous human voice; James Joyce once said that good singing suggests a bird in strong, sure flight. Too, the voice, unlike other musical instruments, can add language to the music.

THE OPERATIC VOICE

The operatic voice generally falls into three ranges: chest tones, middle register, and head tones; and these three ranges apply most clearly to tenors and sopranos, though most operatic voices have these divisions. These three ranges are connected with what is called the *passaggio*—or, in English, the "break" in the voice between these ranges. A great voice should move smoothly through all three of these ranges with the same basic vocal quality and character. Some singers sound as though they had three different voices, all coming from the same throat. This is a technical problem that most great singers have solved, though certainly not all. The smoothness of movement from the bottom, the low notes, to the top, the high notes, with gradual changes in the quality of the voice, typifies the well-trained operatic voice. The voice also should have a lovely timbre, sufficient volume, flexibility, and control.

Sopranos

The soprano voice has generated more adulation than any other musical instrument, and with good reason, for it can do what few other musical instruments can do in terms of beauty of sound and vocal and dramatic expressiveness. The coloratura soprano is the highest soprano, with a range going easily to high C and beyond. Coloratura sopranos are generally the highest voiced and most technically adept of the sopranos. Some roles that demand a coloratura soprano are the Queen of the Night in Mozart's *The Magic Flute*, Lucia in Donizetti's *Lucia di Lammermoor*, and Constanze in Mozart's *The Abduction from the Seraglio*. More recently, Richard Strauss's Zerbinetta in *Ariadne auf Naxos* provides a wonderful and difficult role for coloratura soprano.

Lyric sopranos, as the name suggests, are more *leggiero*, or "lyric," and their major roles include Puccini's Mimì in *La Bohème*, Gilda in Verdi's *Rigoletto*, and Desdemona in Verdi's *Otello*. Beauty of tone characterizes the greatest lyric sopranos, though the beauty of tone must also be put to dramatic purposes for operatic roles.

The spinto soprano, on the other hand, has more difficult roles in terms of vocal demands. The spinto must be able to be more dramatic vocally than the coloratura and the lyric soprano, and she must be able to reach higher and lower notes. Some spinto roles include Leonora in Verdi's *Il Trovatore*, Puccini's Tosca in the opera of the same name, and Giorgetta in Puccini's *Il Tabarro*.

The dramatic soprano's voice, compared to that of the spinto, must be larger and stronger because her parts are longer and even more demanding vocally and dramatically. Some of the great dramatic soprano roles include the title role in Puccini's *Turandot*, Verdi's Abigaille in *Nabucco*, and Santuzza in Mascagni's *Cavalleria Rusticana*.

The Wagnerian soprano is a dramatic soprano who specializes in the most difficult Wagnerian roles: Isolde, Brünnhilde, Kundry —in addition to Leonora in Beethoven's *Fidelio* and the title roles in Strauss's *Elektra* and *Salome*. These roles demand vocal strength, endurance, and power, and a wide and expressive range. The Wagnerian soprano is the rarest of sopranos—often there is just one great one each generation, as with Kirsten Flagstad and Birgit Nilsson. The power of this voice often impresses by its size, large enough to rise above the thick Wagnerian orchestration, but the voice should also be beautiful and dramatically expressive since many of the roles of the Wagnerian soprano are the most dramatically complex and psychologically penetrating of all the operatic roles written for the soprano.

Mezzo-Sopranos and Contraltos

These are the lower female voices. The mezzo-soprano is often difficult to distinguish from the soprano, and indeed some singers have switched from one to the other. But, in general, the vocal color of the mezzo-soprano remains darker than her higher-voiced sister, the soprano. Coloratura mezzo-sopranos need all the agility of the coloratura soprano, but with a darker color and a preference for the lower notes. Most mezzo-sopranos have a high C, but it doesn't come easily and they don't like to sing it very often in public. The great mezzo-soprano roles are the title role of *Carmen*, Eboli in Verdi's *Don Carlo*, Azucena in *Il Trovatore*, and Amneris in *Aïda*.

The contralto, the lowest female voice, possesses an earthy, dark, rich quality. She is Erda in Wagner's *Ring* cycle, and Gilbert and Sullivan wrote some wonderful comic roles for her—for example, Ruth in *The Pirates of Penzance* and Katisha in *The Mikado*. Handel also wrote many fine roles for contraltos in both his operas and oratorios.

Tenors

Tenors remain the rarest of the operatic voices, and opera house directors have the most trouble finding suitable tenors for their performances. Very high tenor voices come primarily from the head register rather than the chest register, and so generate much excitement in audiences. A chronic shortage of tenors has plagued opera houses for the last 100 years or so, despite the many wonderful roles written for them.

An especially rare tenor, the coloratura tenor has the highest and most flexible of tenor voices. He sings roles such as Belmonte in Mozart's *Abduction from the Seraglio*, Count Almaviva in Rossini's *The Barber of Seville*, and Lindoro in Rossini's *L'Italiana in Algeri*.

The lyric tenor has many roles, especially Cavaradossi in *Tosca*, Pinkerton in *Madama Butterfly*, Manrico in *Il Trovatore*, and Alfredo in *La Traviata*. These tenor roles demand a smooth, beautiful sound, but they are not overly taxing in terms of length of singing, high notes, orchestra to sing through, and technical agility. The dramatic tenor (sometimes called the *tenore robusto*) has more difficult roles, at least as far as endurance, vocal range, and dramatic expression are concerned. Of the dramatic tenor roles, the most important are the title role of *Otello*, Radames in *Aïda*, and Puccini's Prince Calaf in *Turandot*.

The Wagnerian tenor, or *Heldentenor* (heroic tenor), remains the most difficult and demanding category of dramatic tenor, and, as the name suggests, the Wagnerian tenor specializes in the difficult Wagnerian tenor roles: Lohengrin, Siegmund, Siegfried, Tannhäuser, Tristan, Parsifal. These roles, especially Siegfried and Tristan, demand tremendous endurance, for they are very long parts with large orchestras and sometimes thick orchestration. Also, these tenor roles require dramatic expression since they are psychologically complex, especially Tristan, Tannhäuser, and Parsifal. Some roles require only that the performer sing beautifully, but this is rarely the case with the Wagnerian tenor roles. Often it is argued that Wagner demanded volume more than anything else from his tenors because they have to be heard over his large orchestra. Wagner did not make impossible demands, but some conductors do. If a conductor controls the volume of the orchestra, the demands are not so impossible. Wagner does not require the many high C's that other composers ask of their tenors, for most of the tenor roles in Wagnerian opera are written for the middle of a tenor's range rather than the top extreme.

Baritones

Baritones are generally considered a hardy, affable lot with sturdy nerves. Although they do not usually affect the box office like their high-voiced brothers the tenors, they can be remarkable on stage and have some wonderful roles. Their voices come primarily from the chest, so their singing sounds more like a speaking voice. Lyric baritones, the highest types of baritones, sing roles such as Figaro in Rossini's *The Barber of Seville*, Papageno in Mozart's *The Magic Flute*, and Guglielmo in Mozart's *Così Fan Tutte*. The lower-voiced heroic baritones, on the other hand, sing the great baritone roles in Wagner: the title role in *The Flying Dutchman*, Wotan in the *Ring* cycle, Hans Sachs in *Die Meistersinger von Nürnberg*, Amfortas in *Parsifal*, Wolfram in *Tannhäuser*, and Telramund in *Lohengrin*. The great Verdi baritone roles consist of Rodrigo in *Don Carlo*, Germont in *La Traviata*, and the title role in *Rigoletto*, perhaps Verdi's most difficult baritone role. These last roles are often called bass-baritone roles as well, because roles like Wotan, Telramund, and Ferrando in *Il Trovatore* demand many low notes in the bass range.

Basses

The *basso* (or "bass" in English) encompasses the lowest male voice, a deep, resonant, dark sound. Wagner's Wotan can be sung by a bass, though bass-baritones do the role as well. Moussorgsky's *Boris Godunov* contains the most famous basso role, calling for the *basso profundo* sound that the Russians seem to produce best. Verdi's *Don Carlo* contains two great basso roles: Philip II and the Grand Inquisitor. Mozart's Sarastro in *The Magic Flute* uses the basso voice as well, with sublime effect. In the Italian repertory, *basso-buffo*s sing comic roles like Bartolo and Basilio in *The Barber of Seville* or, for Mozart, Leporello and Don Giovanni in *Don Giovanni*.

These, then, are the various categories of operatic voices, though you should remember that many singers can cross categories and sing several kinds of roles. Many lyric sopranos can also sing spinto roles, just as many Wagnerian sopranos can also perform dramatic soprano roles in Verdi and Puccini. Also, these categories are not mutually exclusive. Some singers are true wonders and can break through the categories of voice with heroic and impressive ease. Birgit Nilsson sang soprano roles in Wagner, Verdi, Mozart, and Puccini. Geraint Evans sang baritone and bass roles in Mozart, Verdi, and Alban Berg.

VOCAL TECHNIQUE AND BREATH CONTROL

There are several schools of vocal technique, but all agree that breath control is crucial and must come from the diaphragm rather than the chest. Shallow, uncontrolled, and unsupported breathing will not provide the necessary ping or boost that opera singers need to reach an audience.

Lack of audibility and excessive vocal strain result when there is insufficient breath control and support. Another problem is excessive loudness. Loud singers who bark through their roles lack the necessary control to sing beautifully when singing softly. To maintain the same musical quality of sound at either extreme of volume—loudness or quiet—typifies great singing. A well-trained singer should be able to maintain the same audibility and quality of tone throughout his or her entire range—from low notes to high notes, from very quiet to very loud singing.

Control and flexibility especially characterize the singing style necessary for the bel canto singer. Coloratura singing, marked by a beautiful tone and the ability to sing trills and other vocal ornamentation with apparent ease, should characterize all the bel canto ranges: from soprano to basso profundo. The sound must appear effortless to the audience, though of course years of training and daily exercise have gone into the creation of that lovely sound. Effortlessness, the impression that all is being produced easily for the delight of the audience, is the sublime illusion that results when singing is well crafted through a solid vocal technique and proper breath control.

DICTION AND VOCAL COLOR

The voice, unlike any other musical instrument, can create words in addition to musical notes. A singer's clear diction results in the audience being able to understand the words sung—assuming, of course, they know the language being sung. A well-trained singer should have clear diction, though some have made major careers without it. Joan Sutherland was always notorious for mushy diction, even though it did improve later in her career, but her sound was so lovely that her fans (and most other people) forgave her.

The voice should have a varying vocal color as well. Mary Garden was once criticized by an opera reviewer for not having a voice; she haughtily responded that the critic was correct: She did not have *a* voice, but many voices, which she varied for each role she created. Mary Garden was a savvy singer, and part of her success was the varying vocal color she used for each of her roles. A great singer varies the sound for the role he or she is singing. To make Lady Macbeth (*Macbeth*) sound like Violetta Valery (*La Traviata*) or Desdemona (*Otello*) does a violent injustice to all three Verdi soprano roles. Of course, the singer has only his or her voice to work with, but the color of that voice needs to be altered for each of the operatic roles a singer undertakes. Caruso himself said the greatest error a singer could make is to use an unvarying vocal color for all roles.

VOCAL QUALITY AND VOCAL OBSESSIONS

Many opera buffs become obsessed with a particular voice, often a soprano or a tenor, though there are mezzo-soprano, baritone, and bass fans as well. The adulation generated by some voices astounds, and it is partially due to the voice's unique quality. Each great voice generates a timbre that is instantly recognizable. Before recordings, the voice died with the singer, but now, luckily, recordings can preserve something of the vocal quality and beauty of the voice.

Some people also love voices that are not particularly beautiful. Maria Callas's voice immediately comes to mind. While her voice was not pretty in the generally accepted sense of the word, it had a dramatic intensity and excitement that made her truly unique. She was a genius in her use of the language of opera, generally Italian, and her use of the word for theatrical effect created real drama. People who only like pretty, well-controlled voices never liked her singing much, because of her rough timbre and also because of her vocal problems. Many singers have some vocal problems, even the greatest.

VOCAL PROBLEMS

The wobble is probably the most famous vocal problem, and Callas certainly was plagued with one, especially toward the end of her career. The wobble, or *tremolo*, is a singer's inability to keep a note on pitch; instead, the note flutters off pitch. Singing off pitch, whether sharp or flat, is another vocal problem. Singing flat is always bad, but singing sharp can add a certain brilliance and cutting edge to the voice. The great Wagnerian soprano Birgit Nilsson sometimes sang a bit sharp to cut through an orchestra; she knew what she was doing, though, and the effect succeeded and was well worth the slight variance of pitch.

Inaudibility is another problem, or having a "hole in the voice." The "hole" means that there is not much audibility in a particular part of a singer's range. Often the hole, when it appears, occurs in the middle of the voice, but it can occur at the top or bottom as well. Sometimes a singer just cannot hit the high notes properly, or the problem might be that the note is sung but it sounds so strained and uncomfortable that one fears the singer will lose a tooth. An effortful high note does not give the audience much pleasure, though it can create dramatic excitement if it is done at the proper moment. In other words, if a character is caught in a tense situation, a deliberately stressful high note can make the drama of the situation come immediately alive.

As one hears many singers, one develops an ear for good and great singing. One especially listens for the distinctive timbre. A singer can have a wonderful technique and sing all the right notes with a pleasant vocal quality and no apparent strain in the sound, but if the voice lacks a distinctive timbre, it can bore an audience. Though sheer technical brilliance impresses, the distinctive vocal color of the voice, even if that color is not necessarily beautiful, will attract audiences. But, as there are many kinds of opera fans, so too are there many kinds of voice lovers. Some want flawless technique, while others love a particular singer for his or her flaws, or insist that the flaws are compensated for by other things, such as intelligence or dramatic intensity or sensitivity to the text. An opera singer should generate an understanding of the text of an opera, of a character, and not just sing pretty notes. It is best when a singer uses facial expression, body movement, and vocal coloring to bring a role to life.

ACTING WITH THE VOICE

The dramatic aspects of the art need attention as well. Thus, to sing beautifully all parts of the title role of Bellini's *Norma* belies the nature of the character—a woman who needs her lover's love; seeks revenge when she loses it (to the point of considering killing her children to hurt him); and has been unfaithful to her country and her religion. Thus, in the last act, when she sings to her lover "In mia man alfin tu sei" ("You are finally in my hands"), the line should not sound pretty. Revenge is near for her, and she must be contemptuous, angry, and gleeful. The soprano singing the role must communicate the nature of the character and the situation she finds herself in at this point in the opera. It is worthwhile to compare two very different approaches at this moment in the opera, Joan Sutherland's Norma and Maria Callas's. Sutherland sounds sad; Callas sounds angry and revengeful.

Bizet's *Carmen* contains another excellent example of a dramatic situation that should not be sung beautifully. When Carmen sings to Don José "Eh bien! Frappe-moi donc, ou lasse-moi passer!" ("All right, stab me then, or let me go!") during their final confrontation, the line must ooze contempt and daring. If the mezzo-soprano merely sings the line beautifully, the dramatic excitement of the moment evaporates. Of course, some singers possess such ravishingly lovely voices that the audience can be bowled over by the very sound of their instrument, but this reduces opera to a concert in costume—forgivable only if the singing is truly sublime.

Mozart's *Don Giovanni* provides another clever example of the need for acting with the voice. In Act I, the Don's little duet with Zerlina ("Là ci darem la mano") presents the Don at his seductive best. In his attempt to seduce Zerlina, his voice must sing the words so that they sound sexy and enticing. A great Don Giovanni like Ezio Pinza or Ruggero Raimondi can suggest whole worlds of sexual possibilities in this short duet. A Don Giovanni who can sing the duet beautifully but not capture the character's *machismo* is merely mediocre.

OTHER VARIETIES OF OPERATIC LANGUAGE

Singing is not the only operatic language used, since sometimes speaking occurs in opera. The most famous example, the German singspiel, uses a spoken play with musical numbers—such as arias, duets, and ensemble pieces. Beethoven's *Fidelio* and Mozart's *The Magic Flute* are the most sublime examples of the German singspiel on the operatic stage.

In the twentieth century, some opera composers also have experimented with speaking as an operatic language. In Puccini's *Tosca*, for example, Tosca's final line in the second act—"E avanti a lui tremava tutta Roma" ("And before him all Rome trembled")—which she says right after she has murdered Scarpia, is generally spoken rather than sung. Puccini indicated that he wanted the line sung with a speaking tone or spoken. Given that the rest of the opera is sung, the force of this line increases in dramatic intensity when it is spoken rather than sung.

Alban Berg's experiments with operatic language led him to develop what he called *Sprechstimme* for his operas—"speaking-singing." He looked for something between speaking and singing to create a more realistic language for modern opera, a language that combined the realism of speech with the lyric qualities of singing. Thus, the characters in Berg's *Wozzeck* and *Lulu*, especially when they are angry, should sound very unlike typical operatic singers. *Sprechstimme* is difficult to do well, but when the great acting singer can produce this operatic language, the theatrical qualities of Berg's operas become intensified and the vocal style he wanted is created.

VOCAL STYLE

Successful operatic singing requires an awareness of opera's different singing styles. Mozart's singing style demands a refinement, an eighteenth-century elegance, and an avoidance of extremes of volume. Verdi's vocal style changes with the operas, with greater rhythmic energy and vocal extremes in the earlier and middle operas. Wagner's singing style generally demands accuracy, enunciation, and strength. Debussy and Massenet require delicacy and a nuanced approach, while Puccini's lovely sound and *legato* line characterize many of his soprano and tenor roles. Verismo operas such as *Cavalleria Rusticana* and *Pagliacci* need an earthy and sometimes brutal sound for their special dramatic effects.

With proper ability, training, intelligence, and rehearsal, an opera singer can do more than fill (without amplification) a very large theater with music. A real artist can use the operatic voice, opera's unique language, to create both beauty and drama on stage.

Four

Opera as Theater: The Revolutionaries

More than any form of music, opera is an Event.
It brings together many of the arts.

—Harold C. Schonberg,
New York Times

Opera is, more than anything else, a branch of theater, and people who sit at home listening to their opera records are not experiencing opera fully. To appreciate opera's full impact, you must see a live performance. In this chapter we consider how opera is staged, and the changing fashions of operatic production over the years, beginning with the ancient Greeks.

THE ANCIENT GREEK THEATER

Greek tragedies were staged on one set with just a basic backdrop in the rear and in front a graveled pit for a stage. This circular gravel pit, called the *orchestra*, was the center of the Greek tragic stage, and it resembled our thrust stage, extending out into the audience. There was also a *parados*, or aisle, for the players and musicians to enter. Behind the orchestra stood the *skene*, or elevated house for the entrances and exits of major characters. This skene, made of wood and canvas, was sometimes painted to indicate a locale for the particular tragedy performed. From what we know, however, most of the action, especially for the chorus, occurred in the orchestra—as close to the audience as possible.

The Greek stage did not use much scenery, consisting mostly of just a bare stage, an altar to the god, the skene, and a few properties to set the scene. The actors, their words, and the music—these mattered most to the Greeks. (Much later, after World War II, Wieland Wagner used a version of this Greek method of staging in his Wagnerian productions at Bayreuth. Another revival of the Greek method was seen even more recently, in the middle 1980s, when Peter Brook directed and staged his version of *Carmen* in a gravel pit. The opera toured several cities in Europe and America, to wide audience interest and excellent reviews.)

The Greek method makes great demands on the players and on the director, since they get no help from pretty sets or elaborate costumes. But for the audience, everything is immediate; and so the method can provide very successful entertainment. One problem remains: Where to put the orchestra? From what we know of Greek tragedy, the productions used a small orchestra, placed off to one side of the stage in the parados, but this surely caused a visual distraction. On the other hand, the Greek method clearly has advantages since it can be done cheaply and with striking dramatic effect. Above all, it creates immediate contact with an audience. Yet the artifice of the stage presentation is quite apparent since the players use different masks, one for each role played. The masks create an impersonal and eerie effect, emphasizing an artifice on stage that parallels the artifice of the singing. Simple as the Greek method may seem to us today, it represents a highly effective and sophisticated beginning of the tradition of musical theater in the Western world.

THE ROMAN STAGE

The popular interest in theater in ancient Greece certainly continued during the Roman period, and Rome added its own special forms, such as more musical tragedies, which were sung in Latin. Seneca was the most famous of the Roman tragic playwrights, and his plays (each with a musical component) were staged with great success. The Roman stage borrowed some elements from the Greek system, especially the orchestra and skene, but in the Roman theater the skene gradually became more elaborate. What had been a simple enclosure, often marked by plain columns, on the Greek stage, became much taller, often several stories high. In fact, as architectural ornamentation became characteristic of the Roman tragic stage, this decorated skene took its place as a permanent part of the theater. Sometimes the skene was used for the entrances and exits of major characters, at others to represent homes and palaces. Its function varied with the play being performed, yet it remained as a permanent part of the theater. In Roman times theaters also began to be enclosed. Some theaters were built with full roofs and later with walls, so that performances could be staged year-round without regard for the weather. As a result, the acoustics could be controlled and contained much more easily.

THE MEDIEVAL METHOD

Moveable sets built on small wagons made both the secular and religious stages of the medieval period portable, as exemplified especially by the guild productions, such as the York and Chichester cycles of morality plays.

In Italy during the late medieval period a moveable stage, called the *ingegno*, was used for liturgical dramas staged in churches. These units were essentially wagons with canvas or wooden sides, which could be changed to reflect the different settings of the scenes. As the technique spread, ingegno sets soon were adapted to secular dramas, as a renewal of Italian interest in classical drama required new secular staging techniques. Leonardo da Vinci himself designed an ingegno set for a Milan performance of B. Taccone's drama *Danae* in 1496.

The increased flexibility offered by these medieval stage wagons helped to guarantee that they would become an important element of the stage as dramatic art grew more complex. It was during the Italian Renaissance, however, with its humanistic pursuit of classical drama, that enthusiastic audiences began to see the full possibilities of theater as a secular art. From that time, opera again took its place as an important form of theatrical art.

THE RENAISSANCE STAGE AND MONTEVERDI

During the classical revival of the Renaissance, Monteverdi, more than anyone else, brought the new art form to the public. With the opening of the San Cassiano opera house in Venice in 1637, opera was on the boards and before the populace. It was no longer solely an aristocratic entertainment—a change that must certainly be considered revolutionary. Monteverdi's scores represent some of the earliest complete examples for what we now recognize as operas. Luckily both the text and music survived. Much could be said about this composer, but here we are concerned with a single question: How were his operas staged in Venice during the seventeenth century? Briefly, we know that the staging was based on the traditions of the medieval religious spectacles and the secular Renaissance court masques. Thus, from what we know about Monteverdi, ingegno sets were very much a part of the staging.

The staging of Monteverdi's operas was also influenced by Italian Renaissance discoveries in art, especially painting. Alberti's *Della pittura* (1436) had first described the laws of central perspective in painting, and these laws were popularized in the works of another Italian designer, Brunelleschi. What these two discovered in painting was a scientific, mathematical basis for perspective, and these painters (and others) eventually influenced stage design by increasing realism—that is, by allowing the flat, architectural surfaces of the Roman stage to be deepened through the use of illusion. The dim lighting of the stage, provided by candles and oil lamps, heightened the effect of trompe l'oeil. As long as a breeze did not shake the canvas backcloth and cause it to ripple, the illusion created by perspective could be impressive. In addition, trap doors opening to spaces under the stage were added, allowing for the sudden appearances of witches, dragons, and other magical creatures, a common and exciting element in many of Monteverdi's operas.

Also in the seventeenth century, several Italian scene painters, especially Bibiena, Peruzzi, and Serlio, developed greater variety on the stage by the use of large revolving posts painted on three sides. These posts, called *periaktoi*, were based on a similar device in ancient Greek theater, though they were used much more subtly in the seventeenth century. As the posts revolved on stage, the set would be changed, since each of the three sides was painted with a different scene. In addition, Giorgio Vasari and Bernardo Buontalenti added to the effect of realism by painting moveable flats (canvas stretched on a wooden substructure). These flats, painted with perspective, made for greater verisimilitude than did the rotating posts, and they could be moved more easily. Again, by storing the flats in the wings or on the top of the stage (both out of sight of the audience) directors and stagehands could manage a scene change quickly. *A vista* changes, as they were called, were changes of sets done in view of the audience. Then some opera houses developed a small curtain in front of the stage that dropped quickly so audiences would not see any set changes. When this could be accomplished smoothly and without long delays, the audience reacted favorably to the new procedure.

Consequently, painted backcloth and flats became the basic unit for stage sets, both operatic and nonoperatic, until the twentieth century. Given the complex stage machinery used by Vasari, Buontalenti, and other designers in Italy, a proscenium arch was also necessary if all this stage machinery was to remain hidden from most of the audience. Once developed, the setting composed of a proscenium and painted, moveable flats became so standard a system that it served the needs of opera for centuries. Altogether, the system combined the architectural stage of Rome with the greater flexibility of the medieval stage wagon (or ingegno); the results, when lit with candles and oil lamps, could be charming and sometimes even dazzling. More and more of the audience during the seventeenth century actually attended the opera mostly to enjoy the wonderful stage effects—especially in Venice, where Monteverdi's operas brought to the stage gods, goddesses, and dragons.

These early spectacles were gradually coupled with astounding vocal effects created by the singers, especially the star castrati. Now striking in both sight and sound, the opera became the most popular entertainment in Italy during the seventeenth and eighteenth centuries.

Also in the seventeenth century, a permanent curtain was used to hide the stage machinery; it was positioned in front of the setting and immediately behind the proscenium arch. This curtain separated the stage from the audience more than ever before in the history of European theater; contrast, for example, the curtain pulled in front of a modern stage with the open stage of Greek tragedy, or with the moveable wagons of the medieval cycle plays. As you can imagine, the curtain quickly established itself as an effective stage device, and from Italy the use of the curtain quickly spread all over Europe. Plays and directors saw that the permanent curtain offered advantages: For one, suspense could be created immediately since the audience arrived and waited until the action began without knowing what setting they would be seeing—unlike the experience of the earlier Greek audience. The curtain also could be lowered for set changes within an act so that the audience would not have its illusions destroyed by stagehands in full view scurrying to change the set.

Yet another major change occurred during the seventeenth century, and it affected the overall architecture of the theater, but especially its interior. Earlier theaters had also been enclosed, but now the Venetian opera houses of the seventeenth century—the first real opera houses in the world—were redesigned in a new architecture, one that reflected the needs and power structure of the society rich enough to build them. The opera house was built as a rising row of boxes, with the royal box generally placed in the center of the first row. To confirm their status, families rented boxes for an entire season. Of course, the wealthiest and most noble families preferred to be in the same row with the royal box, while the lesser nobility rented the higher rows, and commoners sat in the cheaper seats, which were both lower, on the ground, and higher. A row of boxes, by the way, usually extended right into the stage and behind the curtain, providing a special backdrop for some of the stage action in many of those early opera houses. Thus, in interior architecture, opera houses began to mirror the strata of seventeenth-century society, creating a social connection that would persist for centuries. Also, such a comparatively narrow, high theater was good acoustically and minimized the distance between audience and performers. As a final change during the seventeenth century, the place of the orchestra became established: in front of the stage but at a lower level. In theater design, as well as in the works themselves, the seventeenth century in Italy gave the world opera as we have come to know it.

THE BAROQUE OPERATIC STAGE

The Baroque period, the late seventeenth and early eighteenth centuries, must be regarded as the great period of opera seria. Stage productions became lavish, as money was spent freely to create spectacular effects with painted scenery of great complexity and diversity, featuring an extensive use of perspective. Opera houses of the time often used complex equipment such as wave machines for sea scenes, or a whole array of trap doors that allowed characters suddenly to rise up or drop out of sight. Stage business held a particular fascination, replacing mere realism. In the eighteenth century, not much of an attempt was made to have sets resemble the historical period they were supposed to represent; instead, the Baroque genius for elaborate decoration was devoted to the particular effect that could be created by the painted set. In fact, the theatrical painters quickly became dominant. Some of the great artists and architects of the period, better known for other arts, also painted stage sets: Palladio (among others), for example, designed sets for the opera houses in Venice, and at some private homes he designed sets for the noble families of the Veneto.

One major component of the Baroque operatic stage set was architecture, including an architectural facade. Often a painted set had to be used for the entire opera season, or at least for several operas, so it had to be both imposing and theatrically flexible. (Palladio had a genius for creating sets that were both beautiful and flexible.) Before the use of this architectural backdrop (with cuts in the canvas for entrances and exits), costuming had carried most of the burden of varying the stage picture. Different costumes signaled different scenes and locales.

Baroque operas, like those of the early seventeenth century, were set in earlier historical periods, usually ancient Greece or Rome.

Composers and directors, however, did little research to assure authenticity on the stage or in the production. Greek period sets of the Baroque era look much more Baroque than Greek. Yet the details hardly mattered, for the sets were lit by candlelight, which created a dimness that made Baroque sets take on a hazy, smoky, flickering beauty, though the candles also provided a horrible fire hazard. Not surprisingly, most of the theaters of that period were destroyed by fires, many of which actually began during performances.

The Galli Bibiena family came into prominence during the Baroque period because of their marvelous set designs. This family, over several generations, designed for the theater and opera, and their best work made them famous, first in Italy and then throughout Europe. The founder of this distinguished line of artistic set designers and theater architects, Ferdinando Galli Bibiena, studied with the Bolognese quatrature artists, especially Dentone, Mitelli, and Colonna. These artists, as a group, experimented with perspective to create more subtle and unusual forms—trompe l'oeil, angular perspective, diagonal perspective, the bird's-eye view. Ferdinando Galli Bibiena applied these more subtle and unusual forms of perspective to the stage, so that the straight, square-faced backcloth from Roman times was varied to create impressive new results. Exteriors and interiors now could be presented at an angle, from the sky, and with other trompe l'oeil effects. As we have seen, however, many of these imaginative techniques were rendered less effective because of the feeble lighting available in the theater at the time.

Lighting in the opera house long remained dependent on candles and oil lamps; this would not change until the Industrial Revolution in the nineteenth century. Before that time, chandeliers represented the main source of lighting, both within the auditorium (for the audience) and behind the proscenium (for the stage and singers). Footlights first came into use during the eighteenth century, but before the nineteenth century these were generally tallow or wax candles. More candles or oil lamps were placed along the sides of the stage and along the top—out of sight of most of the audience. These additions did provide more illumination, but also, of course, more heat and smoke to plague the performers and audience. Lighting, for a long time, remained a serious problem.

In 1780, A. Argand designed a new kind of oil lamp that was connected to a concave mirror that enabled the intensity of the light to be controlled and directed (at least to some extent). Argand's invention is regarded as the first spotlight. This primitive spotlight quickly came into use all over Europe because of its improved focus, controllable direction, and greater brightness. Altogether, then, the Baroque theater developed new scenic possibilities. Even if the results remained less than realistic by modern standards, audiences of the time were impressed.

Costuming used in the opera seria, on the other hand, tended to be most unrealistic. Most operatic stars of that time owned their own costumes, which they tried to make as elaborate as possible by displaying as much jewelry as they could afford (or borrow), in addition to feathers, plumes, and striking garments of silk, brocade, and satin. Again, the singer's intent in costuming did not authentically reflect the historical period of the opera; nor did the star performer coordinate costumes with the colors (or periods) used in the rest of the production. Instead, the star sought to be striking, to command as much attention as possible, to stand out from the rest of the cast. Individual celebrity rated higher than consistency in the effect an entire production might create.

Since castrati were especially notorious in this craving for regard, they became natural targets for the satires of the time. In Venice, Goldoni and Sacchi lampooned the castrati by showing how each competed to wear the most dazzling costumes, even if he played the part of Hercules in chains or the abandoned Dido. As a result, while singers with dazzling voices in dazzling costumes often created a great success with audiences, all dramatic verisimilitude was destroyed in the process. In the end, both serious theoreticians and popular humorists found fault with the excesses of the opera seria of the Baroque period, usually because of its preening castrati. Today, we might agree that any form of theater that depended so heavily on castrati could never achieve a high degree of realism anyway; so perhaps the castrati may have had the right idea, for they surely knew their audiences. One popular chant of Italian audiences at the time was "Evviva il cotello"—hurray for the little knife (which had castrated the singer and produced such a wonderful sound).

In part it was the unnatural quality of the castrato sound, and perhaps the existence of castrato singers, that made the Baroque stage so artificial, elaborate, and highly decorated. When these eunuchs were singing (rather than speaking), the artifice became even more ornate since the reigning style of the singing emphasized ornamentation, with each singer vying with the other to achieve a greater number of trills, or to sustain the note longer, or to hit the highest note. Opera began to showcase singers—to emphasize above everything else their attempts to outsing one another and to play to the audience alone—features that still can be seen in opera today. Certainly the absolute core of opera seria during the eighteenth century was the individual performance of the star singer; composers, in turn, provided a general musical outline for the singer to embellish upon as he or she thought best. In the hands of the proper singer, the result of this freedom to improvise became both dramatic and vocally ravishing.

Given the lack of realism inherent in opera, is verisimilitude ever possible on the operatic stage? If it can be achieved at all, is realism worth the considerable cost in time and money, given the essentially unrealistic nature of the art form? These are questions that have reappeared again and again through the history of opera production.

Although it is now fashionable to regard Baroque operatic theater as a bit ridiculous, the fact remains that opera became the most popular form of entertainment at the time in Italy, and one that attracted acclaim in the capitals of England, France, Austria, and the German city-states.

On the other hand, the opera buffa of the late Baroque period was characterized by greater realism. Although this form of opera did not achieve the status of the classical opera seria, composers still lent their genius to the comic opera buffa. Mozart's greatest operas, for example, were all opera buffas, including *The Marriage of Figaro, Don Giovanni,* and *Così Fan Tutte*. These comic gems were not so highly regarded at the time they were written, though they have proved to be enduring favorites with audiences for over 200 years. In fact, their comic realism survived long after Mozart's own opera serias declined in appeal during the early part of the nineteenth century, and opera buffa, more than opera seria, influenced the development of opera in the nineteenth century.

NINETEENTH-CENTURY FRENCH OPERA

Hosting the most impressive and innovative opera productions in the nineteenth century, Paris and the Paris Opéra were (at least for a time) the operatic capital of Europe. Pierre-Luc-Charles Ciceri was the principal designer there for much of the nineteenth century, and he insisted on historical authenticity. When an opera was set in the early Gothic period, Ciceri researched the architecture, costumes, and paintings of that time to ensure that his sets portrayed the period as realistically and accurately as possible. If those same sets, viewed alongside other paintings and lithographs of the nineteenth century, still look a bit Victorian to us, that does not diminish Ciceri's role as a true revolutionary.

Painted flats remained in use at the time, and if lit by modern electrical lighting, such flats tend to look unrealistic. But in the nineteenth century gas was the main source of lighting for the stage, and the dim, flickering light given by gas made those painted flats look very real indeed, though certainly dim by modern standards. The gas mantle lights of the period could create spots of brightness, but they could not light the entire stage brightly.

Not surprisingly then, productions of *I Vespri Siciliani* (1855) and *Don Carlo* (1867) by Verdi and a production of *Tannhäuser* (1861) by Wagner were first staged in Paris (though Wagner's opera did have an earlier Dresden version), where they were given the best productions possible in Europe at the time. That none of these operas proved to be much of a success in Paris tells more about the taste of French audiences during the period than about operatic quality. Native productions, such as the French grand operas of the period, were more popular, especially Meyerbeer's *Le Prophète* and *Les Huguenots*; these titles received their most famous and elaborate productions in Paris in the nineteenth century.

In Paris and elsewhere, many opera composers of the nineteenth century were critical of the Industrial Revolution. Wagner became most vociferous in his denunciations of man's greed for gold, which typified for him nineteenth-century industrialism in Germany—especially in his native Saxony, where mining was one of the principal industries. But industrialism also produced a series of wondrous scientific discoveries that influenced the history of theatrical and operatic production, both during the period and since. Many of these discoveries occurred in England, at the time the most industrially advanced nation in the world, so these developments first affected theaters in London, and then moved quickly on to the Paris Opéra, and later to other opera houses on the Continent and in America.

Both gas and electric theatrical lighting were products of the Industrial Revolution, and both soon influenced opera productions in large measure and certainly for the better. Coal gas lighting was first used for theatrical purposes in London during 1817 at the Drury Lane and Lyceum theaters. Coal gas, because it was not as flammable as either wax candles or oil lamps, made lighting in the theaters less dangerous than in the Baroque period; the gas was also much brighter and less smoky. In 1826 the limelight was invented, which provided the brightest spotlight ever seen in the theater up to that time.

The invention of electric light had even more important implications for opera production. Here the French took the lead, as the Paris Opéra became the first opera house to use electricity when a carbon arc brightened the sun scene of Meyerbeer's *Le Prophète* in 1849. Later, in 1861, Charles Garnier designed a new, larger, and more elaborately decorated Paris Opéra, which opened in 1875— and was acclaimed as the best equipped and most beautiful opera house in the world. In 1881 the new Paris Opéra switched from gas light to electricity, a transition that gradually occurred at every other opera house in Europe and America. Benefits were clear, as electricity proved to be safer than gas and provided a much brighter light that was far easier to control.

Also in the nineteenth century, the panorama, diorama, and partial panorama all were invented and brought into operatic use for the first time. Louis-Jacques Daguerre (inventor of the daguerreotype) applied optical effects such as the diorama and panorama to theatrical productions. Now, pieces of canvas behind the entire stage were painted to suggest entire cities, and lights were used to shine through flats and spaces to achieve greater realism. These advances allowed for spectacular lighting. The effects were aided by the inventions of new lighting equipment, also products of the Industrial Revolution, which improved focus and made lighting changes easier. By the end of the nineteenth century, operatic production had changed drastically from the traditional practices of the Renaissance and Baroque stages. One revolution spurred another.

In addition to new forms of stage practice, changes took place in the design of opera houses during the nineteenth century. The newly built Paris Opéra of 1875 influenced alterations in opera house interiors all over Europe by including not only rows of boxes but also large balconies and fewer box seats. Opera houses now became less aristocratic and more accommodating to the growing middle class, who would be lodged in the large new balconies. In New York the original Metropolitan Opera House, which opened in 1883, did have its famous Golden Horseshoe row of boxes; but the new house also provided several large balconies above the boxes for the use of a less wealthy audience. In addition, nineteenth-century opera houses became much larger to include larger audiences. The Paris Opéra and New York's Met, both built toward the end of the nineteenth century, were enormous theaters that seated over 2,500 people. Such houses needed very large voices to fill them.

Even though Paris and London deserve credit for initiating most of the changes in theater production and design, several of these innovations quickly spread elsewhere. The opera designer Angelo Quaglio worked largely in Germany and Austria, and some of his most beautiful sets were designed for the Wagner premieres and revivals in Munich, Bayreuth, and Vienna. By himself Quaglio ensured that the new technical innovations spread to opera houses throughout Germany. Similarly, Alessandro Sanquirico worked throughout Italy and in particular made La Scala the best of the Italian opera houses. There, many of the Verdi premieres took place in Sanquirico's impressive production designs.

But, overall, the largest number of scenic innovations were made at the Paris Opéra, especially after Garnier designed the new house. One element that helped to solidify the French lead in operatic production was the development early in the nineteenth century of printed production books, published in Paris after an opera proved its success there. The production book for each opera included notes and illustrations on the sets and costumes, what they looked like in the original Paris production, what the lighting requirements were, what the direction was like, and what the vocal requirements were for all the major roles. This book served to guide provincial opera houses; for the composer, it provided a chief reason to wish for, above everything, a success in Paris. The Paris production book ensured a good probability of invitations to produce the opera all over Europe. Of course, Paris had money enough to bring in the best composers, and the Paris Opéra boasted a public that was mad about opera, especially when it included lavish special effects and a ballet, which could not be reproduced exactly elsewhere.

The French opera, then, with its production books as an important source of documentation, enormously influenced nineteenth-century opera and, indeed, the entire history of the opera. The Paris productions became world famous, since concepts of costumes, music, and scenery survived in writing after leaving the Paris stage. Although the vogue for the Gothic dominated much opera and theater during the later nineteenth century, realism also reached new heights as French set-and-lighting designers created beautiful and historically accurate settings for elegant performances that pleased a growing popular audience. In Paris especially, opera was queen of the arts. No evidence of that fact could be more impressive than the careers of the two composer-kings of the time.

WAGNER AND VERDI

These two great operatic composers were revolutionary in the demands they made upon the theater for the productions of their own operas. Wagner, for example, remade opera during his lifetime, in particular by insisting that opera was foremost an art and foremost among the arts. Most people in the nineteenth century did not take opera as seriously as they regarded other art forms. Literature, drama, and painting all were considered more important than opera by many critics and intellectuals of the time—except for Wagner, who insisted that the combination of poetry with music, as in opera, produced the ideal art form. This he called the *Gesamtkunstwerk*, the combination art form that was more significant than any single art form. Wagner wanted theatrical practice altered to reflect his estimation of opera; he wanted the drama in opera to be taken seriously, not just tolerated as an excuse for several good arias from singers and some dazzling stage effects.

So with the help of Gottfried Semper and Karl Bundt, Wagner

designed his own theater at Bayreuth, a small town in Bavaria near Nuremberg. Many of his productions there altered the way opera was staged the world over. That Wagner staged only his own operas at Bayreuth, though indicative of his egomania, does not lessen the importance of what he achieved for operatic production.

One of the first things Wagner did was to dim the lights in the auditorium—the house lights—during the performance. Now we take this for granted, but it was revolutionary at the time, and much resented by certain members of the audience. Earlier audiences were used to chatting during an operatic performance, visiting friends in other boxes, and observing each other—the ladies' clothing and jewelry and the gentlemen's companions for the evening. Wagner insisted that the opera was primary and that the audience's attention should be focused solely on the work. Within ten years every opera house in Europe was following the same practice, bringing happiness to many other opera composers and to the performers.

Wagner not only demanded silence and concentration from his audience, he also wanted hard seats in the theater so that it would not be so easy to doze off. Further, he designed the interior of his theater at Bayreuth so that most of the audience sat on the main floor, which was fan-shaped and without aisles. Entrance to the auditorium was gained through the side doors, which meant no loss of seating space. He avoided the rising tiers of box seats, though there was a very simple central box placed for his royal patron, Ludwig II. In all, the interior of his theater reflected Wagner's concern for a more democratic society; he wanted his opera house to be a home for the people rather than for the bored aristocracy. His theater designs were influential as well; today this seating arrangement is generally called "continental seating" and has been used in many theaters in Europe and America.

Although Wagner's ideas on theater design were revolutionary, his productions, on the other hand, were typical for his time, since he tried to emulate the scenic realism and large, elaborate sets he had seen at the Paris Opéra when he lived in Paris. His use of lighting was also similar to that in the Paris house, though Wagner at Bayreuth lacked the equipment and the necessary stage size to get the same special effects. But he did install a steam curtain behind the proscenium arch, in front of the stage, which produced fogs and mists for the productions, and he placed his orchestra *under* the stage and behind a curved metal lip. With this arrangement, the orchestra could see the conductor, but the audience saw neither conductor nor orchestra but only the all-important stage. Thus, the audience's attention was focused on the stage alone, though they also enjoyed excellent acoustics for hearing the music. This arrangement of the orchestra under the stage allowed the orchestral sound to fill the auditorium beautifully, yet it also helped the singers to fill the house more easily with their voices.

Like Wagner, Verdi drastically changed operatic production—this time in Italy. After he became a famous and much sought-after composer, Verdi demanded that his operas be given historically accurate productions. He wanted costumes, sets, and lighting to be credible, realistic, and especially beautiful. In general, Verdi's concept of beauty was defined by the Romantic artists popular during this time, especially French artists such as Eugène Delacroix and Théodore Géricault. Thus, Italian opera designers such as Pietro and Giuseppe Bertoja worked hard to give him a series of realistic yet visually Romantic productions for his operas at La Scala in Milan. Verdi also wanted a dramatic lead singer—one who not only sang well, in the bel canto tradition, but one who could also act. If given the choice of the lovely voice alone or the not-so-lovely voice combined with some acting ability, he preferred the latter. Verdi developed as well a concept of the *parola scenica*, the "theatrical word." He wanted the dialogue and acting ability of his singers to make the texts of his operas come alive for audiences. Thus, "Forse" and "La pace è dei sepolcri!" from *Don Carlo* are brilliant examples of how dramatic words can be on the operatic stage when sung by singers who act well. Here too the excitement is not just in the lovely arias, which *Don Carlo* does contain, but also in the stage drama and language. Many directors and singers, in order to satisfy Verdi, had to change the way they envisioned opera, since the composer demanded as much dramatic as musical excitement.

In addition to realistic, dramatic productions, Verdi also was one of the first operatic composers to set serious operas in contemporary time. One of the reasons *La Traviata* seemed so strange was that the characters looked like real people, costumed in the clothes the audience recognized. Traditionally, opera had been set in far-off lands during distant periods—such as ancient Greece or Rome, or fifth-century Babylon. Most of Verdi's operas were also set in past historical periods, primarily to get around the censors. But his tendency to set some of his operas in contemporary times, or very close to contemporary times, caused him much grief with the Italian and Austrian censors. Despite such problems, Verdi showed that opera could reflect the problems of contemporary life—it could criticize, satirize, and comment about everything, including political issues such as the unification of Italy. This demonstration of relevance revolutionized the way opera was staged and experienced by its audiences, who were now reminded that they were citizens of the nineteenth century. Earlier, opera had generally insisted upon a distance from the audience. Verdi created a new dramatic immediacy, and with it a special intensity in place of the escape provided by many earlier composers.

Verdi also changed operatic production by insisting on a vigorous schedule of rehearsals to create a truly unified ensemble of acting singers for his productions. Especially toward the end of his life, when he could make large demands at La Scala and get what he wanted, he insisted that his operas receive extensive rehearsal time and that a true theatrical ensemble be created by the director before the opera was presented to the public. His last two operas, *Otello* and *Falstaff*, eliminated the set arias that Verdi was already famous for and instead created a true ensemble for musical drama, a real theatrical experience with the music adding to the drama, rather than stopping the action for an aria or duet, truly a revolution in his time.

THE TWENTIETH CENTURY: ROLLER, THE VIENNA OPERA, AND MUNICH

The twentieth century brought yet another revolution in operatic design, especially through the work of Alfred Roller, who designed primarily for the Vienna Opera during Gustav Mahler's reign there, from 1897 to 1907. Roller became famous for two huge towers, one at each end of the stage, called Roller towers, which could alter the size of the stage by being moved more or less toward its center. Also, they could change sets by being rotated, since they had different scenes painted on different sides, rather like the periaktoi of the Renaissance but much larger. The towers gave the designer enormous flexibility, allowing him to vary the size of the stage and change the set. Often an opera composed to be played on a small stage in a small opera house, instead is mounted in one of the large opera houses, such as the Paris Opéra, the Metropolitan Opera House, or Covent Garden. Mozart's *The Marriage of Figaro, Don Giovanni*, and *Così Fan Tutte*, for example, were written for small, eighteenth-century theaters. Thanks to Roller and his towers, the stage in a big house could be made to seem smaller and more intimate.

Since the Roller towers also allowed for sudden set changes merely by rotating the towers, both realistic and expressionistic stage designs became a more easily achievable reality. In fact, the Roller tower was a marvelous innovation for its time. Roller also introduced other imaginative effects, such as often using color symbolically in stage designs for the Vienna Opera. His famous production of *Don Giovanni* in 1905, for example, was dominated by various shades of red, used to suggest the dominating sensuality of the title character.

At about the same time, Munich's opera houses developed other technical innovations that helped to change the way opera was staged everywhere. The most spectacular of these was Karl Lautenschäger's wonderful revolving stage, first used at the Residenz Theater for a new production of Mozart's *Don Giovanni* in 1896. Here, the ability to change a whole set simply by revolving a huge turntable on the stage made possible instant set changes within acts, instead of interminable delays while the stagehands worked feverishly and the audience fretted impatiently. For Munich, German engineers designed large new motors, powerful enough to turn an entire stage. Also in Munich (and Berlin) early in this century, spotlights mounted on platforms in the auditorium began to replace the traditional footlights. These new, more powerful electrical spotlights could provide either a bright white light or, with color gels, a colored light. This arrangement proved more flexible than the more cumbersome footlights at the base of the stage, since footlights often created unnatural shadows on stage and also obstructed the audience's view of some of the action. Finally, also in Germany, sets began to be placed on trolleys with wheels under them, which allowed for even nonrevolving sets to be moved more easily. Also, some German designers painted sets on plywood instead of canvas, since plywood was more stable and less easily moved by drafts, if a bit more cumbersome.

VERISMO AND THE NEW REALISM

A less mechanical but hardly less important innovation in operatic production began in Paris—verismo. This form of opera originated at the Opéra Comique theater, and it reflected the naturalistic novels of Émile Zola; other verismo operas were written by Italian composers, and these works premiered in Italy. But the earliest verismo productions were staged in Paris by Paris designers. Of these, the most famous and earliest was *Carmen* (1875), for which the new realism required accurate settings of poverty. Earlier opera generally had involved castles, kings, and costumed nobility, usually from the distant past; now the operatic stage demanded believable scenes from the present, often of poor people in squalid surroundings.

Verismo stage designers, especially Meiningen, Jules Draner, and Alfred Grevin, led their profession in the use of realistic properties on the operatic stage. What does a cigarette factory in Spain look like? What machines are used? What do the women who work in these factories wear? These kinds of questions—important for staging Bizet's *Carmen*—led stage designers to a different, more realistic, and more complex use of stage properties for the opera.

When Leoncavallo's *Pagliacci*, another famous verismo opera, was first produced in Milan in 1892, the stage had to look like the outskirts of a poor Calabrian village. Here, a very important property was the wagon and props of a group of traveling commedia dell'arte actors and actresses. Suddenly, opera required not its traditional stage properties—scepters and crowns—but instead wagons and whips. In fact, the play within a play, the central conceit of *Pagliacci*, revolutionized the theatricality of opera and with it the demands made upon its designers, directors, and audiences.

ADOLPHE APPIA AND THE
THEATER ARTS MOVEMENT

Around the turn of the century the Englishman Gordon Craig (1872–1966) and the Swiss Adolphe Appia (1862–1928) used new theories and designs for the stage to change further the traditions of operatic production. Both hated the traditional painted backdrop or flats used everywhere in opera houses and theaters in the nineteenth century. As a result, they minimized the number of both sets and costumes, rejected the traditional obsession with perspective, and instead maximized lighting and light effects. Appia especially felt that lighting was the visual equivalent of music, so he designed abstract, nonrealistic sets that were meant to be lit very subtly. Most of Appia's designs were for Wagnerian opera, and few were ever staged in his lifetime, though they did become very influential after World War II. Arturo Toscanini invited Appia to design a new production of *Tristan und Isolde* at Milan's La Scala, and the production appeared in 1923 to critical if not popular success; this was Appia's only opportunity to stage an opera at a major house.

Both Craig and Appia preferred a symbolic, antirealistic, and modernistic stage design. As real modernists, these designers despised the merely "pretty," which dominated nineteenth-century theater design. To replace prettiness, which Craig and Appia dismissed as kitsch, they wanted the stark and the simple. They feared kitsch more than cholera.

Today we might ask what made those old painted flats appear so ugly to these two stage innovators. The answer depends in large part on understanding the impact of the industrial age and modernism on the practices of the theater. Before electricity, gas lights were typically used to light a stage, but electricity changed the way the audience saw the stage. A painted flat for *Tannhäuser*, for instance, might look like a lovely fairyland or a magic castle in the dimly flickering glow of the gas lights. Once an electric spotlight plays on those same flats, however, they can lose all magic and simply look ridiculous. As a result of electrical lighting, then, the theatricality and the artifice of opera became much more obvious. Clearly, designers needed to find new ways of designing sets and properties that would make opera work for an audience with modern sensibilities. The modernistic aesthetic apparent in painting and sculpture began to affect opera production as well. Craig and Appia were two of the first designers who accepted this challenge and used new techniques to create a nonrealistic, sleek, modernist look for the opera stage. In fact, their vision of what opera productions could look like gradually affected what an audience did see, and even what it learned to enjoy. The nineteenth century had exhausted the possibilities of the "pretty." Many modern stage designers now sought to create for opera a concept of the beautiful that steadfastly avoided the "pretty."

OTHER TWENTIETH-CENTURY OPERATIC INNOVATIONS

The German Bauhaus art movement and the Italian Futurist style, both dating from the early decades of this century, also exerted particular influence on operatic design. Settings and lighting were largely affected, and both movements in their turn expressed a debt to the nonrealistic (in fact, antirealistic) Impressionist and Expressionist painters who preceded them. Of the Impressionists, Georges Seurat proved especially important to opera; his insistence on lighting as the primary determinant of what we see could not be ignored by others. In fact, the Impressionist interest in how changing light alters colors and so alters the viewer's perception generated a new concern in theater and operatic production with stage lighting and especially with the far more sensitive handling of variable light on stage. In America David Belasco produced plays that featured dazzling lighting effects—dawns, sunsets, lightning storms. In fact, Belasco staged a play called *Madame Butterfly* as a series of special lighting effects, with a very realistic sunset, evening vigil, and subsequent dawn. Puccini saw this production and was so impressed that he wrote one of his most famous operas with these lighting effects in mind. When his own *Madama Butterfly* (1904) premiered in Milan, it included striking lighting effects, but they alone were not enough to please the audience, for the Milanese did not like the music, jeering the opera off the boards. Later, with some minor changes, Puccini's opera reappeared and became a huge success.

Meanwhile, the Belasco-Puccini connection continued in the form of Puccini's famous *La Fanciulla del West*, whose premiere relied on a Belasco production. The opera was first staged at the Metropolitan Opera House in New York in 1910, where its Belasco-inspired sets, especially for the California redwood forest in Act III, and special lighting effects helped to make the opera very successful. Puccini more than any other modern opera composer was sensitive to light and lighting effectiveness for the stage. His operas contain many stage directions referring to the lighting effects he wanted, and he composed music to reflect those effects. David Belasco was only one influence on Puccini's desire for changes in the way his operas were staged and lit.

Puccini was also influenced by the Futurist theories of art, especially those of Marinetti and Severini. These men (among others) called for nonrealistic, wholly modern stage design; their ideas about what was modern derived primarily from the Expressionist painters such as Henri Rousseau, Toulouse-Lautrec, and Van Gogh. Many of their paintings suggested dreamlike, nonrealistic visions and employed a bold use of primary colors; these characteristics now appeared in the staging of operatic works as well. For example, in Puccini's final opera, *Turandot* (1926), an Expressionistic, dreamlike décor was used for the entire opera, with bold colors predominating in the sets and lighting. The audience could not miss the signal that something new had been added to operatic production.

In Germany the more local Bauhaus movement, and especially designers such as Walter Gropius and Mies van der Rohe, developed a modern, antiperspective, flat, mechanistic, geometric, antirealistic aesthetic for all the plastic arts, and this influence would also show up in German opera, especially since many of these designers also worked in the theater, primarily for plays and ballets but sometimes for operas as well. Members of the Bauhaus group were especially fond of Offenbach's *Tales of Hoffmann*, primarily because of the great diversity of settings represented in its four acts and the immense scenic possibilities they allowed. Bauhaus designs for this opera contributed a new, modernistic, antirealistic setting for opera in general. Everywhere audiences were enthralled; in particular, László Moholy-Nagy's famous designs for a production of the opera at the experimental Kroll Opera in Berlin in 1929 sustained a strikingly geometric, modernistic effect throughout the work's prologue, three acts, and epilogue.

Also in Germany, the 1920s brought the premiere of the very popular Brecht/Weill work *The Threepenny Opera* (1928), to be succeeded in 1930 by *The Rise and Fall of the City of Mahagonny*. These were landmark productions since both works made use of most unusual stagings. Both were staged in Berlin as cabaret operas, on a bare stage with only a few rear projections. These didactic operas were parodies of traditional opera, an effect that worked against the audience's conventional expectations. In the finale of *The Threepenny Opera*, for example, the plot dictates a last-minute rescue of the rascally Mack the Knife, at the same moment when other characters are singing that these last-minute rescues occur only in opera and not in real life.

Parody and anti-opera opera did not dominate the operatic scene in Germany during the early decades of the twentieth century, however. At the same time, a more traditional method of staging opera continued, especially in the popular works of Richard Strauss and Hugo von Hofmannsthal. Their first collaboration, *Elektra*, opened in Dresden in 1909, directed by Georg Toller with sets by Emil Rieck and costumes by Leonhard Fanto. This Dresden production was staged traditionally, as were many other operas of the period, as if to ignore the radical changes being called for by some revolutionaries. Toller produced the Dresden premiere of the next Strauss/Hofmannsthal collaboration, the extremely popular *Der Rosenkavalier* (1911), which was filled with gracious eighteenth-century interiors, beautifully produced by the famous designer Alfred Roller. Later, in 1919, symbolic and unrealistic décor was used for another collaboration, *Die Frau ohne Schatten*, which opened in Vienna. Roller's décor for this production did show a recognizable influence of Expressionist art, especially in its use of bright colors and Expressionist dream-visions—a perfect approach to staging an opera of fairy-tale fantasy.

The autocractic Max Reinhardt directed the premiere of *Ariadne auf Naxos* for Stuttgart in 1912, but the work was not a popular success; so Strauss and Hofmannsthal completely reworked it for a new premiere in Vienna (1916) with a different director. Reinhardt, one of the most famous directors working in Germany at the time, became well known for his theories about the primacy of the director and the director's vision in every production of a composer's work. In the seventeenth and eighteenth centuries, the singer had been considered the single most important element in opera. Then in the nineteenth century, composers such as Wagner and Verdi asserted loudly that they were the controlling force in opera. Now, in the twentieth century, Reinhardt, by creating the era of the director, hoped to demonstrate that the director's vision of the opera is fundamental to every successful production. In fact, Reinhardt's view and the new power of the director springing from it became a dominant theory of opera production in the period after World War II.

Also early in the twentieth century, certain Russian designers worked out their own special scenic aesthetic for opera—again connected in several ways to the widely influential theories of French Expressionist painting. These Russian theater designers quickly gained international exposure, primarily through Sergei Diaghilev's Ballets Russes, which because of its extensive touring in Europe and America, attracted a mixed European and American audience of wealthy aristocrats as well as the intellectual and artistic avant-garde. After Diaghilev saw the enormous success of his Russian ballets, he began to stage some Russian operas, primarily in Paris and London; these too were accorded an instant popularity, as the public enthusiastically endorsed what Diaghilev put in front of them. Among the most influential of his Russian operatic productions was Moussorgsky's *Boris Godunov*. Its first staging outside Russia was in Paris in 1908, where the opera was directed by M. Sanine, with sets and costumes by Yuon, Anisfeld, and Bilibine. Cosmopolitan European audiences were delighted by the savage splendor of the work as it developed from the production's use of bright primary colors, huge and vibrant choruses, and the exaggerated, intense acting styles of the principals.

In the following year, Diaghilev brought to Paris Borodin's opera *Prince Igor*, and again the primitive quality of its sets and costumes impressed European audiences. For a jealous London, Diaghilev staged Rimsky-Korsakov's *Le Coq d'Or* in a colorful and lavish production by N. Gontcharova. In fact, the London audiences for those performances in 1914 saw nothing less than a new way of staging opera. Diaghilev combined for the first time many elements of modernity: the bold use of primary colors, dreamlike and unrealistic sets and lighting, and a direct, prominent use of large choruses. Many members of the audience understood that the visual effect of these Russian productions was related to that created by paintings from recent masters, such as Van Gogh, Chagall, Picasso, and Matisse, and that the best European opera composers were consciously attempting to define a new form of opera theater. Here, again, Puccini deserves mention. In particular, his last opera, *Turandot* (1926), exemplifies many of the elements he borrowed from the most successful of the Russian operatic productions.

CONCLUSION

Operatic components such as plot, character, situation, and conflict—in both comic and tragic operas—help to fill the framework of each particular production, whatever its style or time. These elements always deserve our attention, and they offer their special rewards. Yet what we hear and see as an audience at the opera is not controlled by the composer alone; the set designer, director, and lighting director also contribute to the opera's total effect on its audience. Opera, since its inception in the age of the ancient Greeks, has been staged in many different ways, each of which succeeded for a time in meeting the expectations of audiences and composers.

In this chapter we have examined that rich history and lengthy tradition so that as opera-goers we can approach each particular performance within its context. In all, the history of opera is a story of theatrical revolutions. In fact, as we shall see in the next chapter, the biggest and the most dramatic of the operatic revolutions is just now occurring, a revolution we can actually see and hear in opera houses today.

Five

The Current Opera Scene:

Production Since World War Two

The stage is as nothing and worse than nothing if it is not marvellous. It must be the dream of dreams or else it is a wooden pillory on which the imagination of the poet is foully prostituted.

—Hugo von Hofmannsthal

Since World War II opera production has continued to change in important ways. These changes will be discussed in this chapter, but we should begin by noting briefly some reasons for change, especially the technical and mechanical advances and the key directors and designers who have altered opera production so considerably in recent times.

THE NEW TECHNOLOGY AND OPERA

Today, opera comes to us through both videotaped and live television broadcasts, which seem far more satisfactory than recordings of the music alone. Contemporary opera productions, taking advantage of a communications revolution that has superseded the Industrial Revolution of an earlier century, can now reach more people than ever before, and of course this technology itself has profoundly influenced the experience of enjoying an opera.

The recording of a complete opera, while introduced before World War II, had been an awkward and expensive affair—all of *Die Walküre* or *La Traviata* on dozens of 78 r.p.m. records, every one of them easily breakable. But with the development of the long-playing record, a listener could hear complete operas on three or four unbreakable records (or five or six in the case of Wagner's operas) with improved fidelity to the original sound. Although records were not able to reproduce the visual aspects of opera, they did multiply opportunities to enjoy its sound and, perhaps even more important, helped to introduce opera to many new listeners. Audiocassettes, which were easier to handle than records and not so fragile, became popular for opera recordings in the 1970s. Today's compact disk is the most recent improvement in opera recording. Using a laser beam rather than friction between a record and a needle, the compact disk reproduces music with greater fidelity in a much more durable medium.

Today, with opera on television and compact laser disk, the telecasting of live opera via satellite, and the videotaping of performances for later replay, millions of people can enjoy both the visual and aural aspects of opera right in their own homes. One recent telecast of Wagner's *Ring* cycle, for example, showed the *Ring* to more people at one time than the total of all audiences at Bayreuth since the *Ring*'s premiere there in 1876. Such a potential to reach viewers remains awesome. For with every television event come new viewers, who then become new audiences, interested enough to want to go to an opera house and experience at first hand what opera can be within the theater.

In the opera house itself, technical advances have also affected the performance of opera. Here the computer has played a key role, especially in providing more sophisticated control of lighting boards. On the stage, new plastic-based paints have made painting sets easier, with brighter, longer-lasting colors that dry in a shorter time. Also, plastic and latex rubber molds have been used to facilitate property construction and handling. Fiberglas can also make properties such as draperies easier to handle, and much less flammable. For example, old "stone" staircases used to be made of plaster or wood—both quite heavy and cumbersome. Now, they are generally made of plastic, so that they weigh less yet look far more realistic. Stage chandeliers used to be made of tin or plaster and glass. Now designers more often use plastics, so that the final production is lighter, more durable, and looks better on stage—more like the genuine article. Papier-mâché used to be used to construct many properties for opera; now that plastics and Fiberglas are used instead, less effort is required to achieve better results.

Additionally, in modern operatic productions, scrims have come increasingly into use, especially for outdoor scenes such as those in operas by Wagner and Verdi. Scrims had been used since the nineteenth century in opera, but they were hung in the rear of the stage for special effects such as the eerie appearances of ghosts. Modern scrims, however, thin pieces of gauzelike covering for the entire stage, can create several unusual theatrical effects. First, they are generally used to control lighting, since they can be either opaque or transparent, depending on how they are lit. A fire that is supposed to engulf the entire stage, as in the last scene of Wagner's *Die Walküre*, can be easily represented on a scrim that covers the stage with projections of a flickering fire. At the same time, the scrim does much to unify and harmonize the whole range of colors in a production by giving them a gentle patina. On the other hand, scrims can make the entire stage look very dark when shadowy beauty may be what the director and stage designer intend for the production. In fact, an unvaried somber darkness, created all too often by scrims, has generated frequent audience complaints about overwhelming murkiness. Also, scrims are often hated by singers, who find it more difficult to see the conductor; some singers even argue that scrims make it more difficult for their voices to reach the audience. But even so, scrims have made possible far more dazzling scenic effects, especially by imaginative use of modern lighting.

Since World War II, projectors have also been used in many ways to control and alter the opera stage. Rear projectors can reproduce whole scenes on a cyclorama, placed in back of the stage, thereby substituting for constructed and painted scenery. Modern projectors can also replace properties and real items on stage, as a way of achieving greater verisimilitude. A flowing waterfall, a flickering fire, branches shaken by the wind—these natural motions can all be generated realistically with the help of stage projectors, which have to be considered as important modern innovations in staging operas.

Modern projectors can also reproduce on stage some very realistic *changes* in lighting effects. Light, after all, is not static, but rather something that is constantly changing as the French Impressionist painters first insisted—changing, for example, from a bright high noon to a glowing sunset, a gradual fading twilight, into a starry night. Projectors can even create on stage the sense of approaching dawn or gradual sunset, in addition to the dappled light of a forest or the reflected bright light of a seashore. Shadows, which used to be painted into the flats, can now move (as they do in nature), thanks to projectors.

Before the modern period, stage lighting in opera was concerned primarily with visibility—making sure that the audience could see what happened on stage. But with powerful equipment like fresnel lights, more subtle effects like the movement of light become the concerns of the lighting director. Projectors have enabled the lighting director to create some of these special effects. Modern stage projectors come in two general categories: slide or movie, the first for stationary effects, and the second for effects involving motion. Stage lighting, lenses, and Linnebach projectors make possible unusual kinds of special effects for opera: a waterfall, the movement of trees in the wind, the flickering light of a dense forest, the pale light of the moon, and the blinding light of noon. Different kinds of fresnel lights and projectors can create these special effects.

Another, newer use of projectors in opera enables subtitles to be projected over the stage. Variously called "surtitles," "supratitles," and "supertitles," this system makes it possible to project an English translation over the stage, which allows an audience not familiar with the opera to know immediately what is happening and what the characters are saying. While some of the more knowledgeable among the audience have been unhappy with surtitles, most opera-goers have responded enthusiastically to them. This device, of course, was inspired by subtitles used for foreign films.

Contemporary operatic production has often been called opera's age of cinematic production. Timing and visual effects are often adapted from the movies or television. In fact, with a scrim, the entire stage can be made to resemble a movie screen. And, of course, many contemporary opera designers and directors have also worked in movies and/or television.

Movies themselves have sometimes been used as parts of opera productions, and one of the most important examples of this since World War II is Sarah Caldwell's 1967 production of Alban Berg's *Lulu*, which included films of the seductive Lulu's mouth and body. Some of these techniques were first used experimentally in Germany during the 1920s; today they are widespread on opera stages around the world. Thus, instead of a painted forest scene, a photograph of a forest can be projected on the cyclorama, a huge piece of canvas that curves around the entire back of the stage. Or, different stages in the life of a character can be presented together, as Frank Corsaro did in the film strips used for his striking production of Leoš Janáček's *The Makropoulos Affair*, where we see the fascinating heroine at several moments in her long life. Combinations of stage, film, and screen techniques have influenced opera production enormously, and will continue to do so.

Another, very different, aspect of popular taste has altered the nature of opera houses in our own time, to make them increasingly a museum for productions of "the classics," or what is called "the standard repertory." In an earlier time, opera audiences demanded primarily new operas—this was especially true of eighteenth- and nineteenth-century audiences. But at present most opera audiences seem very suspicious of contemporary works, and they generally prefer performances of the classics only, primarily the works of the Big Five: Mozart, Verdi, Wagner, Puccini, and Strauss. So the opera diet has in recent years become less varied, which can be stultifying. Recently, in response, more modern works have been introduced gradually into the standard repertory, especially operas by Benjamin Britten and Alban Berg.

More generally, as opera audiences have continued seeing the standard repertory operas over and over again, directors have responded by changing, sometimes radically, the ways opera classics are staged. In fact, our own age of opera production has been hailed as the age of the director, and the director (sometimes called the producer as well) has risen to preeminence in the opera house.

Opera on Film

Some directors have wanted to expand opera itself beyond the opera house, onto film, thereby generating a broad new exposure for the art form.

Besides the videocassettes mentioned earlier, since World War II several major film directors have turned opera more directly into a cinematic experience by filming operas for commercial release in movie theaters. One of the earliest and more successful of these was Ingmar Bergman's filmed version of Mozart's *The Magic Flute*, filmed in Swedish in the famous Drottningholm Castle Theater in Sweden. Making no attempt to film the opera on realistic locations, instead Bergman filmed the opera as a theater piece. The film begins with an audience filling a small eighteenth-century opera house, and while characters are singing on stage, we see others waiting behind stage for their cues. Such a technique solved a basic problem of filming opera: Opera's artificiality, juxtaposed with the realism of the other medium, can very easily make the singers look silly on film. Bergman never tries to convince us that the opera is actually occurring in real life, with the characters singing instead of speaking. Instead, Bergman's solution is to present opera as theater, and the approach produced a brilliant film experience.

More traditional approaches have been taken by films such as Joseph Losey's *Don Giovanni*, where the stately architecture of Palladio in the area of the Veneto around Venice produced a gorgeous backdrop for Don Giovanni's attempted but always frustrated seductions. The eighteenth-century background of the opera was emphasized by the lovely period architecture, and settings were created for the music that could never have been duplicated in a theater. Franco Zeffirelli used this same approach in his lovely film version of Verdi's *La Traviata*, and his cinemagraphic imagination created for the film some gorgeous and colorful visual effects that likewise would not be possible in the opera house. Francesco Rosi's *Carmen*, with Plácido Domingo and Julia Migenes-Johnson, used another realistic approach, going on location in Spain to produce authentic backgrounds for the singers. A new kind of realism was created, though the singing undercut much of that realism. Yet the authenticity of the setting and the acting ability of the main singers created a gripping and successful operatic film. Götz Friedrich's film version of Strauss's *Elektra* created an ugly, brutal realism that brilliantly reflected the opera's major themes.

Hans-Jurgen Syberberg's *Parsifal* employed a more extreme approach to filmed opera. Here, little attempt was made to produce a realistic version of Wagner's opera; instead, the film became the director's vision of the opera—complete with a sex change for the major character in the middle of the film. Syberberg has defended his approach by saying that his film has little to do with Wagner's *Parsifal*; instead, Syberberg is using Wagner's opera to present his own version of the Parsifal myth. The result includes much visual excitement and some striking footage, which sometimes reflects Wagner's intentions and sometimes violates them.

That opera has attracted major directors to make films based on operas adds a new musical dimension to cinema and a new potential for operatic expression in film. Some highly creative directors have given opera, through film, another mode of communication. So now let's move on from film production to the most influential operatic directors and examine their theories about how to stage opera in unique and striking ways.

THE MAJOR DIRECTORS

Wieland and Wolfgang Wagner

Born in 1917, Wieland Wagner continued, but at the same time radically altered, his family's tradition of opera production at Bayreuth's Wagner Festival, where his innovative productions have influenced Wagnerian staging around the world. The grandson of the composer, Wieland Wagner, along with his brother Wolfgang, assumed control of the festival as a result of a legal settlement. His mother, Winifred, had been a friend of Hitler's and had tried to make the festival an arena for some Nazi ideas. During World War II performances were discontinued, largely because of bombing and war damages, but after the war a German and American court agreed to let the family restart the festival—on the condition that Winifred Wagner have nothing to do with it. So the directorship passed to her two young sons, Wieland and Wolfgang.

When they formally reopened the Wagner Festival in 1951, the brothers expressed a radically new vision of the festival. In Bayreuth, they hoped to present experimental new productions; even though an older generation of Wagnerians had come to think of the theater at Bayreuth (designed by the composer himself) as a classic shrine for traditional and definitive productions of the master's great works, the brothers were determined to change things. In the process they shocked and irritated the festival's tradition-minded audience. Yet the Wagner brothers succeeded in making Bayreuth a place of novelty, experimentation, and excitement, all resulting from their operatic staging. If some older fans were lost, many new Wagnerians were gained as Wagner's works were produced in a new, exciting way. While both brothers staged their grandfather's operas, Wieland became identified as the true genius in their generation; his productions created a sensation, with much scandal, more excitement, and, later, widespread veneration and imitation. In fact, Wieland altered the way we think about Wagnerian opera, and his alterations have changed staging at opera houses around the world.

In general, Wieland Wagner designed abstract, nonrealistic sets that conveyed his modernistic vision of Wagnerian opera. He dismissed the realism that had been preferred in the 1920s and 1930s as simply fascist kitsch. He also found that realistic productions of Wagner seemed to trigger too many associations with Nazism; they made contemporary German audiences uncomfortable. Instead of presenting a Romantic, legendary German past, Wieland wanted a timeless effect in his productions, something that did not represent either authentic or legendary medieval German culture. He also felt that, since opera is a nonrealistic art form to start with, the most effective sets should reflect the very nature of the form.

Possibilities for novel lighting especially obsessed Wieland Wagner because he felt, like Adolphe Appia, that lighting should be considered the visual equivalent of music. In this new approach lighting is a spiritual, intangible reality, as changeable as the music in opera; thus nothing could be more important to the opera than a sensitive use of lighting. Over and over again, Wieland Wagner repeated that it is lighting in the hands of the lighting designer that governs what the opera audience sees. A costume designer may design a magnificent, colorful costume for Brünnhilde, but no one in the audience will see much of it if the figure and the costume are not properly lit. To produce striking and intelligent effects, then, the lighting designer and director must work harmoniously, creating together a unified vision of the entire work under production. That vision, moreover, should be the director's vision overall, for the clever use of light can make a large stage seem small or a small stage seem larger, because the spotlight can focus the audience's attention on the central character, or the central dramatic conflict, or the incident or decision that most controls the action. All of this can be effected by lighting, but coordinated only by an understanding director.

In addition to Appia's interest in lighting and abstraction in Wagnerian production, Wieland Wagner found useful ideas in his study of the Greek stage and especially its approaches to staging ancient Greek tragedies. Most audiences felt that if his sets and costumes looked like anything definable, they suggested Wieland Wagner's profound interest in Greek tragedy. In particular, his sets and costumes sometimes resembled simple, modern versions of ancient Greek designs for the tragic stage, with most of the acting occurring in the circular *orchestra*. A certain classic quality was retained in most of Wieland's productions.

Turning his back on tradition, however, Wieland got rid of the prettily painted backdrops, the iron brassiere and helmet for Brünnhilde, and the plumed helmet and patched eye that ordinarily costumed Wotan. Wieland's *Ring* productions eliminated all the typical trappings of Wagnerian opera in use since the nineteenth century. Instead, the stage seemed almost bare; the overall look was plain, stark. In the director's mind, the *Ring* and all great opera was about the timeless conflicts of humanity. With that rationale, Wieland justified his productions and denounced nineteenth-century Romantic sets as operatic kitsch.

But what guidelines for production did Richard Wagner himself leave behind at his death? Wagner, in fact, was very specific in detailing what he wanted on stage for his operas in terms of sets, properties, and style of acting. Against the weight of this legacy, Wieland Wagner argued that each generation has to find its own solutions to the problems of opera production, that his grandfather had told his children to make something new for the arts; thus, they should not merely repeat the same things over and over again, until predictability and boredom became characteristics of Wagnerian productions. Richard Wagner had wanted his theater at Bayreuth to be always fresh, an exciting, innovative place rather than a shrine to dead traditions. And his grandsons, especially Wieland, understood these intentions and worked to make Bayreuth a home for innovative staging and experimentation in Wagnerian productions.

As we might expect, Wieland's abstract, nonrealistic approach quickly gained authority and spread to productions of non-Wagnerian operas as well. His results were sometimes quite effective when he produced non-Wagnerian operas away from Bayreuth. Wieland did famous productions at Stuttgart of *Fidelio* (1954) and *Salome* (1962)—which showed that his abstract, subtly lit sets could work for a wide range of operas. When Wieland died in 1966, a few months before his fiftieth birthday, he had dramatically altered the conventions of opera staging and left a legacy of his own.

In a style very similar to Wieland, his brother Wolfgang has staged most of the Wagnerian operas at Bayreuth as well. But while Wieland often used bright light, Wolfgang concentrated more on shadows and the beauty of moving shadows on the stage, created primarily through the subtle use of projectors. Wolfgang's staging of the *Ring* in 1974 emphasized the murky, shadowy quality of the tragic cycle through a production that was dark, abstract, and dominated by menacing shadows. If the darkness sometimes got excessive, the tragic grandeur of the tetralogy and a dark, gray beauty impressively dominated the stage.

Luchino Visconti and Franco Zeffirelli

Where Wieland Wagner was abstract and symbolic, Franco Zeffirelli is concrete and realistic. At the same time that Wieland was busy dismissing realism as a dated medium for opera in the twentieth century, Franco Zeffirelli worked to create his own style of beautifully realistic productions. One of his earliest successes was his 1956 production of Verdi's *Aïda*, staged at La Scala in Milan. The sets were not only realistic, but they looked like old daguerreotypes of nineteenth-century productions of the same opera. Zeffirelli clearly was using the very nineteenth-century approach, complete with the painted sets, elaborately ornamented costumes, and perspective, that Wieland Wagner had dismissed as kitsch. Yet Zeffirelli's *Aïda* was a great success with its Milan audiences, and it established him as an internationally famous opera director.

What governs Zeffirelli's approach to opera is a strong desire to make opera fantastic, beautiful, theatrical, yet basically realistic. His use of colors is always daring, though rarely garish, and his revival of old-fashioned techniques like painted sets, exotic settings, deep perspective, visual splendor, and, even more, his desire to bowl the audience over, characterize his productions. Of course, one important consideration is that Wieland Wagner and Franco Zeffirelli have worked in different repertories—Wagner primarily designing for German opera, while Zeffirelli usually restricts himself to Italian opera. But the two men display differences in temperament as well. While Wieland Wagner saw the theater as a holy place, a temple of truth and enlightenment, much as the Greek tragic playwrights did, Franco Zeffirelli treats the theater as a place of enjoyment, of spectacle, of dramatic excitement, where one goes not for religious enlightenment but for an evening's entertainment—as the Roman comic playwrights saw theater. These temperamental differences are sometimes represented as a stereotypical conflict between the idealistic German and the realistic, if not cynical, Italian.

Zeffirelli absorbed much of this realism during an apprenticeship with his mentor, Luchino Visconti, who became world-famous for directing Maria Callas in a series of famous productions at La Scala in the 1950s. Visconti's ability to direct Callas so that both their geniuses were apparent on stage influenced the way Zeffirelli saw theater—what it could do, what it could be, how opera could be realistic while still true to itself, and how theatrical techniques could work in the opera house.

For Visconti, subtle, realistic gesture best revealed character, and Callas became famous for what she could do with a look, a movement of the hand or arm. A simple walk upstage could be an eloquent statement of character and dramatic situation—when *she* was doing the walking. Altogether, Visconti's direction helped and guided her intuitive ability to handle characterization and dramatic intensity, and Visconti taught Zeffirelli much as well. For example, Visconti changed the historical periods of operas in some of his most famous productions: his *La Traviata* with Callas at La Scala was placed in the Belle Époque period, instead of in the Second Empire, the time in which it was composed. The director claimed that he did this because Callas looked especially beautiful in gowns of the Belle Époque. In addition, Visconti's eye for the theatrical effect shows up in his films as well as in his opera productions.

Like his mentor Visconti, Zeffirelli also works in film, and produced famous cinematic versions of Verdi's *La Traviata* and *Otello* and a filmed-for-TV version of his famous La Scala production of *Pagliacci*. In addition, Zeffirelli has done such nonoperatic subjects as films of Shakespeare's *Romeo and Juliet* and *The Taming of the Shrew*. Both men (but especially Zeffirelli) have keen visual senses, well suited to film. Their operatic productions display this cinematographic quality—again, especially Zeffirelli—which annoys some members of the opera audience but delights most of them. In any case, Zeffirelli has proved his ability to keep stages as large as those of the Metropolitan Opera, Covent Garden, and La Scala in constant motion, filled with colorful details that are visually interesting, true to the period of the opera, and dramatically relevant as well.

Especially successful in America have been his Metropolitan Opera productions of *La Bohème*, *Otello*, *Falstaff*, *Cavalleria Rusticana*, *Pagliacci*, *Don Giovanni*, and *Tosca*—the last of these operas done in sets that replicate the actual locations in Rome. His use of exterior scenes has received special applause because of broad, dramatic skies, a Zeffirelli trademark. Where Wieland Wagner was satisfied with a few gray clouds, Franco Zeffirelli requires a blazing sunset or a star-filled night. Of course, his efforts to bring the dramatic, the exciting, and the spectacular all together on the operatic stage and in a realistic way have been denounced by some as hokum or kitsch; but for the most part his productions are visually impressive and dramatically exciting. A modern audience is well served by Zeffirelli's work.

Walter Felsenstein

Another very provocative, highly original, and often successful approach to directing opera was taken by Walter Felsenstein. Although born in Austria, he quickly came under the influence of the famous Russian director Stanislavsky and many of his theories about opera. Working primarily with the Komische Oper in East Berlin (he was made director of the company in 1947), and using Marxism and Communism as his ideological bases for theater and opera, Walter Felsenstein directed striking productions of operatic classics. Using mainly the Marxist belief in class conflict as a basic element of operatic production, he reexamined many operas in the standard repertory, concentrating always on their political and ideological bases. Felsenstein always insisted on extensive rehearsals and working intensely with each of the solo singers. He said that he never imposed an interpretation of a role, only coordinated the production. He insisted that for an interpretation to be credible for an audience it must come from the personality of the artist singing the role. Felsenstein became especially famous for a very original production of *Carmen* (1949), which emphasized the poverty and downtrodden condition of the characters. His production of *Der Freischütz* (1951) also won wide acclaim for the dramatic intensity of the portrayals of the major roles—whose palpable reality grabbed audiences by the throat.

Felsenstein became known not only for the political and ideological elements in his approach, but also for his significant uses of detail and the direction of the minor characters and chorus. For example, his choruses never lined up in a semicircle, standing around the major characters looking like so many tombstones. Instead, for Felsenstein they were *das Volk*, the common people, who were treated as the most important characters on stage. His use of the chorus emphasized the individuality of its members, each presented as a unique individual rather than a part of the masses. His productions of *Don Giovanni* (1966) and *Fiddler on the Roof* (1971) used crowd scenes as a way of telling us much about how the common people lived during the periods in which these operas were set. Finally, he insisted on a forceful, realistic drama, and that intensity of character interaction was evident in much of his work.

Felsenstein, like Visconti in Italy, sometimes changed the periods in which operas are set—often for political reasons—to emphasize certain ideological and social aspects of the opera, and to make such conflicts seem more relevant, more real, and more contemporary to modern audiences. If opera is to interest contemporary audiences, Felsenstein insisted, it must reflect the concerns and problems of contemporary humanity.

Götz Friedrich

One protégé of Walter Felsenstein's has already achieved his own fame in the West, Götz Friedrich. Born in East Germany, Friedrich came to national attention (if not national notoriety) in West Germany for his iconoclastic production of *Tannhäuser*, at Bayreuth in 1973. Rejecting the traditional view of the opera, he presented the Landgrave and his retainers and minstrels as a group of crypto-fascists, and Elisabeth as the naive woman who becomes the fascists' prize for obedience to their ideals. Jeered and whistled at by the first-night audiences for this production, Götz Friedrich toned down his original version for subsequent performances, which received much better critical responses the following summers from both German and international critics.

Earlier Friedrich had been dismissed as a slanderer; now much of what he presented in the opera was seen as a slight exaggeration of what the composer himself had subtly suggested in the text. Of course, there is something awesome and powerful about the Landgrave, and when Tannhäuser disagrees with the Landgrave's view of love, he and his knights and minstrels threaten to kill him—and would do so except for the protection of Elisabeth. Equally famous was Friedrich's production of the entire *Ring* cycle for London's Royal Opera at Covent Garden. Setting the *Ring* in a science fiction never-never land and using only one basic symbol, a central piston to control a square platform that revolved or tilted for each of the scenes in the vast and complicated tetralogy, Friedrich created an impressive new vision for a work monumentally difficult to stage, with the help of his brilliant stage designer, Josef Svoboda. Friedrich also provided some interesting new insights into the central characters and their relationships. For example, Friedrich presented Loge as a weird isolate who manipulates the gods and Froh as a drag queen with tendencies to hysteria. While some of Friedrich's conceptions of characters may seem bizarre and even contrary to what the composer intended, others work quite well (depending on the singer in the role, of course), providing the viewer with a fresh insight into a great work of operatic art.

Does a director have to do what the composer intended? Götz Friedrich and some other post–World War II directors argue that the director's job is to create an interesting operatic experience for a contemporary audience, and that eighteenth- and nineteenth-century composers could hardly be expected to know the needs and interests of twentieth-century opera-goers—or, for that matter, about the stage effects possible in contemporary theater. Few opera-goers today could endure a nineteenth-century opera produced in the style of the nineteenth century, or so these new directors claim.

Götz Friedrich has been one of the most successful of these new directors, providing interesting productions based on his own theory of operatic staging. That his theory is despised by some modern opera-goers but adored by others is testimony to the continuing vitality of contemporary audiences.

Josef Svoboda

The Czech stage designer Josef Svoboda, while rarely active as a director, has designed sets and lighting for some of the most controversial and impressive productions in Europe and America since World War II. He designed the sets and lighting for the famous Götz Friedrich *Ring* cycle at Covent Garden, which appeared there initially from 1974 to 1976. He used a square wooden platform, like the ingegno wagon used for medieval comedies, with a piston under the platform so it could be raised, lowered, tilted, and revolved; this platform and piston provided settings for the entire four operas of the tetralogy.

What made the use of this platform and piston so engrossing was Svoboda's brilliant variations of the central image—varied primarily through movements and lighting. Using everything from laser beams and mirrors to high-intensity spots, and from white light to bright colors, Svoboda turned this *Ring* production into a brilliant scenographic experience through his creative variations on the central image. In addition, he designed an important *Tristan und Isolde* for Bayreuth with the director August Everding. Using luminous lighting with colored slides, often projected on long cords suspended from the top of the stage, Svoboda created an impressive and tangible texture of light for the production. This technique served to give the light a palpable form and interesting depth. Combined with projections on a rear cyclorama, the effect created a uniquely beautiful world for the obsessive lovers.

With the director John Dexter, Svoboda created two impressive productions for the Metropolitan Opera: Verdi's *I Vespri Siciliani* (1974) and Smetana's *The Bartered Bride* (1978). Svoboda is very fond of using staircases in his productions, and a vast staircase dominated the production of *I Vespri Siciliani*; the staircase became the dominant symbol of the production, and an embodiment of the desire of the Sicilians for liberty and freedom from French rule. The staircase was lit brightly and luminously, especially during the famous massacre scene, and provided an effective background for the action of the opera.

For the Smetana opera, often staged in a kitschy-folksy way, Svoboda used a revolving stage and a cyclorama behind the revolving stage to create striking lighting effects. In his and Dexter's production, the opera became not a cute folk tale but a symbolic confrontation of man and nature, male and female, and sky and earth. Svoboda's use of light, abstract forms, and symbolism characterizes the genius of his work for opera.

Günther Schneider-Siemssen and Otto Schenk

Less radical than some of the directors already mentioned, Günther Schneider-Siemssen became famous as the lighting designer for some of Herbert von Karajan's renowned productions at the Salzburg Festival during the 1960s. What he showed there, especially his interest in subtle and dramatic lighting effects, has remained characteristic of his later work.

Although usually regarded as basically a realist in operatic production, unlike Wieland Wagner or Josef Svoboda, Schneider-Siemssen has often used realism in an unusually abstract and symbolic way, often to create impressive, cinematographic effects on the operatic stage. His *Ring* cycle for Salzburg (and later at the Metropolitan Opera), while offending some critics, still presented its audiences with wonderful moments of dazzling lighting and scenic splendor. With the director Otto Schenk, Schneider-Siemssen designed a very conservative production of *Tannhäuser* for the Met that had been hailed by many critics then as the greatest and most beautiful staging of that opera, largely on the grounds of its scenic realism and dramatic appropriateness. In approach, the production displayed a cyclical view of the opera: The spring scene in Thuringia in Act I looked somewhat autumnal, while the autumn scene in Act III displayed indications of the coming spring. In all, the opera became a series of recurrent cycles, like the cycles of nature itself, and like nature, the scenes became interlocked, just as Tannhäuser is joined to both Venus and Elisabeth. Tannhäuser's conflicts then come to represent the cyclical conflicts of all men between the controlled sexuality of marriage and the uncontrolled sexuality of the bordello.

Clearly influenced by Wieland Wagner, Günther Schneider-Siemssen particularly values projections and the special capacity of lighting to capture the imagination of the audience, as well, of course, as the intensity of powerful music. The designer's *Ring* cycle, done with Herbert von Karajan, emphasizes the vastness of the tetralogy, the dazzling colors of nature, and every possibility of symbolism inherent in the mythology of the work. While avoiding the extreme abstraction of Wieland Wagner, and the extreme realism of so many late nineteenth- and twentieth-century directors of the *Ring*—people like Theodor Pixis, Joseph Hoffmann, Carl Emil Doepler, Paul von Joukovsky, and Heinz Tietjen—Schneider-Siemssen has tried to steer a middle course. He often produces on stage a recognizable reality that is nevertheless abstract, colorful, and full of dramatic symbolism.

In his productions the intrapersonal relationships between characters are often remote from those of real people. His *Ring* characters rarely touch, instead maintaining an almost classic reserve, Nordic in its intensity, yet also Greek in its stately calm. His *Ring* cycle, as a result, emphasize the mythic, classic aspects of the work.

Günther Schneider-Siemssen has often worked in collaboration with Otto Schenk, a well-known Viennese director, on some very successful productions. Schenk has directed a wonderful *Tales of Hoffmann* for the Met, in which Schneider-Siemssen designed the sets and lighting. Both men dictated a realistic approach for this impressive production, and Schenk's direction went further to emphasize the humanity of each character, and especially the despair, grief, and eternal frustration of the poet Hoffmann. Schenk also directed a very realistic *Tosca* for the Met as well as an interesting *Elektra* for the Vienna State Opera; in both these productions a modern realism, often stark in its approach, characterized Schenk's direction.

Günther Rennert

Working primarily at the Bavarian State Opera in Munich and the State Opera in Hamburg and from there getting international recognition, Günther Rennert specialized primarily in the operas of Mozart and Strauss. Though not a designer of sets or costumes, Günther Rennert was nonetheless a great director, and certainly he worked very closely with the persons directly in charge of the visual elements in each of the productions he directed.

Rennert's reputation rests on the critical claim that he brought a new intimacy and humanity into the staging of Mozart's operas. His direction turned the composer's characters into real people, as it were, rather than treating them as eighteenth-century puppets. In fact, with this approach to character, among other things, there was a quiet charm and subtlety about Rennert's direction that made his work especially appropriate for television. Indeed, many of his productions were taped in live performance and later broadcast on television, among the most successful being his Mozart operas. Rennert staged acclaimed productions of *The Marriage of Figaro, Falstaff, Salome, Don Giovanni, The Magic Flute*, and the *Ring* cycle—a remarkable record for anyone in modern operatic theater. Yet Rennert was a traditionalist in that he always reminded his audience that the opera being staged was set in a definite historical period—the one specified by the composer. Overall, Rennert tried to follow the stage directions laid down by the composer while still bringing the opera to meaningful life for contemporary audiences. Our view of Mozart's operas as intimate and delicately human has been due in great measure to his skillful direction of them. At the same time, renewed popular interest in many less well-known operas—for example, Richard Strauss's *Die Schweigsame Frau, Ariadne auf Naxos*, and *Elektra*—may also be credited in part to Rennert's successful early stagings of these works, which he effectively reentered into the opera canon for our time.

Although most of Rennert's work was in Germany, one of his best productions was a famous *Magic Flute* for New York's Metropolitan Opera. The sets and costumes for this production were designed by the renowned Russian artist Marc Chagall. Ravishingly beautiful and marvelously reflecting its fantasy world, the sets and costumes created a colorful fairy-land setting for Mozart's opera. But Rennert ensured that the show did not become a gallery exhibit. His direction of the characters and their dramatic situations focused our attention on the important human elements in Mozart's child-like, fairy-tale opera. Rennert's realistic, focused direction of the characters revealed this opera for the sublime human comedy it is.

Jean-Pierre Ponnelle

This French director established an international reputation in the last twenty years, based mostly on certain striking productions at opera houses in both Europe and America. One of the things that typified Ponnelle's work was a striking visual and dramatic image on stage—a single image that dominated a whole production. For example, in his famous production of Wagner's *Tristan und Isolde* for Bayreuth in 1980, he used a huge tree for all three acts. As that tree dominated the stage, it became the central symbol for the entire production and, functionally, a dramatic image representing the tenacious force of the love of Tristan and Isolde. He also used a tree as the dominant symbol in his lovely production of *Pelléas et Mélisande* in Munich in 1973.

Ponnelle's famous production of *Turandot* for the San Francisco Opera in 1977 was dominated by a huge statue of a female Buddha. The statue recurred in the production as a symbol of Turandot herself and her fanatical chastity; the statue wept tears of blood when Turandot finally submitted to the love and rule of Calaf.

For the Metropolitan Opera in 1975 Ponnelle directed a won-derfully comic production of Rossini's *L'Italiana in Algeri* with a symbolic central courtyard. Here, much comedy derived from a well-directed chorus of eunuchs who trembled whenever their au-tocratic Mustafà entered the courtyard. Ponnelle's direction of both major and minor characters added to the fun of Rossini's comic gem. The central courtyard was a symbol of the public nature of the relationships of the central characters.

In another vein, Ponnelle directed a series of original productions of opera serias dating from the seventeenth and eighteenth centuries. This form of opera is usually dismissed as a dated bore by most audiences, but for the Salzburg Festival, the Bavarian State Opera, and the Metropolitan Opera, Ponnelle created striking productions of some of these operas, and these productions have been very popular with sophisticated audiences. His stagings of Mozart's *Idomeneo* (New York, 1982) and *La Clemenza di Tito* (New York, 1984) have especially succeeded. Rather than trying to make such an artificial form of opera seem modern and realistic, Ponnelle used instead a very Baroque approach to these works. Sets and costume designs reminded the audience that the operas presented a Baroque view of Greek and Roman history, rather than stage realism. By emphasizing the artificiality of the form, Ponnelle generated new interest in opera seria, and he encouraged audiences and critics alike to reevaluate past judgments that had condemned the form as static and uninteresting. Ponnelle's fondness for the dominant central image showed up in these stagings as well. One especially striking image was the huge head of Neptune seen in his *Idomeneo* productions—conveying a Baroque view of the powerful Greek god who controls the lives and actions of the characters on stage.

Another way Ponnelle created new audiences for opera was through his work in film and television. For television he directed a marvelous videotape of Puccini's *Madama Butterfly* that starred Plácido Domingo and Mirella Freni. These two singers were well directed by Ponnelle, and the result impressed many skeptics who had doubted the viability of opera for television. Ponnelle did not tape the opera as a stage work; instead, he made it as a realistic film and used some interesting photographic techniques to dramatize the heroine's situation. Another production taped for television was his Salzburg Festival staging of Mozart's *The Magic Flute*, in which he made an amphitheater function as the central symbol; this, however, was definitely the taping of a theater piece. The Baroque quality of the sets, costumes, and properties, and the action on the central graveled stage, all helped to dramatize many of the conflicts in the opera: good versus evil, light versus dark, male versus female, and noble versus common. A major force in the contemporary period, Ponnelle directed opera successfully around the world.

Patrice Chéreau

Yet another Frenchman has reached the top tier of operatic directors in recent years. Patrice Chéreau began in theater rather than opera, although his first notable success was in French opera in an impressive production of *The Tales of Hoffmann* for the Paris Opéra. The outstanding element in that production was Chéreau's use of exterior architectural settings for most of the scenes in the opera; the effect seemed rather like the Baroque theater's obsessive interest in architecture to provide the dramatic setting for opera.

Chéreau gained more international attention when he was selected to design the centennial *Ring* production at Bayreuth in 1976. Earlier Bayreuth audiences had grown used to the elegant, shadowy, and highly symbolic *Ring* productions of Wolfgang Wagner, but instead of following this lead Chéreau along with his set designer Richard Peduzzi designed a highly realistic, architectural, and brightly lit *Ring*—a departure greeted with boos and bad press notices when it premiered in 1976. In the summer of 1977, however, the Chéreau/Peduzzi production rated a better press, especially when it was filmed for television. Finally, in this form it reached a worldwide audience who celebrated its merits. Almost as important, the whole *Ring* cycle suddenly became available on local television, and of course some viewers taped the Chéreau *Ring* cycle for their private videotape collections.

A closer look at the productions shows that Chéreau's *Ring* boldly mixes periods and styles: Sometimes we are placed in a vaguely prehistorical Germany; at other times we find ourselves in the Germany of the nineteenth century, at the time Wagner wrote his *Ring*; at other times we are in contemporary, modern Germany. Again, while some characters wear loincloths, others are costumed in modern tuxedos or nineteenth-century gowns and business suits. Incongruities are everywhere, yet the mixture is saved from being ludicrous by the intense drama and interaction between characters. For example, Chéreau makes the attraction between Siegmund and Sieglinde during the first act of *Die Walküre* electric and sensual. Mime, who has generally been presented as a grotesque dwarf, is brilliantly portrayed as a shrewd peddler, while Alberich fascinates us with his wheeling and dealing, as does his relative, Loge. This is purposeful eclecticism and outstanding video opera. As a master of the form, Chéreau does a brilliant job of directing the singers so that each major character seems amazingly real as a person, instead of remaining merely historical, a noble but distant creature of mythology.

When Chéreau directed, Wotan was not presented as an exalted god, but rather as a wealthy yet tired old man, a Victorian businessman in appearance. Wotan and Alberich thus become very similar, almost like business colleagues chasing the same juicy contract. They did not relate to each other as god and dwarf. Again, the intense love of Brünnhilde and Siegfried was portrayed as an adolescent boy's first sexual encounter—just what Richard Wagner originally intended. Yet Chéreau has dramatized many important political ideas in this *Ring* as well: a rejection of nobility and heroism, the search for reactions from the common man, the modern feeling that the *Ring* remains an unfinished work, and that we the audience must find our own meaning to complete it. Even with all this, for Chéreau the *Ring* was treated as a product of its time, nineteenth-century Germany during the period of German industrialism, laissez-faire capitalism, and imperialism. By using an anti-heroic, anti-abstract, and strongly political and realistic approach, Chéreau builds fascinating moments into the *Ring*. As a result, its influence (as well as his own) has become simply immense, largely because of the power of television. Still, the originality and perceptiveness of Chéreau's approach to opera must not be overlooked, for they have singled him out as one of the great new French opera directors, a master of his own age.

August Everding

As a director, Everding has specialized in the German repertory, primarily Wagner and Strauss, and within that repertory he has created some impressive and innovative productions. Like Wieland Wagner, Everding requires a complex lighting structure as a fundamental element of opera production, and he uses lighting and color symbolically. His famous production of *Tristan und Isolde* for the Metropolitan Opera was dominated by the grand sails of Tristan's ship throughout the first act, the spectacular, celestial lighting effects representing the starry night in Act II, and the burning light of noon in Act III, ending with another starry night for Isolde's "Liebestod."

But unlike Wieland Wagner, Everding remains at heart a realist who uses lighting, symbolism, and set design within the theater to present a real ship, a real castle, and a real (although abstract) fort for Tristan in the last act. Everding wants lighting and sets to create new and impressive realities for opera, but he also wants those realities to be seen as parts of a unified vision of the opera so that the audience will not merely gape at the technical achievements possible on the modern stage. Instead, he wants the audience to understand that even spectacular lighting and staging effects remain for him thematic: They are present to reflect and underscore the human drama of the opera on stage. Everding's achievement is that he can cleverly tie the grandest spectacle that the stage can produce, at least in his capable hands, to the dramatic conflicts and thematic suggestions of a particular opera. Such an artistic unity characterizes his most successful productions.

Scenic flexibility plays its part in his work in the theater as well, for Everding refuses to repeat the old familiar scenic formulas. For example, when he directed two very different *Lohengrin* productions for two distant theaters, Everding refused to repeat his ideas. For the Bavarian State Opera in Munich, he designed a lovely, Romantic, fairy-tale *Lohengrin*, which placed the opera scenically in the Romantic décor of the nineteenth century. For the Metropolitan Opera, on the other hand, he designed (along with Ming Cho Lee) another *Lohengrin* that challenged the first. Brutal and stark, it was a candid reflection of the early medieval period in which the opera is set. While both productions seemed basically realistic in that stage properties and backgrounds looked real rather than purely abstract, and certainly both were effective, the two productions were very different in their operative conceptions of a single complex work. By keeping possibilities open, Everding gave evidence of his artistic flexibility, as well as of an intense sense of theater, color, and lighting. His rich mixture of skills and perceptions has generated overall widely divergent but still valid and always effective productions of familiar operatic classics in the German repertory.

Sarah Caldwell

A student of Walter Felsenstein's, Sarah Caldwell began directing opera by starting her own company in Boston, a town then without an opera company. During the 1960s and 1970s she made her company an innovative new voice in opera that had to its credit an impressive number of firsts. In 1968 her production of Berg's *Lulu* was the first use of film on the operatic stage in America, a technique she also employed in an outstanding production in 1970 of Kurka's *The Good Soldier Schweik*. Her interest in the political and class conflict aspects of opera was evident in her 1965 production of Luigi Nono's *Intolleranza*, an American premiere that also was the first opera to use television images projected on the operatic stage.

In addition to *Intolleranza*, Caldwell staged the first productions in America of the following operas: Prokofiev's *War and Peace*, Roger Sessions's *Montezuma*, Michael Tippett's *The Ice Break*, and Glinka's *Russlan and Ludmilla*. This impressive track record of premieres is matched with creative, imaginative productions of opera classics as well. Her 1983 staging of Bellini's *Norma* presented the opera as the embodiment of the spirit of Italy's *Risorgimento*. The Druids under Roman rule in the opera became in her production the Italians under Austrian rule, plotting for freedom and political self-rule. Caldwell's interest in a political approach to opera has generated productions of both the opera classics and unusual works that have often succeeded through her imaginative stagings—and usually with very low budgets.

Outside Boston, Caldwell has directed a clever production of Strauss's *Ariadne auf Naxos* for the New York City Opera. Emphasizing the Baroque theatrical aspects of the work, the backstage set for the opera's prelude revolves to reveal the front of a lovely Baroque stage for the opera itself. Caldwell's direction of the characters and her clever use of sight gags for the commedia dell'arte troupe in the opera resulted in a lovely and witty production. Caldwell has remained one of America's most creative operatic directors who has succeeded in giving American premieres of important new works as well as original stagings of opera's standard repertory.

Frank Corsaro

The American opera director Frank Corsaro, working primarily with the New York City Opera and other American opera companies, has generated great excitement among critics and audiences alike, based on his impressive productions of both the operatic classics and some unusual repertory. His association with the New York City Opera has been especially successful; they have together managed to create notable operatic theater, as in a production of *La Traviata* with Patricia Brooks in the title role. Under Corsaro's direction, the City Opera's *La Traviata* became a towering achievement, because it provided a perfect mechanism for displaying

Brooks's genius as an acting singer; at the same time, the production showed its audience a whole range of new possibilities for development in opera. By himself, Corsaro has displayed a special talent for being able to work within the small budgets available at most regional companies, while using these modest financial resources so wisely that they underwrite artistically successful results.

As a signal demonstration of his talent, Corsaro distinguished himself with an innovative production of Bizet's *Carmen* (1983), first for the Philadelphia Opera and later moving it to the New York City Opera in 1984. His setting the opera in the Spain of the Spanish Civil War (1936–1939) made Carmen into a La Pasionaria figure, part gypsy but also an emotional defender of the Loyalist cause, firmly placed in political opposition to Francisco Franco and the Fascists. Thus, Carmen's call for "la liberté" becomes the political cry of a united people determined to fight Fascism. Although it may seem somewhat difficult to adjust to the 1930s settings and costumes for this staging, the opera audience came to see *Carmen* in a new light, and to understand the central character in a larger, more defensible way, as a result of the political subtext of the opera created by Corsaro's staging.

With less familiar operas, Corsaro has also been notably successful. He has directed several of Leoš Janáček's operas for the New York City Opera, and these have made audiences aware of twentieth-century additions to operatic literature that had lacked sufficient recognition. As an example, *The Makropoulos Affair* was built around slides and projections designed to remind the audience of the constantly shifting time sequences in the life of the fascinating central character, Emilia Marty. Corsaro directed *The Cunning Little Vixen* around the wonderful sets of Maurice Sendak, and the result displayed the power of a fairy-tale opera that connects the forces of nature with common human experience. Corsaro and Sendak also produced a wonderfully comic and clever production of Prokofiev's *The Love for Three Oranges* for both the Glyndebourne Festival and the New York City Opera. Usually working with tiny budgets and in small theaters, Frank Corsaro has defined rich possibilities for current opera production, just as he has suggested new directions for the responses of sensitive modern audiences.

Other New Voices

In addition to these major figures, by the 1980s opera had begun to distinguish an even newer group of talented opera directors, many of whom have already created successful productions for contemporary audiences. Among them are: Peter Hall in London, Peter Brook in Paris and New York, Elijah Moshinsky in London, Andrei Serban in New York and Munich, Harry Kupfer in Germany and England, Giorgio Strehler in Italy, Ulrich Melchinger in Kassel and Berlin, and Tito Capobianco in New York and California. These directors have shown striking ability, mostly in impressive productions that display distinctive new visions. From this group will come the internationally celebrated opera directors of the future. For the sophisticated opera audience, part of the fun comes from watching new talents grow and mature. For the modern designer, the challenge is to create visually and dramatically exciting new productions which also work well acoustically—i.e., the operatic set should be designed to help the singer's voice project to the audience.

CONCLUSION

There was a time when going to the opera usually involved looking at ridiculous productions, populated primarily by very fat people who surely could not act. In our own time, much has changed, and now productions have become much more intelligent and engrossing. An enlarged concern for artistry, informed production values, and the obvious popular success of some contemporary opera have all worked together to make the theatrical component as interesting as the musical component in opera has always been. Here, staging and especially direction have made an important difference. So whether based on the traditional approaches of a Zeffirelli, Schneider-Siemssen, or Ponnelle, or the more radical vision and techniques of a Chéreau, Svoboda, or Götz Friedrich, opera now manages to do far more to fascinate. It is a stage spectacle and a theatrical event as well as a musical offering. Modern audiences stand to gain much, for, if golden ages exist at all, the Golden Age of opera production must be the present. The age of the director is now.

Six

How the Conductor Controls What We Hear

There is one factor of vital importance in conducting—to achieve the most complete and eloquent expression of the inner spirit of the music and all the potentialities lying dormant on the printed page of the score. These dormant potentialities are like seeds which sometimes lie for years in the soil until the right combination of sun and water, the right minerals and fertilizing elements within the soil, awaken the life in the seed so that stems and leaves and flowers and fruits unfold themselves. A conductor should fully express all the potentialities of the music he is conducting. Often there is much more in the music than is expressed by a performance that is technically perfect, but mechanical and unimaginative.

—Leopold Stokowski

Never underestimate the power of a conductor in an opera house. Most people go to a performance to see a particular opera or hear a particular singer, and the conductor seems like such a humble fellow down there in the pit—one barely notices him. But it would be a mistake to underestimate the conductor's importance or his responsibility for the whole performance.

THE RESPONSIBILITIES OF THE CONDUCTOR

One of the main duties of the conductor is to ensure that the opera is being performed correctly, which means ensuring that all the notes are played accurately. The conductor must have a good enough ear so that he or she knows when the violins are going flat or the horns are cracking. The conductor must see that the notes are played as written in the score, which means often correcting players during rehearsal and hoping they hit the right notes during performance. For this responsibility the conductor really should have perfect pitch. The conductor's responsibility also extends to the singers, some of whom are notorious for singing inaccurately. Some conductors will insist that only the notes written in the score be sung, though others are more flexible. There are certain traditional notes, generally optional high notes, which singers use or omit depending on whether they can hit the note comfortably. Audiences love these sustained high notes. But, sustaining such a note, called a *fermata*, when the composer indicates it in a score, has to be done with taste if it is going to be done at all. Here, too, the conductor must ensure that the singer, if he or she uses some optional embellishments—for the Baroque and bel canto operas— does not distort the composer's intentions.

Holding the musical elements together also demands much of the conductor. Keeping the whole show on the same beat is very difficult, especially for some particularly complex operas. Think of the first act of Berlioz's *Les Troyens*, for example, where the conductor must hold together a very large orchestra, a large chorus, five soloists, and even cue the ballet in.

The conductor, in most opera performances, controls much of what the audience hears because he or she is also responsible for tempo, balance, and possible interpolations. It is the conductor who takes overall control of the performance, who shapes and interprets it. A good conductor can make a mediocre opera sound interesting, while a mediocre conductor can make a great opera sound boring. A Wagnerian performance can seem interminable if it is not conducted properly. Also, the conductor can form the opera into a unified whole that works, or create an imbalance and a series of fragments out of the score. Some conductors are notorious for drowning singers out. The orchestra sounds wonderful and there is a lot of excitement coming from the pit, but the singers have to yell to be heard, and only the biggest voices can penetrate the dense orchestral sound.

Then there is the opera conductor who merely accompanies the singers and keeps things moving along in a pedestrian way. Because the singers remain the primary focus, the orchestral sound never impresses.

In addition to finding a successful balance between singers and orchestra, a conductor has to find the musical balance for the entire opera. The conductor not only decides when to begin and how to begin, but also how to balance the orchestral sound by listening and adjusting volume levels when several instruments are playing at the same time. The same passage from *Aïda* can sound gorgeous or brassy, depending on who conducts. The conductor also controls dynamics, or volume levels. The composer indicates the dynamics in the score, but it is the conductor who interprets them, and the dynamics will also sound different depending on the acoustics in the particular opera house where the work is being performed. What does a Puccini *piano* sound like, and is it similar to a Wagnerian *piano*? The conductor has to decide how soft is *piano* and how loud is *fortissimo*, and know enough about the acoustics of the theater he is working in so these dynamic levels reach the audience as he and, one hopes, the composer intend.

The conductor decides on rhythm and timing for the work being performed. The same passage from *The Tales of Hoffmann* can sound bouncy or langorous, depending on how it is conducted. The "Triumphal March" in *Aïda* can sound either ponderous or peppy, depending on how the conductor controls the rhythm.

Even more important, the conductor controls the overall musical interpretation of the work. This interpretation is something all the participants should agree with or at least be able to live with. If the conductor of *Don Giovanni* sees the opera as essentially a tragedy, but everyone on stage is playing it as essentially a comedy, a disorganized mess will result. The conductor must not only have an interpretation of the work, but he must impose that interpretation on the singers, or at least convince them that it is the right interpretation for this performance.

A poorly executed interpretation can destroy much of the work of the greatest singers. If the bouncy, brilliant score of Rossini's *The Barber of Seville* is conducted by someone who approaches it with all the solemnity and ponderousness of *Tristan und Isolde*, the greatest singers in the world cannot add much sparkle to the evening. If the conductor thinks Beethoven's *Fidelio* is just a light comedy, what are the singers to do with the more dramatic and philosophical sections of the opera? Many a singer has complained of a ruined performance because of an inept conductor, and conductors have been just as quick to blame singers for ruining their sublime interpretation of a particular score.

In reaching his interpretation, however, the conductor must breathe life and excitement into a performance. It is not enough that the score is followed and the performance is accurate; the performance should also be exciting and interesting. Academic conductors are sticklers for following the score, and the resultant performance becomes an accurate, balanced, faithful rendition of the score—a rendition which is also boring and predictable. A great conductor makes an evening in the opera house exciting, interesting, a revelation of the score, a revelation of the opera being performed—in short, a musical and theatrical Event. If the conductor can marshal his players and his power and imagination, the result will be an artistic success, a great operatic performance, what the composer had envisioned. Balancing accuracy with inspiration, the conductor's responsibility is similar to a military general's; in the case of a defeat he gets most of the blame, but in victory the singers will claim the major credit.

Another of the interpretive responsibilities of the conductor is being realistic about what an orchestra and particular group of soloists can do. The conductor must compromise his ideals for a performance with an honest assessment of the forces at his disposal. I remember one Wagnerian performance where the conductor wanted a quiet, subdued orchestral sound that would be restrained, beautiful, and not drown out the singers, some of whom had rather small voices for Wagnerian singing. Such an approach is valid, but it depends upon controlled playing from an orchestra; alas, this particular orchestra could not play well when it was reined in. The horns cracked and the woodwinds went flat because it is much more difficult for an orchestra to play accurately when it has to play quietly. The easiest thing for most orchestras to do is play *mezzo forte*—or rather loudly—in other words, to just blare out the music. This particular conductor, who was mercilessly booed for the performance, would have been wiser either to demand more rehearsal time or compromise his interpretation with what he could realistically hope to achieve given the quality of the orchestra with which he had to deal. When the trumpets crack and the cellos go flat, it is the conductor who is booed rather than the culprits who hit those wrong notes.

THE PROBLEM OF WHICH SCORE TO USE

The conductor also has the responsibility of deciding which score to use for a particular performance since some operas have several possible versions. If the house administration has decided to stage Bizet's *Carmen*, which *Carmen*? Originally, the opera was an opéra comique, which meant it had spoken dialogue with musical numbers. After Bizet's death, the composer Ernest Guiraud used other works of Bizet to put the spoken text of *Carmen* to music as well. So, is the original opéra comique version or the Guiraud version with musical dialogue to be used? After consulting with the house management and the cast, the conductor must decide. Another problematic opera for variations of scores possible remains Moussorgsky's *Boris Godunov*. Traditionally, the opera has been performed in Rimsky-Korsakov's orchestration, he being a dazzling orchestrator and Moussorgsky traditionally considered not very good as an orchestrator. But, more recently, musicologists have produced an edited version of Moussorgsky's original orchestration, which they argue is much better than the Rimsky-Korsakov version. So which score is to be used? The conductor must decide.

Within a score, some sections or arias have traditionally been cut, such as the elder Germont's cabaletta in the second act of *La Traviata*. Wagnerian scores have often been cut as well because of their Wagnerian lengths. The conductor has to decide whether to perform the score completely as written or with the traditional cuts, some of which have been approved by the composers.

VARIETIES OF POSSIBLE INTERPRETATIONS: WAGNER

Conductors can use a variety of approaches for the more complex operas, and the result can make one wonder if the same score was used. How accurate are opera scores, after all? Going from score to performance demands re-creation and interpretation, and here the conductor must make a work come alive; several interpretations are sometimes possible. The same score can sound very different in the hands of two different conductors, and both interpretations can be equally valid and equally successful. This is especially true of Wagner's operas, where the orchestra is most important and the works are especially long. With the large, Wagnerian orchestra, the conductor carries a heavy burden.

For example, there are three famous recordings of Wagner's *Ring* cycle—Georg Solti's, Herbert von Karajan's, and Wilhelm Furt-wängler's—and these three different interpretations can be compared and contrasted. Solti's is certainly the most direct, dramatic, and exciting of the three because of his lively tempos, his dynamic control of the orchestra, and his sure sense of the dramatic excitement of the work. One feels that Solti makes the most of each of the dramatic scenes in the work: the Rhinemaidens' loss of their gold, the love of Siegmund and Sieglinde, the conflicts between Wotan and Bruünnhilde, Siegfried's forging of his sword to fight Fafner, the love music of Siegfried and Brünnhilde, the death of Siegfried, and the immolation scene. But the orchestra is so forceful that sometimes it drowns out the singers, who often have to battle with that driving orchestral sound and intense conducting.

Herbert von Karajan uses a very different approach, so that the orchestra itself often sounds like a chamber group. His is a quiet, underplayed, lovely-sounding approach, which makes Wagner's music seem lyrical and free of all bombast. The singers can always be easily heard, and they don't sing *forte* very often. Quiet, beautiful, and subtle phrasing and singing characterize Karajan's recording of the *Ring*. The tempos also tend to be slower than Solti's, and the singers clearly get more attention from this conductor. His is a more relaxed, subtle, and less frantic approach to the *Ring*, but on the other hand much of the drama and excitement of the work are lost under Karajan's baton.

Finally, Furtwängler's *Ring* has a subjectivity about it, a sense of the conductor's brooding consciousness over the whole work. Also, the tempos tend to be slow and there is a greater variability of beat. When Furtwängler conducts Siegfried's funeral music, for example, one feels that Siegfried's death had a profoundly sad effect on mankind; when Solti conducts the same music, however, one feels the horror of the dramatic event. While Solti's approach seems objective, Furtwängler's feels and sounds much more personal, less driven by the score and the drama on stage, more driven by the emotional responses of the conductor. Furtwängler's very subjectivity, however, creates a brooding, philosophical dimension that adds intensity to the whole tetralogy.

So which is the correct version? Which is the recording to buy? Well, it's difficult to say because much depends on your theory of what a conductor should do with a score. Some scores can only be conducted well or badly, but the greatest scores, such as Wagner's *Ring* cycle, can be conducted with several different interpretations, all of which seem valid. The greatest music can support different interpretations, and here the conductor's power is most important because he must have an overall approach and make that interpretation an exciting artistic experience for the audience.

VARIETIES OF POSSIBLE INTERPRETATIONS: VERDI AND PUCCINI

Variations in interpretations are also apparent when you listen to Solti's recording of Verdi's *Don Carlo* and then listen to Carlo Maria Giulini's. Both are fine recordings, but Solti's has a dramatic intensity and excitement that result from his forceful orchestral direction and generally dramatic and intense tempos. Giulini's recording is not as dramatic but is more beautifully sung and played. He lets the melodies breathe, and their rhythms are not as driven. He gives his singers more leeway so that they can vary the notes and phrases to create a more lovely and subtle vocal interpretation. Singers must enjoy being conducted by Giulini, because he keeps the orchestra quiet, and as a result they can sing more quietly and subtly. Some of the dramatic excitement of Verdi's opera, however, is, to a degree, lost with Giulini. This variation in interpretation is a product of one of the oldest conflicts in opera: Is it theater or is it music? Of course it is both, but either the musical or the theatrical aspect of an opera can be emphasized, given the approach of a particular conductor, and if the sound is lovely to hear, then maybe some of the theater may be lost—though certainly not always.

There are two famous recordings of Puccini's *Tosca* that also indicate the tremendous variations possible with the same operatic score. Georges Prêtre's recording with Maria Callas and Tito Gobbi is great theater with some very inaccurate and ugly singing, while Herbert von Karajan's recording with Katia Ricciarelli and Ruggero Raimondi has the more beautiful sound and the quieter, more accurate and controlled singing. In Karajan's recording the orchestral sound is absolutely a revelation because the orchestration sounds so interesting and subtle; one hears music in the score one had never heard before. But much of the theater of the opera and most of its dramatic intensity are lost when contrasted with the blazing conflict of Maria Callas and Tito Gobbi under Prêtre's direction.

The musical approach also indicates overall interpretation. A great conductor does not move from one aria to another; instead, he or she conducts the opera as an organic whole and unifies the sound of the score so that the totality of the piece comes through. The conductor should not just beat time and wait for the prima donna's cue to begin an aria. He must control the overall sound and flow of the music, all within an exciting and valid interpretation. Musically, the opera must mean something, must add up to something, must have a point of view—something possible in all the greatest operatic scores—and only a conductor can do all this. The end of the entire *Ring* cycle should be shattering and exalting, the end of *Don Carlo* must be tragic and enlightening, the end of *Tosca* should be ironic and grotesque, all of which is possible with a great conductor in control of the performance.

THE CONDUCTOR, INTERPRETATION, AND CAST

The conductor must have an interpretation for the scene, for the act, for the character, and for the opera as a whole. And that interpretation must govern his approach to the score, but of course he has to work with singers, and singers are the bane of many a conductor's career. To illustrate, a conductor might be conducting Mozart's *Così Fan Tutte* and have a definite interpretation of Dorabella: He sees her as a lazy, sensuous woman and wants her part to be sung slowly and languorously. But the soprano singing the role may see the character as essentially passive, comic, and not too bright, and want faster tempos for Dorabella's arias. Well, in this case, conflicts between conductor and soprano are going to occur. If the conductor is a real autocrat and insists on his approach to the character (part of his overall approach to the opera because he sees the two sisters, Fiordiligi and Dorabella, as conflicting halves of woman in general), and if during rehearsals those slow tempos and that languorous tone he wants for Dorabella begin to sound awful because the soprano cannot sustain those notes without singing flat or wobbling, conflicts will intensify. The singer may want the livelier approach in part because it is easier for her to sing. Also, her view of the character may make it easier for her to act on stage, while it is very difficult for her to produce the conductor's vision of the ideal Dorabella. Clearly, this performance will be a confused failure unless compromises are worked out. The conductor must work with the singers and production at his disposal rather than insisting on his own interpretation and vision of the opera. Opera, after all, remains a performing art and a joint venture of many artists.

THE CONDUCTOR AND STYLE

Another prime duty of the conductor involves an awareness of a composer's style. Mozart's musical style involves a lovely tone, an avoidance of extremes in volume, and some embellishments correctly made in his style. Verdi's early style demands rousing rhythms and an immediate dramatic intensity, whereas his late style includes subtlety of rhythm and a more complex dramatic intensity. Puccini's style includes a lovely tone for the soprano and tenor and some crescendo effects, especially at the end of arias.

A competent conductor has to be part musicologist, that is, aware of the characteristics of the various operatic styles. The further back the style goes, the more of a historical awareness the conductor must possess, since older scores generally have fewer directions in them.

Handelian style is certainly different from Mozartian, and contemporary opera conductors should be able to handle both composers. Often these stylistic elements are not written into the score since the composer may have assumed that conductors and singers would know the basic elements of his style. Also, musical style changes with the age. Our grandfathers were used to hearing much more portamento and legato in their operatic performances, while current audiences generally prefer a more direct and unambiguous approach.

So, too, there are various styles of singing that should be under the conductor's control. Soprano A, for example, may be very proud of her ability to sing *piano* and *pianissimo*, and want to sing softly so often that this becomes an affectation that conflicts with the composer's directions in the score. Or Tenor B may be famous for his loud, sustained high notes and want to sing everything loudly and interpolate high notes that are not in the score. His sustaining these high notes, while bringing him much audience approval, will disfigure the shape of the music. The conductor must control these variations of voice style so that a uniform, consistent style of singing and instrumental playing unifies the performance. A weak conductor will fail to produce a real ensemble, will fail to unify the singing and playing styles of a particular performance.

Opera composers have been very aware of this difficulty and have often written a role for a particular voice. Mozart, for example, had to work with a soprano who had an impressive top voice and an impressive lower voice but not much of a middle range while he was composing *Così Fan Tutte*, so he wrote the music accordingly. "Come scoglio," Fiordiligi's big aria in the first act of that opera, is written for a soprano with an impressive top voice and bottom voice but not much in between. Verdi purposely wrote the part of Lady Macbeth for a soprano with an ugly voice, and he wanted the part sung by an ugly voice since he felt this sound was appropriate for Lady Macbeth's evil character.

Musical style, then, is something the great operatic composers were very aware of, both as it pertained to a particular era and a particular singer. Contemporary conductors must be equally aware of operatic style so they can create a musical and vocal style appropriate to the opera being staged and the singers available for the roles.

A Brief History of the Conductor in Opera

Someone, of course, has to beat the time in music, and in that sense there has always been a conductor in the opera house, but until comparatively recently, conductors did not have much power. The idea that the conductor was an important person in opera production reached Europe and America only about 150 years ago with Wagner's insistence on the importance and even primacy of the conductor. Before then, the conductor was taken for granted, and the soprano or castrato or other major singer demanded and got much more attention and much higher fees. The conductor was viewed rather as an accompanist, the quiet fellow who followed the singers and listened to their demands about tempo and volume for their particular performance.

According to *The New Grove Dictionary of Music and Musicians*, beating time is as old as music itself and has been done in various ways. In ancient Greece stamping the right foot on the ground at the beat held the performance together. Medieval musicians sometimes clapped hands as a way of keeping the time. And in the Paris Opéra until the eighteenth century the conductor beat the time for the operatic performances with an audible thud of a stick on the ground. In Germany until the end of the seventeenth century stamping on the ground was a way of keeping musical time in many churches.

But somehow musicians in the later Middle Ages and in the Renaissance developed inaudible indications of rhythm and time in music, primarily through hand gestures. Some Italian manuscript illuminations and paintings of the sixteenth century indicate the first recognizable conductor in Western music, generally using his hands to indicate the beat for a church performance. During this period short sticks in addition to hands were used to keep a choir together, especially in some of the more harmonically complex pieces of the period. The complexities of polyphonic music necessitated a regulated beat, and so a conductor was necessary to keep the performance from falling apart.

In the seventeenth century some writers on musical subjects insisted that the tempo should not always be strictly in time; for purposes of elucidating the text, the tempo should fluctuate for greater emphasis or clearer meaning. And so the performance of madrigals in Italy during this period, often with texts of beautiful poetry, demanded that a conductor know the text well enough to vary the rhythm so that the meaning of the words was either clarified or dramatized. Thus the first conductors in the Renaissance were those madrigal conductors who had to know both music and text to make the madrigal performances successful. By the end of the seventeenth century, of course, Europe had rediscovered operatic performances through the efforts of the Camerata Group in Florence.

Also in the seventeenth century, opera became popular in Paris, especially at the court of Louis XIV, where Jean-Baptiste Lully was both court composer and court conductor. He conducted with a large wooden staff that he pounded on the floor to create an audible beat. Such pounding, according to his biographers, was in fact responsible for Lully's early death because at one performance he hit his own foot instead of the floor and the wound became gangrenous. Perhaps because of this gruesome incident, in addition to the distracting sound of pounding during a performance, conductors began to look for more subtle ways of keeping control of their orchestral and vocal forces.

When Gluck performed his own *Il Trionfo di Clelia* in Bologna in 1763, he conducted from the harpsichord with his hands, a practice generally followed by Mozart as well. This method also allowed the composer to play the recitativo secco on the harpsichord between the arias and other musical numbers. By the end of the eighteenth century, the conducting in opera could come from three possible sources: (1) the keyboard; (2) the principal violinist, or concertmaster, who often used his bow to conduct; or (3) a standing conductor who used a violin bow, a staff, a rolled piece of paper, his hands, or sometimes even a baton.

The development of the modern conductor began with the insistence of several composers on the primary importance of the conductor for operatic performances. Before then, as was mentioned earlier, conductors were considered less important than the starring singer. The one exception to this in the eighteenth century was the composer, who was normally responsible for conducting the first few performances of any new work. Thus, when Mozart was commissioned to write an opera, the contract also stipulated that he rehearse the company and conduct the first performances. But, in the nineteenth century, as recitativo secco and harpsichord were replaced by full orchestra playing throughout the opera, the conductor, as we know him, came into being.

The modern conception of the conductor, as distinct from the composer/conductor, gradually became a reality. This was partially the result of the increasing complexity of operatic scores of the time, especially in Paris, where French grand opera developed. That style called for a huge orchestra, a large chorus, a large group of soloists, and a ballet. A real maestro was needed to control all the musical troops demanded in the score. Operas by Auber, Meyerbeer, Spohr, and Spontini in the early part of the nineteenth century demanded these large musical forces.

Also, Romantic music tended to avoid a regular beat and, as a result, a more subtle and professional conductor was necessary to modulate the beats and to interpret the drama on stage. Interpretation became much more important as Romantic opera developed and scores became more complex rhythmically, harmonically, and melodically. Spontini became famous for the effective conducting of his own and other composers' operas in Berlin early in the nineteenth century, as did Weber in Dresden during the same time, and these composers were also very rigorous conductors who demanded extensive rehearsal time and, as a result, produced impressive performances. In Italy, Verdi insisted on the importance of the conductor, wanting his friend Angelo Mariani to conduct the premieres and subsequent performances of his operas.

But it was Wagner in Germany and Berlioz in France who established the modern role of the conductor. Wagner especially insisted that the conductor must be responsible for overall interpretation of the opera being performed; the conductor, Wagner asserted in a series of important essays on the subject, must not just brainlessly beat the time and keep the operatic ensemble together. Wagner argued that operatic music must sing, and the conductor must find the melody—or *melos*, as he called it—in the score. As a result, the rhythm and beat indicated in the score were only vague guidelines; the conductor must have a profound understanding, almost a spiritual rapport, with the opera being performed and so understand the inner melos, and make that melos apparent for the audience.

Berlioz in France during the same period also developed some of the practices of the modern opera composer. He also deplored audible time beating, but he followed the score more rigidly than Wagner. He also insisted on many rehearsals for his performances and rehearsed singers and chorus separately from the orchestra. At his orchestral rehearsals he demanded precision and clarity. He especially sought clear diction and a dramatic interpretation of the lyrics from his singers. Something that Berlioz did which would strike most opera-goers as very strange now was his insistence that the conductor have his back to his orchestra in the theater and conduct from the edge of the stage in front of the singers so he could control and direct them more easily. Though this was common practice in France and Vienna at the time, by the twentieth century this was abandoned in favor of placing the conductor in front of all his musical forces, as Wagner had recommended.

In the twentieth century the composer Gustav Mahler was in charge of the Vienna Opera from 1897 to 1907 and his conducting there made him world famous. The rigor yet the beauty of his performances, especially of Mozart and Wagner, continued the Wagnerian tradition of flexible conducting. Richard Strauss also conducted many operas at Vienna, Dresden, Munich, and Bayreuth, and he became renowned as a conductor of his own scores and of Mozart's. More recently, two very dynamic though radically different approaches to operatic conducting were practiced by Wilhelm Furtwängler (1886–1954) and Arturo Toscanini (1867–1957). The German followed the Wagnerian approach, with irregularity of beat, great subjectivity, and a philosophical and lyrical approach to the music, while the Italian insisted on following the score as objectively as possible to produce great clarity, dramatic intensity, and musical objectivity in his performances.

TECHNIQUES OF THE MODERN CONDUCTOR

The modern operatic conductor has a variety of jobs in an opera house and controls what we hear in several important ways. First, it is at rehearsals that the conductor has the greatest effect on the performance, for it is here that he shapes the musicians into an organized whole and can control their performances and thereby create an organic interpretation that will both please the audience and be true to the work.

There are several kinds of rehearsals, and the conductor should be effective in all of them. First are the rehearsals with the soloists at the piano, and here the conductor needs to know how the singing voice works and how it can be helped. If a singer has a vocal or intonation problem, the conductor should be able to offer practical advice. A great conductor should help singers to sing their role more expressively and more beautifully. Is the singer following the score accurately? The conductor should be able to correct and shape the singer's performance so that the final result will be more accurately what the composer wanted, as well as we can know this.

The conductor should be able to tell a singer performing the title role in *Carmen* when her voice carries into the house and when it does not; when she is dramatically convincing and when she is not; when she is mispronouncing the text and when her timing is wrong. A conductor should be able to tell a singer doing the title role in *Don Giovanni* when he is not following the score accurately, when he needs to sing more quietly, when he needs more volume, when he is drowning out his soprano during a duet, and when his portrayal of the character needs more intensity. The conductor also has to work with soloists for arrangements such as duets and trios, for example, to ensure that their voices blend well and their diction is clear.

While rehearsing soloists, the conductor also has to be aware of certain realities that require variance from the score as written by the composer. If a singer cannot easily hit certain notes in a section of the opera, he or she will ask for key changes, or for the lowering of the key a tone or two to make the notes more comfortable. The composer himself may or may not have approved of such changes to accommodate a particular singer, but opera composers tend to be practical people who want their operas performed even if the greatest singers are not available. So conductors have to adjust keys sometimes and then rehearse the orchestra so that they know that they are not to play the notes they see in their copies of the score, but to lower or raise them a tone or two for a particular singer. Variance from the printed score is also necessary for vocal ornamentations like trills, added grace notes, and arpeggios, for example—especially for Handel and the bel canto composers. These vocal ornamentations should be performed tastefully and in the style of the piece, and the conductor is responsible for guiding the singer's use of ornamentation during rehearsals at the piano for optimum effectiveness in the theater. Here, again, the conductor has to be a musicologist, familiar with the ornamentation styles of earlier periods.

The conductor also needs to rehearse the chorus, even when the opera company has a chorus master. It is very easy for choruses to be too loud, to have poor and unclear diction, and to have an ugly and unmusical tone. The great operatic chorus has a musical sound, clear and clean diction, and can sing beautifully and clearly whether it is singing softly or loudly. The subtle variance of dynamics, the interpretation of the text, and the making of a beautiful sound are what the opera conductor should try to get from the chorus during the piano rehearsals. Sections of the choral music in Wagner's *Tann-häuser*, for example, must be sung *a cappella*—that is, without any orchestral accompaniment. It is very difficult for the chorus to stay on pitch without orchestral support, so rehearsals are very important here. Some of the choral sections in the first act of *Carmen* demand a divided chorus and a quick interchange between the two. Singing quickly, remembering cues for entrances, and trying to act at the same time demand much from a chorus.

Simultaneously working with soloists and chorus, the conductor must begin orchestral rehearsals. With a great opera orchestra, and there are not many, and with an opera the orchestra knows, not many rehearsals are needed. But the orchestra may be playing a phrase in a traditional way that may diverge from the printed score. Mahler used to say that "Tradition ist Schlamperei" (tradition is sloppiness), for he felt that the opera conductor had to ensure that the score was being followed accurately rather than allowing the traditional cuts and mistakes. Also, the orchestra may play a score as its last conductor wanted it played, which will probably conflict with the interpretation of a new conductor. These problems have to be resolved during orchestra rehearsals. In addition, there are particular passages in many operas that are difficult for the orchestra. Can the overture to Mozart's *The Marriage of Figaro* be played with the proper balance and quiet beauty of tone? Can the horn passages in *Fidelio* be played without cracking? Can the solo flute passages in the mad scene in Donizetti's *Lucia di Lammermoor* be played quietly and limpidly to blend well with the vocal timbre of the soprano singing the role?

The conductor at last brings all the forces together for several rehearsals to ensure that everything works well together and that the balance is right. Orchestra, soloists, and chorus might not work well together—one element can lose audibility or become too loud unless the conductor can control his forces. Simultaneously, the stage director has been rehearsing the singers and chorus for the theatrical aspects of the drama on stage, so the conductor and the stage director must work together and confer regularly so that their interpretations are the same. If they have different interpretations of the opera, a confusion will surely result. If the stage director sees the lead in *Carmen* as essentially childlike and innocent, but the conductor portrays her music in a strident, staccato manner, what will happen to the poor singer doing the role on stage? All must be coordinated, which is accomplished when conductor and stage director confer on their understanding of scenes, acts, individual characters, and the opera as a whole. If the opera also contains a ballet, a choreographer must be in charge of the dancers. And through all these different kinds of rehearsals, the conductor must also be careful to avoid the problem of over-rehearsal, when the opera is rehearsed to the point where the performance lacks vitality and sounds only correct and routine. Rehearsals should not result in boredom for the musicians but increased musical challenge and excitement.

Finally, the conductor calls for on-stage rehearsals for orchestra, chorus, dancers (in many operas), and soloists, which lead to the dress rehearsal, with everyone in costume, and the opening night performance. If the conductor is skilled and if he is lucky with his performers and stage directors, the reviews will be good and artistic success will result. Operatic success is often a wonderfully noisy event, with elegantly dressed people in the audience bellowing like fans at a rock concert. The naive general public often thinks of opera as a quiet, genteel, dignified affair, but anyone who has ever been to a really successful operatic performance knows how thunderous and raucous a group of opera fans can be when they are happy. It is the conductor who is responsible for much of the thunderous approval, though he does not always get the credit due him. It is the conductor who has ultimate responsibility for an operatic performance, and sophisticated and aware opera audiences know whom to blame or praise for much of what they hear.

OPERA CONDUCTING SINCE WORLD WAR II

Since the war, Georg Solti and Herbert von Karajan have done the most opera recording and have had the largest influence on operatic conducting. While the first tends to be dramatic, intense, and precise, the second was quietly aristocratic, beautiful-sounding, and understated in approach. In addition, the Austrian conductor Karl Böhm, having studied his art under the tutelage of Richard Strauss, made a specialty of conducting the Strauss scores—to great success. The Italian Carlo Maria Giulini has conducted sublime performances of the Mozart and late Verdi operas, especially *Don Giovanni* and *Falstaff*. Colin Davis, presiding over London's Royal Opera at Covent Garden, specialized in the Mozart and Britten operas and has also revived several of the Berlioz operas, thereby encouraging several other opera companies to perform these wonderful works as well. In Munich, Wolfgang Sawallisch has conducted solid and impressive performances of the German repertory—Mozart, Wagner, and Strauss.

In the 1970s, another generation of young conductors has succeeded with operatic audiences. From Italy, Claudio Abbado, Giuseppe Patanè, Riccardo Muti, and Giuseppe Sinopoli have specialized in the Italian repertory, primarily at La Scala, and from there have conducted that wonderful repertory around the world. From America, Leonard Bernstein and Lorin Maazel have presided over exciting performances of the standard repertory operas. In New York, James Levine, who studied at the Juilliard School, was soon put in charge of the Metropolitan Opera and quickly proved himself the *Wunderkind* of his generation. His successful conducting of Verdi, Puccini, Wagner, Strauss, and Mozart impressed audiences with the breadth of his knowledge and the dramatic excitement of his approach to these scores. From East Germany, Kurt Masur, Klaus Tennstedt, and Marek Janowski specialized in the German repertory and were soon conducting all over Europe and America. From Holland, Bernard Haitink has conducted wonderful performances of Mozart's operas. From South America, Carlos Kleiber has led some fabulous performances of Verdi, Strauss, and Wagner.

Many successful conductors have appeared since the 1950s to carry on a great and important tradition in opera: the essential, effective, and creative conductor who can turn a composer's written score into a sublime musical and dramatic experience for the audience.

Seven

The Great Singers: Opera's Vocal Tradition

God sent his Singers upon earth
With songs of sadness and of mirth.

—Henry Wadsworth Longfellow

Was there ever a golden age of singing? Vocal connoisseurs often refer to this or that "golden age," but all ages have some great voices, and since all great voices are unique, it is easy to say that the golden age has ceased when your favorites retire. There are too many ambitious, impressive, and talented new singers for that conclusion to be valid. Yet old connoisseurs like to impress the young with all the wonderful old voices they have heard that the young fan will never be able to hear, though luckily now voices can be preserved on recordings. Of course not all performers are recorded, but generally the most popular opera singers record their best roles these days, which gives us a semblance of a permanent record. Although recorded sound has certainly improved markedly in the last fifty years, the sound of the voice in the opera house has yet to be exactly duplicated.

To appreciate voices and the beauty of a particular soprano or tenor voice, one must know something about opera's great vocal tradition. This tradition in opera includes audience awareness of the great operatic singers of the past, and how the singers' approach characterized a particular style or a particular period's taste, or indeed altered that taste by providing a sound so new and startling, yet so captivating, that taste and style themselves underwent a change. I have listed below short biographies of the greatest singers in the history of opera (at least, this critic's view of them), plus commentaries on how their vocal style made them famous and whether they altered the history of opera's great vocal tradition.

To become a real cognoscente of the operatic voice, one must have an awareness of opera's vocal tradition, and one must listen to many singers and many recordings. Years of serious listening with a trained ear will result in a true understanding of what one is hearing and how it fits into the great vocal tradition, how it borrows from that tradition, or how it alters the tradition. Chapter Three, "The Operatic Voice," gives the reader the necessary terminology concerning, for example, the kinds of sopranos, tenors, and baritones that exist. Now let us examine the great singers themselves. You will undoubtedly notice that sopranos and tenors will be getting the most attention.

Sopranos and tenors have, with some notable exceptions, been the most recurrent stars in opera. Audiences tend to get more excited about great tenor and soprano singing. Why? Actually, they produce the most unnatural sounds, they are the high-wire acts. Although mezzo-sopranos, baritones, and basses produce sounds more like the normal speaking voice, sopranos and tenors produce sounds that are more exciting because they are more unnatural. In turn, tenors and sopranos generally get the best roles, though of course there are important exceptions—the title role in Bizet's *Carmen* and Rossini's Rosina (*The Barber of Seville*) were written for mezzo-sopranos, the title role in *Boris Godunov* was written for a bass, and Wotan in Wagner's *Ring* cycle was written for a bass-baritone. But most of the best, biggest, juiciest roles in opera were written for sopranos and tenors, and these are the singers who will get the most attention in the following discussion of opera's vocal tradition.

The voice itself is one of the things that one must love to be an opera enthusiast. The sound of a great voice, uniquely beautiful and expressive, will move most opera fans to ecstasies because of its beauty, its power, and its dramatic and expressive ability, or—most unusually—all three. Some voices excite by their sheer beauty, others by their power and strength to penetrate a dense orchestral sound, still others by their dramatic intensity and ability to portray the character being performed. Below, I have listed the singers according to their centuries so that the various periods and their vocal tastes would become more apparent. After reading this chapter, in addition to much serious listening, you can become a connoisseur of the operatic voice, something that will add hours of enjoyment to both opera-going and to discussions with fellow opera lovers.

SEVENTEENTH AND EIGHTEENTH CENTURIES

Antonio Bernacchi (1685–1756)

Most of the great singers of the seventeenth and eighteenth centuries were castrati (singular: castrato), male singers who sang male or female roles but with the voice of a soprano, mezzo-soprano, or contralto. Antonio Bernacchi, one of the first of the great acting castrati, studied voice in his native Bologna, making his debut there in 1706. He soon succeeded with operatic audiences in both Bologna and Venice. His acting was always praised, but the control, flexibility, and size of his castrato voice impressed even more. His specialty was improvised *fioritura* (ornamentation) on the vocal line, which he could do for long periods, thereby keeping an audience entirely captivated.

Handel was especially fond of Bernacchi's contralto voice and took him with him to London, where he appeared in 1717 in a successful revival of Handel's *Rinaldo*. He also created the title role in Handel's *Lotario* and Arsace in *Partenope*. By the end of his operatic career, in 1730, Bernacchi was esteemed as a great teacher, in addition to being a very wealthy man. He retired comfortably to his native Bologna, and was in part responsible for the career of another great castrato, Farinelli.

Faustina Bordoni (1695–1781)

Bordoni was the great rival of the soprano Francesca Cuzzoni, and in fact their professional rivalry began the operatic tradition of two divas competing for the greatest public favor. The two singers often appeared in the same city at the same time, which of course added to the publicity both received. These two sopranos were shrewd publicists in addition to being talented singers.

Faustina Bordoni was one of the first female opera singers to gain a European-wide reputation. She first sang in Venice, where she was an immediate success, making her debut in Pollarolo's *Ariodante* in 1716. Her Venetian debut led to offers from other opera houses in Italy. In 1726, Handel brought her to London, where she became very popular with the English audiences. She was able to compete with the castrati at the height of their fame, and audiences liked the fact that she was a female singer playing a female role. But her greatest successes were in opera seria, the home ground of the castrati singers, rather than in comedy, where the castrati were never as popular since greater realism in acting was needed for opera buffa. Bordoni retired to Venice, where she married the opera composer Johann Hasse.

Caffarelli (Gaetano Majorano) (1710–1783)

Caffarelli took the name of his great patron and teacher, Domenico Caffarelli. He then studied voice in Naples with Nicola Porpora, the most famous voice teacher in the eighteenth century. After his debut in Rome in 1724, Caffarelli was one of the most sought-after male sopranos in Europe. He sang briefly in London in Handel's operas in 1738, but his major career was in Naples and the other Italian opera houses. Caffarelli is one of the few opera singers actually mentioned in an opera; in Rossini's *The Barber of Seville* Don Bartolo mentions Caffarelli when discussing the great music of his youth. Caffarelli was also a great favorite with Handel, who wrote several important roles for him.

While the singer Farinelli communicated a sweetness of disposition both on and off the stage, Caffarelli was a nasty, neurotic, temperamental man, but his performances succeeded because of what the castrati were generally wonderful at: impressive vocal power, control, and display. His voice could do runs, trills, and other fioritura, and he could sustain high notes softly, a very difficult feat for a singer. His control of his impressive and beautiful instrument was awesome, his technique was amazing, and he had a long and successful career as a result. But it was punctuated with many screaming matches with other singers and directors. Caffarelli was once jailed for his behavior in the theater, and he also fought a duel with a French poet over the values of Italian versus French music. Luckily no one was killed, though the castrato did wound his opponent.

Caffarelli's fortune from his tempestuous singing career gave him a very comfortable retirement. He even managed to buy a dukedom in his native Italy and lived there in quiet and splendid retirement.

Cusanino (Giovanni Carestini) (1705–1760)

A product of the Bolognese school of singing, Cusanino was a great soprano and then later became a great contralto. He excelled in opera seria, and in Rome he succeeded admirably at his debut in 1721 in Bononcini's *Griselda*. Handel especially admired his voice and brought him to London in 1733, where he remained for several seasons and sang in many of Handel's opera serias. As a result of this collaboration, Cusanino and Handel had several great operatic successes in London. Cusanino's voice deepened as he matured, and he became one of the great contraltos of the eighteenth century.

After his years in London, Cusanino returned to Italy to acclaim in all the major Italian opera houses. In Berlin he had another great success in Graun's *Orfeo* (1752). After singing successfully in St. Petersburg for several years, he retired to Italy in 1758, to his native town of Monte Filottrano near Ancona.

Francesca Cuzzoni (1698–1770)

The first female singer to gain international status, Cuzzoni had to compete with enormously popular castrati during her career, but she competed well and gained real celebrity status. She began her career in Italy, making her premiere in her native Parma in 1716, and then singing primarily in Venice and Bologna, but quickly her success spread to other countries where she was invited to perform. She had significant success in London as well as Vienna and in some of the German city-states. She first appeared in London in 1723 in Handel's *Ottone*. After that success, she was given leading parts in other Handel operas. But her admirers were soon quarreling with those of a rival diva, Faustina Bordoni—beginning the tradition of rival sopranos. On June 6, 1727, the two singers actually got into a scuffle on stage during a performance. This scandal became the basis of the Lucy versus Polly fights in Gay's satiric *The Beggar's Opera*.

Cuzzoni's gifts as an actress, and the fact that she was a female playing a female role, added to her popularity, especially with the more literal-minded English. But she squandered her money foolishly and ended up in the poorhouse in her old age, dying in Bologna in extreme poverty.

Farinelli (Carlo Broschi) (1705–1782)

The most acclaimed of the castrati, Farinelli became famous first in Naples, which by the middle of the eighteenth century rivaled Venice as the operatic capital of the world. Its schools produced some of the greatest castrato singers, of whom Farinelli was the most famous. He made his debut in Naples at the age of fifteen and soon succeeded there, in addition to Rome and Venice later, in many of the opera seria soprano roles. After he studied voice in Bologna with another great castrato, Antonio Bernacchi, Farinelli's singing became truly great. His finest performances took place in London, Vienna, and Madrid.

He became even more famous in the Spanish court of King Philip V, who had to have Farinelli sing him to sleep at night. The king suffered from severe depression, and only Farinelli, singing the same four songs, could quiet the king so he could nod off. For twenty-five years, starting in 1737, Farinelli remained in Madrid's royal court, and helped to establish an Italian opera company in Madrid in 1750. After Philip V died, Farinelli also served his successor, Ferdinand VI, but Farinelli did not get along very well with the new Spanish monarch, Charles III, so he continued his wildly successful operatic career elsewhere. His sweet, temperate personality flew in the face of the stereotypical temperamental and demanding castrato, and his disposition won him many fans, though not as many as those attracted by his vocal prowess. He retired in Bologna, a very wealthy and well-liked man who occasionally taught voice.

Baldassare Ferri (1610–1680)

The first of the great castrato singers of the seventeenth century, when they first dominated the opera stage, Ferri was born in Bologna, a city that produced many fine singers. Ferri had all the attributes of the great castrato singers: a large, beautiful, pure voice in the soprano range with all the power of a man. His first operatic successes were in Venice and Florence, after which he went to Poland to sing for three successive Polish kings.

In 1655 Ferri was invited to sing in the court theater in Vienna. Remaining there for twenty years, he provided Vienna with great singing and acting. He retired to Perugia, another immensely wealthy man.

Gaetano Guadagni (1725–1792)

Born in the small town of Lodi, near Milan, in northern Italy, Guadagni had vocal and dramatic talent since his earliest youth. He made his operatic debut in Parma in 1747 as a contralto, but then sang soprano roles and soon became a great and sought-after singer. Handel quickly brought him to London, where he sang in *Samson* and *Messiah*. He achieved his greatest role as Orfeo at the premiere of Gluck's *Orfeo ed Euridice* in 1762, and his simple and unornamented rendition of the famous aria "Che farò senza Euridice" made him the most famous castrato of his generation. Guadagni's dramatic success particularly gratified Gluck, because this simplicity of vocal expression was precisely the reform he was seeking for opera.

Indeed Guadagni's dramatic ability was in some ways more famous than his voice. His performances could even make orchestra players weep, and they are a notoriously hard-bitten lot. He had a very long career, singing until the 1780s, when he retired in Italy.

Michael Kelly (1762–1826)

A lively Irish tenor who began his singing career in 1779 in Dublin as the Count in Piccinni's *La Buona Figliuola*, Kelly then went to Naples to continue his vocal training and to further his career. After successes in many Italian opera houses, he went to Vienna, where he sang with the court opera and met Mozart, who was very fond of his acting and singing talents. Mozart cast him as Basilio and

Curzio for the premiere of his *Marriage of Figaro* in 1786, and Kelly had great success in these roles. His Irish tenor voice, combined with his miming ability, made him wonderfully successful in the comic roles of older men despite his youth.

After Vienna he traveled to London and appeared in opera there, eventually becoming an impresario and directing an opera company in which he was the leading tenor. His final operatic appearance occurred in Dublin in 1811, in one of his own popular operas, *The Bard of Erin*. In 1826, Kelly published his two-volume *Reminiscences*, a lively account of operatic practice in the eighteenth and early nineteenth centuries.

Gertrud Schmeling Mara (1749–1833)

Under her husband's Italian name, this woman became the first German singer to attract attention all over Europe. Mara's soprano singing was excellent, which allowed her to compete successfully on stage with the most conceited castrato.

Mara's debut was in Dresden, where she was immediately recognized as a major voice. In 1771, Frederick II engaged her for the Berlin Opera, and by 1780 she was also singing in Paris and Vienna. In 1787 she had a great success in London as Cleopatra in Handel's *Giulio Cesare*. The rest of her career was primarily in Munich and Vienna, and some of the lesser German states, where she appealed to the German fondness for realism. She sang in some singspiels while in Germany, but most of her career was in serious opera. Toward the end of her career, Mara traveled to Russia to sing and liked it so much she settled there permanently, singing first at the court opera in Moscow and later teaching and living comfortably from her savings.

Gasparo Pacchierotti (1740–1821)

Pacchierotti studied voice in Venice, and his soprano singing was soon in demand in many of the Venetian opera houses. One of the last of the truly great castrati, Pacchierotti had a divine voice in full technical control plus wonderful acting ability. Even orchestral players were reportedly affected by his acting and singing in many of the opera seria roles. Pacchierotti's dramatization of the grief of heroes and gods was considered unparalleled in his own day, and his singing in London, starting in 1778, made him and Handel the toasts of the city. His consummate artistry, in fact, increased the demand for castrati all over Europe in the eighteenth century.

In addition to singing in London, Pacchierotti also sang successfully at both of the most famous Italian opera houses: La Scala in Milan and La Fenice in Venice. His voice was considered one of the very greatest of the time, and when he came out of retirement in 1796 to sing for Napoleon, reports indicated that his singing was still superb.

Ann Storace (1766–1817)

Often called Nancy as well as Ann, Storace was an important English soprano of Italian descent. She went to Italy for vocal training and began her career there in 1776. After some success, she and her brother Stephen, also a singer, traveled to Vienna, where Mozart was very fond of her pert appearance and lovely soubrette singing. She originated the role of Susanna in Mozart's *The Marriage of Figaro* in 1786, and both the critics and the public appreciated her voice and her wonderful comic acting ability.

Because of her comic talent, Storace's greatest successes remained in the soubrette roles. She then followed her brother to London, where she had additional acclaim in a variety of roles. She generally succeeded most with light, clever parts, and she usually appeared in popular English operettas, frequently those composed by her brother for her. The combination of Ann Storace and Michael Kelly in the operettas of Stephen Storace provided London with much entertainment at the end of the eighteenth and the early years of the nineteenth centuries.

NINETEENTH CENTURY

Emma Calvé (1858–1942)

This French soprano made her debut in Brussels in 1882 as Gounod's Marguerite in *Faust*. Calvé, however, continued to study voice with the famous teacher Mathilde Marchesi, and after appearances in London and Paris she became a real diva. One of the greatest dramatic sopranos for the French repertory, Emma Calvé became the most exciting Carmen of her generation. At a time when most sopranos were playing the role of *Carmen* with silk and satin costumes, she played her primarily in a gypsy's simple black dress and an old shawl. Her dramatic instincts made her Massenet roles memorable experiences because of her sympathetic portrayals of these characters, especially Anita (*La Navarraise*) and the title role in *Sapho*.

These same parts can be dull in other hands, but in Calvé's hands the characters had a humanity and an affecting quality that made Calvé memorable and made the operas themselves seem better than they are generally given credit for. The French repertory has not produced many great interpreters, which is unfortunate given some of the wonderful roles available in French opera.

Angelica Catalani (1780–1849)

One of the great prima donnas of the early nineteenth century and the highest-paid singer of her time, Catalani began her career in Venice in 1797. Her voice impressed many musical critics of the time because of its range and power, and she was one of the people who put the castrati out of business. She sang some Mozart roles, appearing in London in 1812 in one of his last opera serias, *La Clemenza di Tito*, and some of her greatest successes were in the Italian operas of Mozart. She was the first London Susanna in Mozart's *Figaro* in 1812. She sang most comfortably in her native Italian.

Hers was a truly pan-European career: She began in Italy, singing primarily in Venice, Rome, and Naples, but was soon invited to sing at the other operatic stages in Europe. She succeeded admirably in England, primarily because of her voice and her good looks on stage. After England, she received acclaim in some of the German states and in Austria, primarily Vienna. But she retired from opera in 1819 to her native Italy and spent her final years there, founding a vocal school in Florence. She died in Paris of cholera.

Jean De Reszke (1850–1925)

A Polish tenor, De Reszke began singing—and singing beautifully—as a baritone in the title role of Mozart's *Don Giovanni* and Valentine in Gounod's *Faust*. His voice impressed because of its range, its ringing high notes, and its size. But his brother, the famous bass Édouard De Reszke, was convinced that Jean was really a tenor, and he was right. In 1884 Jean sang the tenor role of John the Baptist in Massenet's *Hérodiade*, and the premiere was very successful. Jean De Reszke was the first tenor to sing the lead in Massenet's *Le Cid* in 1885, and that made him famous in Paris and eventually around the world. His acting also worked to the advantage of his performances, as in his famous portrayal of the title role of Gounod's *Faust*.

Toward the end of his career, De Reszke did an amazing thing by becoming a heldentenor and switching to the Wagnerian tenor roles. He was considered at the time the best Lohengrin, Walther, Tristan, and Siegfried. This daring move, at the end of his career, added to De Reszke's fame as a great tenor. He retired to Nice, where he became a revered voice teacher.

Domenico Donzelli (1790–1873)

One of the great tenors of the bel canto era, Donzelli's singing especially impressed Rossini, who wrote several roles for him. Donzelli is connected with the earliest period of French grand opera, and he sang in many operas by Auber, Rossini, Halévy, and Meyerbeer in Paris. Bellini was also very fond of Donzelli's singing, and Donzelli created Pollione in *Norma* at La Scala in 1831. His was a historic tenor sound, and he could hit high notes without resorting to falsetto, instead producing a uniform quality of notes from his chest.

One of Donzelli's specialties was the role of Otello in Rossini's *Otello*, where both his fioritura and his dramatic acting made him much admired. His was one of the earliest of the large tenor voices, and as a result his career blossomed at a time when audiences and a new generation of composers wanted the dramatic verisimilitude of the tenor and to avoid the artificiality of the castrato. Donzelli was the first of the great tenors for the new Romantic age of opera and the first great dramatic tenor.

Gaetano Fraschini (1816–1887)

One of the earliest of the great Italian tenors, Fraschini made his debut in 1837 and was the tenor lead for the premiere of Donizetti's *Caterina Cornaro* in 1844. Verdi became obsessed with Fraschini's voice and stage presence and wrote several important roles for him, specifically in *Alzira* (1845) and *Il Corsaro* (1848), in addition to the more famous Riccardo in *Un Ballo in Maschera* (1859). Verdi wanted him to sing all his major tenor roles and Fraschini often did, in Italy, Paris, and London. What Verdi liked most about Fraschini's stage presence was the nobility of his bearing and his fine diction—he was the perfect tenor for Romantic opera, in other words. As a result, many of Verdi's roles for tenor in his early and middle periods involved a noble tenor who was forced to do evil because of circumstances. This was the role that Fraschini played to perfection.

His influence on Verdi marked Fraschini as a great man with audiences as well. His was not one of the greatest tenor sounds of the nineteenth century, yet his singing made a significant contribution because of his intelligence and dramatic talents. To make opera both a musical and dramatic experience is not allowed to many singers. After a final operatic performance in 1873, Fraschini retired to Naples.

Manuel García (1775–1832)

One of the greatest tenors of his generation, the Spanish Manuel García was especially impressive in the Donizetti and Rossini tenor roles, and he excelled in both comedy and tragedy. He also started a dynasty of opera singers. His wife sang, and his two daughters and his son all became international celebrities as singers: Maria Malibran, Pauline Viardot-García, and Manuel García II.

Manuel García was also an impresario and was the first singer/impresario to lead an operatic tour of the United States, which was then virgin territory in terms of opera. In 1825 he first presented Italian opera in New York, with Mozart's librettist Lorenzo Da Ponte in the audience, for Da Ponte had emigrated to America and was a professor of Italian (the first) at Columbia University. The New York season was a great success, and García decided to tour other American cities with his company. He had many adventures, recounted in his memoirs, including making quite a bit of money while touring Mexico and then losing it all to bandits on a road near Vera Cruz.

Manuel García settled in Paris in his retirement, instead of his native Spain, since Paris had become the operatic capital of Europe. In Paris, García wrote several important books on operatic singing for his own pupils, and these manuals remained central for nineteenth-century singers and are still studied by voice students and teachers today.

Luigi Lablache (1794–1858)

Although his heritage was French, Lablache was born and trained in Naples and became a great bass who excelled in basso buffo roles. He made his debut in Naples in 1812, then was engaged by the opera house in Palermo and by Milan's La Scala. Lablache originated Giorgio in Bellini's *I Puritani* as well as Don Pasquale in Donizetti's *Don Pasquale*, since both bel canto composers were very fond of his singing and acting. An especially comic Don Bartolo in *The Barber of Seville*, he sang many of the basso buffo roles in Rossini.

His was a long career, baritones and basses often enjoying longer careers than their higher-voiced colleagues, and during that time both his acting and singing were admired. He established the style of both Italian basso buffo singing and acting for the bel canto period, in addition to singing many of the French baritone and bass roles in French grand opera. He sang primarily in Paris and London, and was for a while Queen Victoria's singing teacher.

Lilli Lehmann (1848–1929)

One of the great German sopranos of the nineteenth century, Lehmann debuted in Prague in 1865 and soon made appearances all over Germany. She was one of the Rhinemaidens at the premiere of Wagner's *Ring* cycle in Bayreuth in 1876. Her first Isolde occurred at Covent Garden under Hans Richter in 1884 and was well received. After 1885 she introduced most of the Wagnerian soprano roles to America through the Metropolitan Opera in New York. She had a large voice and real acting ability, and it was through her portrayals that the new world came to know Isolde (*Tristan und Isolde*), Brünnhilde and Sieglinde (*Ring* cycle), Elisabeth (*Tannhäuser*), Elsa (*Lohengrin*), and Kundry (*Parsifal*). She helped to popularize Wagnerian opera in America.

Lehmann also sang these roles in Europe, primarily in her native Germany and in Austria, where her appearances in Berlin and Vienna were much prized. But she also sang the title role in Bizet's *Carmen* and Verdi's Violetta in *La Traviata*, yet despite her wide range of roles she was most memorable in the Wagnerian soprano repertory. After she retired, she gave recitals until the 1920s, then became a very famous teacher. Geraldine Farrar and Olive Fremstad were among her pupils.

Jenny Lind (1820–1887)

The "Swedish Nightingale," as she was called, Jenny Lind was the most famous soprano of her generation. She was born in Stockholm and made her debut there in 1838 as Agathe in Weber's *Der Freischütz*. Her first great success occurred in the title role of *Norma* in Berlin in 1844, and she then sang all over Germany, Austria, and Scandinavia. After singing to popular acclaim in Europe, she toured America under the sponsorship of P. T. Barnum, giving recitals in many American cities.

Lind sang primarily in the German and Italian repertory, succeeding especially as Amelia in Verdi's *I Masandieri*, Alice in Meyerbeer's *Robert le Diable*, and in the title role of Bellini's *Norma*. The limpid beauty of her voice and her acting ability made her the preferred singer for many of the great soprano roles of her time. After her operatic career ended in 1849, she sang in concerts and oratorios for another ten years. Hers was a lovely, girlish, sweet-sounding voice, a type the nineteenth century was especially fond of. In her last years she became professor of singing in England's Royal College of Music, a position she began to hold in 1883, and she taught singing in England for the rest of her life.

Maria Malibran (1808–1836)

A daughter of the legendary Manuel García, Maria Malibran was one of the great acting sopranos of the early nineteenth century. She made her professional debut in London in 1825 as Rossini's Rosina in *The Barber of Seville*. She excelled in roles that demanded vocal grandeur and drama, including all the Rossini and Mozart soprano roles, and especially her greatest role, the title role of Bellini's *Norma*.

Malibran's voice always had serious vocal problems, despite the help she received from her father, who was also a famous voice teacher. Still, the theatrical excitement of her performances amply compensated for any vocal defects. During an American tour she married the French banker Malibran, a marriage that soon ended in divorce. Her second marriage, to the Belgian violinist De Bériot, was quite happy until she died tragically and prematurely from injuries sustained from a fall from a horse.

Amalie Materna (1844–1918)

This Austrian soprano was born in St. Georgen, Austria, and began as a soubrette, often singing in Viennese operetta. But an initiation into Wagner's operas changed all that, and Materna became the first great Wagnerian soprano. She originated Brünnhilde in the three *Ring* operas that include this character at the *Ring*'s premiere in Bayreuth in 1876. She was also the first Kundry (*Parsifal*) in Bayreuth in 1882. Under Wagner's coaching and conducting, Materna also sang Wagnerian roles in London. That a soubrette could have become a Wagnerian soprano is indeed amazing, but with Wagner's coaching she underwent a transformation. She also sang the first Brünnhilde in America, at the Metropolitan Opera in New York in 1885, conducted by Damrosch.

Materna established the style and sound of Wagnerian soprano singing; and, of course, she reflected the standards of the composer who trained her in these roles. Hers was a steady, large, powerful voice, but its sheer size did not preclude vocal beauty. Although her acting did not generate many sparks, the beauty of her voice and dramatic expression made her the first great Wagnerian soprano, and she has had few successors, despite the fact that she was a voice teacher in Vienna in her last years.

Victor Maurel (1848–1923)

Born in Marseilles, Maurel studied voice in Paris and made his debut there in 1868. He was one of the great French baritones of the nineteenth century; Verdi wrote his *Otello*'s Iago with his voice in mind, and Maurel sang and acted brilliantly in that role at *Otello*'s premiere in 1887. Verdi also wrote his final opera, *Falstaff*, for him, and Maurel was a great Sir John at the La Scala opening in 1893, and in subsequent performances of the role.

Maurel also succeeded in the Wagnerian baritone roles, becoming a great Telramund (*Lohengrin*), Wolfram (*Tannhäuser*), and Dutchman (*The Flying Dutchman*). In both Wagner and Verdi his performances brought to the opera stage a large, lovely voice and excellent diction in both Italian and German. His final performances were given at the Metropolitan Opera in New York, where he retired in 1899 to become a voice teacher.

Nellie Melba (1861–1931)

One of the great sopranos of the last quarter of the nineteenth century and the early years of the twentieth, Melba triumphed in many roles. After studying voice in Paris with the famous Mathilde Marchesi, she made her debut in Brussels in 1887 as Gilda in Verdi's *Rigoletto*. After that premiere, she rarely returned to her native Australia. Melba began as a coloratura, excelling as Lucia in *Lucia di Lammermoor*, Rosina (*The Barber of Seville*), Violetta (*La Traviata*), and Gounod's Juliette (*Roméo et Juliette*). After successes in London, she sang in New York and elsewhere in Europe. Melba succeeded in many coloratura roles, but then she switched to Wagner, excelling as well in the role of Elsa in *Lohengrin*. She also sang in the Italian dramatic soprano repertory, singing beautifully in the title role of *Aïda* and as Desdemona in Verdi's *Otello*.

Melba was especially admired by the great French chef Auguste Escoffier, who created several dishes for her, the most well known being the ice cream dessert called "Peach Melba." As Melba gained weight, Escoffier designed "Toast Melba," to help her diet. After she ended her career, she wrote her autobiography, *Melodies and Memories*, published in 1925. Toward the end of her life she returned permanently to her native Australia.

Lillian Nordica (1857–1914)

Despite her Italian name, Lillian Nordica was born in Farmington, Maine, as Lillian Norton. She was one of the first Americans to have an international career as an opera singer, and she was the first American to appear at Bayreuth, as Elsa (*Lohengrin*) in 1894. She quickly became a great interpreter of the Wagnerian soprano roles of Elsa (*Lohengrin*), Brünnhilde (*Ring* cycle), and Isolde (*Tristan und Isolde*), but she could also sing a lovely Violetta in Verdi's *La Traviata*. What was most impressive about her voice was its size and power, in addition to its technical accuracy. She achieved great fame in Wagnerian roles, once singing *Tristan und Isolde* with Jean De Reszke in New York at the Metropolitan Opera. New

York and London audiences were also privileged to hear most of her wonderful performances.

Nordica has been called "America's first diva," and in many ways she truly was. She often sang with the greatest singers of her day—Caruso, Melba, Patti, and the De Reszke brothers. During a world tour in 1914, she was shipwrecked off the coast of Java. Although eventually rescued, she died of a fever in Java. There is a museum and memorial to her life and career in her birthplace, Farmington, Maine.

Adolphe Nourrit (1802–1839)

One of the earliest of a string of great French tenors, Nourrit specialized in the tenor repertory provided by the French grand opera composers, primarily Halévy, Meyerbeer, and Auber. He also sang in several of Rossini's French operas, and was an excellent Arnold in *William Tell*. His major successes were as the leading tenor of the Paris Opéra, where he created the roles of Robert in *Robert le Diable*, Eléazar in *La Juive*, and Arnold in *William Tell*.

Nourrit also sang in Italy with some success, though not as much as in Paris because he was most comfortable singing in the French language. His voice was not naturally one of the most beautiful of vocal instruments, but his acting has been described by contemporary critics as riveting, which compensated for his comparative lack of a great voice. His career was cut abruptly short by his suicide in Naples in 1839. He had suffered from recurrent depression, which finally drove him to take his own life.

Giuditta Pasta (1798–1865)

Pasta was one of the legendary divas of the nineteenth century, making her debut in Brescia in 1815, then singing in London and Paris, where she had her greatest triumphs. One of Bellini's favorite sopranos, she was the first Norma in the opera of that name. Donizetti also much admired her singing and wrote for her the title role of *Anna Bolena*. What these composers, and audiences, admired about her voice was its beauty, control, and dramatic intensity. She was one of the great divas of her day; despite some vocal problems, she had an international career, even performing in Russia, where the czar was particularly fond of her singing.

Rossini also admired Pasta, and she excelled in some of his operas, particularly as Desdemona in *Otello*. Pasta's greatest triumphs were in London, Paris, and St. Petersburg. She died in Blevio, near Lake Como, after a long and glorious singing career.

Giovanni Battista Rubini (1794–1854)

One of the greatest tenors of the bel canto period, Rubini originated many of the tenor roles in Bellini's operas, a composer he worked especially closely with and who was especially fond of him. Rubini sang the tenor leads at the premieres of *Il Pirata*, *La Sonnambula*, and *I Puritani*. Donizetti wrote the tenor lead in *Anna Bolena* for Rubini as well.

Rubini's acting and singing were both admired, and he seemed able to communicate to his audiences real enjoyment in the very act of singing. Rossini admired this quality and was always pleased to have Rubini sing his tenor roles. Toward the end of his life, the czar offered Rubini an important teaching position in St. Petersburg. He taught very successfully there for many years, and eventually retired to Italy with a substantial fortune earned from his singing and teaching.

Ludwig Schnorr von Carolsfeld (1836–1865)

One of the earliest heldentenors, Schnorr von Carolsfeld was a fine, intelligent singer with acting ability in addition to his large and wonderful voice. He made his debut in 1858 and soon became a famous, and great, performer of the title role of *Lohengrin* in all the important German opera houses. Wagner much admired his interpretation of the role, and the tenor appeared in Wagner's *Tristan und Isolde* in Munich in 1865 as the first Tristan, and his wife, Malvina, was the first Isolde. Overjoyed to find such a wonderful pair of singers, Wagner had coached them both extensively in these very difficult parts. Tragically, after the greatness of these first *Tristan* performances, Ludwig Schnorr von Carolsfeld died soon after the premiere, which served to give the role a reputation as a "killer of tenors."

Wagner long mourned the loss of this great heldentenor, for in a real sense there were no successors to him for thirty years. Meanwhile, Schnorr von Carolsfeld's widow grew increasingly unbalanced, becoming involved with spiritualists and resorting to séances in her desperate attempt to communicate with her dead husband.

Wilhelmine Schröder-Devrient (1804–1860)

A great dramatic soprano for the German repertory, Schröder-Devrient was one of Wagner's inspirations as a young man. Wagner relates in his autobiography, *Mein Leben*, that seeing Schröder-Devrient as Leonora in Beethoven's *Fidelio* showed him how opera could be both a musical and theatrical experience and made him decide to become a composer. In addition to her Leonora, she was also a famous Romeo (traditionally sung by a mezzo-soprano in Bellini's version) in Bellini's *I Capuleti ed i Montecchi*.

Wagner wrote for Schröder-Devrient the roles of Adriano in *Rienzi*, Senta in *The Flying Dutchman*, and Venus in *Tannhäuser*, and she excelled in all these parts. Her ability to move on stage and act convincingly made her performances true music dramas in the Wagnerian sense. She made her debut as Pamina in Mozart's *Magic Flute* in Vienna in 1821 and retired in 1847 after twenty-five wonderful years, in a glorious performance in Gluck's *Iphigénie en Aulide*.

Marcella Sembrich (1858–1935)

By birth a Pole, but with an international career, Sembrich was one of the great coloratura singers at the turn of the century. She made her debut in Athens in 1877 as Elvira in Bellini's *I Puritani*. But her career really skyrocketed in London, where she sang from 1880 to 1895. After her initial successes in London, she made her debut in New York in 1883, captivating audiences there too.

Although she specialized in the coloratura roles, especially Lucia in *Lucia di Lammermoor*, Marguerite de Valois in Meyerbeer's *Les Huguenots*, and Rosina in *The Barber of Seville*, she got bored with these roles and started to branch out, becoming a significant Mozart singer and doing many recitals of Italian songs and arias. In fact, Italian was the language in which she was most comfortable singing. After her retirement from opera in 1909, she taught voice in New York City until her death.

Teresa Stolz (1834–1902)

Stolz, a Czech, was one of Verdi's favorite sopranos. She made her Italian debut in Bologna in 1864 and moved to Milan's La Scala the next season, where Verdi first heard her. She became the mistress of Verdi's favorite conductor, Angelo Mariani. Verdi insisted in her singing the La Scala premiere of *Aïda*, and Stolz also sang Elisabetta (*Don Carlo*), Leonora (*La Forza del Destino*), and the soprano solo for Verdi's *Manzoni Requiem Mass* when it was performed at La Scala and later all over Europe.

What Verdi admired most about Stolz was her ability to sing dramatically with superb diction. She made the Italian dramatic soprano a reality on the Italian (and international) operatic stage with her clear diction and ability to direct her large voice to dramatic purpose. Her genius in presenting a character on stage ensured her success in the Verdi soprano roles, and, in fact, the Verdi soprano really began with her interpretations of the title role in *Aïda*, Desdemona in *Otello*, Leonora in *Il Trovatore*, and Elisabetta in *Don Carlo*. After the death of Verdi's wife, Giuseppina Strepponi, in 1897, Stolz lived with Verdi to help and comfort him in his remaining years.

Francesco Tamagno (1850–1905)

Tamagno studied voice in his native Turin and made his operatic debut there in 1873 in Donizetti's *Poliuto*. His next great success was in Palermo in 1874 as Riccardo in Verdi's *Un Ballo in Maschera*. From 1877 onward he sang most often at Milan's La Scala. This great dramatic tenor was the original interpreter of Verdi's last dramatic roles. He sang the tenor lead in the revised *Simon Boccanegra*. Verdi wrote the title role of *Otello* for Tamagno, and the composer was immensely satisfied with his portrayal of the jealous Moor at the opera's premiere in 1887. Tamagno had an exciting stage presence that generated fear as well as interest in an audience, and his large voice filled large opera houses quite easily. Also, Verdi admired Tamagno's fine diction and his ability to give the words dramatic meaning rather than just a lovely sound. His portrayal of Otello, at the premiere in 1887 and for twenty years afterward, repeatedly captivated audiences.

In non-Verdi roles Tamagno excelled as John in Meyerbeer's *Le*

Prophète, and in French grand opera tenor roles in general. He met with success in Italy, as well as London, Paris, Chicago, and New York. He retired from the stage in 1902, one of the first great dramatic tenors of the Italian repertory.

Enrico Tamberlik (1820–1889)

One of the earliest Italian dramatic tenors of the Romantic age, Tamberlik made his debut in Naples in 1841 in Bellini's *I Capuleti ed i Montecchi*. Verdi was very fond of his voice, and Tamberlik excelled in many of the early and middle Verdi operas, Manrico in *Il Trovatore* being one of Tamberlik's specialties. He created the tenor role of Alvaro in Verdi's *La Forza del Destino*.

Born and trained in Italy, despite his German-sounding name, Tamberlik had a large voice with a dark color that carried very well. As a result he could sing the Rossini and especially the Verdi tenor roles with real expertise. His high notes were especially popular with the public, and Verdi liked their timbre as well. Tamberlik could interpolate high notes and still remain within the style of the opera being performed. Verdi also wanted credible acting, and Tamberlik was one of the great operatic actors of his day. After he could no longer sing, he retired in Paris and became a voice teacher and vocal coach.

Antonio Tamburini (1800–1876)

Born in Faenza, Tamburini became one of the greatest Italian baritones of the nineteenth century. He made his operatic debut in Cento in 1818 and was soon engaged in all the important Italian opera houses. In 1832 he made his London and Paris debuts, and his phenomenal technique quickly earned him thousands of fans, especially in Paris, where his greatest successes occurred. While in Paris he sang Riccardo in the premiere of Bellini's *I Puritani*, and he also sang Malatesta at the premiere of Donizetti's *Don Pasquale*.

Tamburini's next great triumphs were in London, where his wonderful baritone singing enabled him to perform many roles, among them his famous Don Giovanni in the opera of that name. He also introduced to London many of the new bel canto operas then recently composed: He was London's first Riccardo in *I Puritani*, first Alfonso in *Lucrezia Borgia*, first Earl of Nottingham in *Roberto Devereux*, and first Enrico in *Lucia di Lammermoor*. Because of his immense popularity in London, a second Italian Opera House was opened in 1847 in Covent Garden, the site of the current Royal Opera Company. At his last public appearances, in 1859, his lovely baritone still sounded glorious. He retired to Nice, where he taught occasionally.

Giovanni Battista Velluti (1780–1861)

Velluti was one of the last great castrato singers, and by the middle of his career, audiences were already tiring of the castrato's unnatural sound and lack of dramatic verisimilitude. He sang beautifully in London in 1825, but was considered freakish by the English. In Italy, however, Velluti still held audiences' attention at the height of his career because of his wonderful voice and his embellishments. One of his earliest successes occurred in 1813 in Rossini's *Aureliano in Palmira*, an opera seria in which the castrati were accustomed to excel.

Stendhal admired Velluti and wrote frequently about the singer's sway over his audiences because of his excellent singing. Napoleon heard him in Venice and was also impressed with his lovely sound. Although Velluti's acting was never impressive, his sweet soprano singing was. His career was centered in Venice and other Italian cities, but it never became truly international because the age of the new Romantic opera had arrived, and this new form of opera had no roles for the castrati—then considered an old and decadent aspect of the aristocratic eighteenth century. Velluti lived into his eighties in retirement in Venice, a lingering antique of a former age.

Pauline Viardot-García (1821–1910)

This French mezzo-soprano was from a famous musical and operatic family; Viardot-García's father was the great Manuel García and her sister was the legendary Maria Malibran. She studied voice with her father, one of the great voice teachers of the nineteenth century; she studied piano with Liszt, among others; and made a mediocre vocal debut in Brussels in 1837. Her London debut as Rossini's Desdemona (*Otello*) in 1839 failed as well. Her Paris debut in 1839 was her first real success. And Paris remained her central city—where she was born, where she had her greatest operatic successes, and where she died. In Paris she created the role of Fidès in *Le Prophète* at the composer Meyerbeer's insistence, and after his excellent coaching in the role. She was also the first London Azucena in Verdi's *Il Trovatore*, and here at last she had a real success in London.

With Berlioz's encouragement, Viardot-García sang the role of Euridice in Gluck's *Orfeo ed Euridice* at the Paris Opéra's famous revival of that "reform" opera in 1859, following this triumph in 1861 with a revival of Gluck's *Alceste*. Married to the opera impresario Louis Viardot, she later became the mistress of the Russian writer Turgenev in her retirement. During her retirement she also sang for friends, painted, composed, wrote poetry, and occasionally taught voice.

EARLY TWENTIETH CENTURY: 1900–1945

Lucrezia Bori (1887–1960)

The Spanish soprano Lucrezia Bori's career falls neatly into two categories: pre-nodes and post-nodes. Her very successful early career came to an abrupt halt with the discovery that she had nodes on her vocal cords, which threatened her singing career. She went to the same Milan surgeon that Caruso went to with the same problem, and she too had the nodes removed. Then, on her doctor's recommendation, she rested her voice for a year, barely speaking. During that time, many, including Bori herself, wondered whether she would ever be able to sing again. After a tentative but successful performance in Monte Carlo in 1919 that was well reviewed, she returned to the Metropolitan Opera in 1921 to rave reviews, and she continued to sing there (and elsewhere) until her retirement in 1936.

Bori's operatic debut occurred in Rome in 1908 as Micaëla in Bizet's *Carmen*, and this role remained one of her best. In addition, her Mimì (*La Bohème*), Manon (*Manon Lescaut*), and Juliette (*Roméo et Juliette*) succeeded both before World War I and after her throat operation until her retirement from the operatic stage in 1936. She dominated these roles in New York and several other houses in Europe because of her distinctive vocal style and wonderful technique. She did not sing much in her native Spain after her successes in Italy and the New World, especially in New York, where audiences were blessed with most of her wonderful performances.

Enrico Caruso (1873–1921)

A short, fat man from the slums of Naples, Caruso was to become synonymous with opera in America and many parts of Europe. He was *the* Italian tenor of the early part of the twentieth century. While he sang in all the major opera houses, his career was centered primarily in America, and there and in Italy he made many famous recordings. His recordings and superb performances made him the great tenor of his time.

After his successful debut in Morelli's *L'Amico Francesco* in Naples in 1894, Caruso quickly became a sought-after tenor all over Europe. He created the role of Dick Johnson in Puccini's *La Fanciulla del West* at the Met in 1910, and Puccini greatly admired his singing. In addition, Caruso created Maurizio in Cilèa's *Adriana Lecouvreur* and Loris in Giordano's *Fedora*. Although Caruso was not a very good actor early in his career, his singing was always gorgeous and pleased audiences. His acting, however, soon improved, especially in the comic roles: he was a superb Nemorino in Donizetti's *The Elixir of Love*. His final performances, in Halévy's *La Juive*, were moving because of his fine acting in addition to his wonderful singing. He, like Bori, had nodes on his vocal cords and had to have surgery, and as a result of the operation his voice darkened. Beginning as a light, high tenor, his voice deepened after his surgery and as he aged, prompting him to sing more dramatic roles by the end of his career. Caruso's Canio in *Pagliacci* was considered definitive at the time and remained his most famous role in the mind of the general public. He died where he was born, in Naples, and is buried there. His sudden death from bronchial pneumonia added to his legendary quality, for no audience ever heard him in vocal decline.

Feodor Chaliapin (1873–1938)

The first of the great Russian basso profundo singers to make an international career, Chaliapin first sang in Europe with Sergei Diaghilev's touring production of *Boris Godunov*. Chaliapin's beautiful and deep basso voice and his superb acting produced raves from both audiences and critics. His most famous role always remained Boris, and his singing of the part elevated *Boris Godunov* into the standard repertory. After the Diaghilev tour, his career was centered in Europe and America rather than Russia, where he did not want to return after the Bolshevik Revolution.

In addition to Boris, Chaliapin was a famous Méphistophélès in Gounod's *Faust* and Boito's *Mefistofele*. He sang many other roles in French opera, achieving particular success in the title role of Massenet's *Don Quichotte*. His acting was often more impressive than his singing, especially toward the end of his career, for he created theatrical excitement in opera. He wrote two books of memoirs in his retirement, *Pages from My Life* (1926) and *Man and Mask* (1932).

Giuseppe De Luca (1876–1950)

This great Italian baritone enjoyed a long and productive career, and also sang many important premieres in both America and Europe. He started as a baritone in Piacenza in 1897 and soon sang at La Scala and other major Italian opera houses. He was the first Gianni Schicchi at the premiere of Puccini's *Il Trittico* in New York in 1918, and he established the comic and sardonic style for performing the part. He also premiered the role of Sharpless in Puccini's *Madama Butterfly*, the first to sing the part in both Europe and America. His acting ability was legendary in both serious and comic roles, and De Luca captivated opera audiences with both the beauty of his rich baritone voice as well as his acting. His singing was often called bel canto because of his wonderful technique, control, and flexibility.

De Luca always remained within his repertory, the Italian baritone roles, and he had a long and exciting career. He retired from the operatic stage in 1940 and taught singing at the Juilliard School in New York for the final ten years of his life.

Emmy Destinn (1878–1930)

The great rival of Geraldine Farrar, Czech soprano Emmy Destinn was certainly the better actress although her voice was not as beautiful. Destinn's fans appreciated the theatrical intensity of her performances. She sang Minnie in the world premiere of Puccini's *La Fanciulla del West* in New York in 1910, and her dramatic excitement in the role, in addition to her vocal accuracy if not vocal splendor, created a sensation with the audience and the press.

Destinn generally sang the more dramatic Italian roles: Santuzza in Mascagni's *Cavalleria Rusticana*, Minnie in Puccini's *La Fanciulla del West*, and the title role of *Madama Butterfly*. She also sang the first Senta in Wagner's *The Flying Dutchman* at Bayreuth in 1901, and she created the title role of *Madama Butterfly* at London's Covent Garden. Hers was a remarkable stage presence on the operatic stage at the turn of the century, and her acting and singing brought her to audiences in Europe and America and created important new roles that became part of opera's standard repertory.

Geraldine Farrar (1882–1967)

One of the great American sopranos, Geraldine Farrar was a real star with all the accompanying publicity that that title suggested in the years before and after World War I. She made her operatic debut in Berlin in 1901 as Marguerite in Gounod's *Faust*. Specializing in the Italian and French repertory, she sang the title role in the American premiere of Puccini's *Madama Butterfly*, among others. Her singing was sometimes criticized for not being totally accurate, but her fans were adamant in her defense. She had a charming stage presence and was a beautiful woman with a lovely figure, something rare in opera, especially during that period. At the Met in New York, her home base, she became a house idol.

Farrar soon specialized in the Italian soprano roles—the title roles of *Tosca* and *Madama Butterfly*—and also as Bizet's Carmen, and she sang them beautifully. When she retired in 1922, at the height of her career, her farewell performance was the main event of that Metropolitan season. She left in peak form, and she never sang in public during her vocal decline, which added to the legendary status of her career. But she did make over twelve films and wrote an autobiography, *Such Sweet Compulsion* (1938).

Kirsten Flagstad (1895–1962)

Born in Norway and trained there, Flagstad made her debut in Oslo in 1913 to mediocre reviews. She appeared only in Scandinavia until 1933 and was about to give up her career when she was engaged to sing at Bayreuth. Her appearance there in 1934 as Sieglinde in *Die Walküre* led to her Metropolitan Opera debut in the same role the following year, which made her an international star overnight. She soon became the great Wagnerian soprano of the 1930s and 1940s, and her performances with Lauritz Melchior became synonymous at the time with great Wagnerian singing. Her interpretations of Sieglinde, the three Brünnhildes of the *Ring* cycle, Isolde, and Kundry were considered definitive, and some critics would say that her recordings of them are still definitive. Her voice was not only very large, it was also accurate and beautiful. The warmth of her singing added immeasurably to the success of the Wagnerian performances in the 1930s. It has been said, in fact, that her Wagnerian performances with Melchior in the 1930s saved the Metropolitan Opera from collapse during the horrible days of the Great Depression, when few Americans could afford opera tickets. Her non-Wagnerian roles included Mozart, Gluck, and Purcell parts.

Flagstad retired from live performances in 1954 but continued to record. During the last few years of her life, she was the director of the Norwegian National Opera, where she succeeded admirably as an administrator until her sudden death from cancer.

Olive Fremstad (1871–1951)

Olive Fremstad was born in Stockholm but raised in rural Minnesota. She received much vocal training in Boston, where she made her debut in 1890 in Gilbert and Sullivan's *Patience*. After further vocal study with Lilli Lehmann in Berlin, Fremstad made a second debut in Cologne, in 1895. This marked the real beginning of her operatic career, thanks in part to Lilli Lehmann's help, and she quickly specialized in the German soprano roles. She gained notoriety in America for singing the difficult title role of Richard Strauss's *Salome* at its New York premiere in 1907; the opera was withdrawn after one performance because it was considered too morally shocking. But Olive Fremstad was a great dramatic soprano, and her talents were quickly recognized and glorified when she sang Isolde in *Tristan und Isolde* at the Metropolitan Opera and elsewhere: Her voice and acting ability made hers the definitive Isolde at the turn of the century. In her *Ring* cycle roles, her Brünnhilde, Sieglinde, and Kundry also succeeded because of her fine voice and convincing acting.

Fremstad sang in the Wagner theater at Bayreuth to wide audience approval, but most of her career was spent in New York and London, where she had many successes. Her farewell performance in New York in 1914 was greeted with twenty-one minutes of ovations. Her career inspired Willa Cather to write *The Song of the Lark*, a fictionalized account of Fremstad's life.

Amelita Galli-Curci (1882–1963)

One of the great coloratura sopranos of all time, Galli-Curci had a small, thin voice that could do amazing things because of her control and phrasing. Her high notes were her bread and butter, and she sang high C's, D's, E's, and even F's. Moreover, she could sing these amazingly high notes accurately, sustaining and shaping the note without apparent strain, which always impressed audiences. (Sometimes a singer can hit these notes, but the sound suggests that the singer might lose a tooth from the effort.)

Galli-Curci made her operatic debut in 1906 in Trani, Italy, as Gilda in *Rigoletto*. Soon after, she sang in opera houses all over Italy. She made her American debut in Chicago, and after that her career remained primarily in America, especially in New York. Her greatest roles were the great coloratura soprano parts: the title role of *Lucia di Lammermoor*, Violetta (*La Traviata*), Gilda (*Rigoletto*), Elvira (*I Puritani*), and the title role of *Dinorah*. She stayed primarily within the Italian coloratura repertory, in which she excelled, creating a vocal style that was limpid, flexible, and beautiful. Also, since she was willing to record during the pioneer days of sound recording early in this century, she left a substantial recorded legacy. Her career ended abruptly in 1936 from a throat ailment, and she retired to California, where she taught.

Mary Garden (1874–1967)

Although Mary Garden was born in Scotland, her family moved to Chicago when she was a child, and there she received most of her vocal training. She started singing in opera quite early, making a very successful debut in Paris in 1900 in the title role of *Louise*. She quickly became an international celebrity despite the diminished and unspectacular quality of her voice. Her instrument was never considered particularly gorgeous, but it did have a distinctive timbre that audiences could recognize. Moreover, her legendary acting ability compensated for her lack of a spectacular voice.

Garden excelled especially in the French repertory, singing the title roles in *Manon*, *Thaïs*, and *Louise* with great success. She created the role of Mélisande in Debussy's *Pelléas et Mélisande* at the Paris premiere in 1902, and this role became one of her most popular vehicles. Her diction was always admired, since it is very difficult to sing well and with good diction in French. Hers was excellent, and the result was real theatrical excitement when she was performing any of her great French roles.

After Garden's success in Paris, she became manager of the Chicago Opera from 1919 to 1920, but here she succeeded only when she was on stage. Her inability to handle money or other singers resulted in huge losses, but her career went on after a millionaire admirer covered them. She continued to sing until 1931 when she retired to her native Scotland, where she wrote her notable autobiography, *The Mary Garden Story* (1951).

Beniamino Gigli (1890–1957)

Gigli's early career suffered by proximity to the skyrocketing career of Enrico Caruso. Gigli studied voice in his native Rome and first got attention when he won a prestigious vocal competition in Parma in 1914, whereupon he quickly made appearances all over Europe and then in America. By the 1920s he was considered Caruso's successor as the great Italian tenor. He dominated many of the lighter tenor roles in the late 1920s, 1930s, and 1940s, and he was considered one of the greatest Italian tenors of his time because of the beauty of his voice, although his acting was only mediocre.

Gigli's was a light tenor sound, and his voice excelled in the lyric and spinto tenor parts; his greatest roles included Nemorino (*The Elixir of Love*), the Duke of Mantua (*Rigoletto*), Des Grieux (*Manon Lescaut*), Cavaradossi (*Tosca*), and the title role in Giordano's *Andrea Chénier*. He sang often in New York, but left when the Great Depression forced pay cuts. After that, he sang primarily in Italy, and he died in his native Rome.

Frieda Hempel (1885–1955)

The great German soprano of her generation, Frieda Hempel had one of the widest vocal ranges of any soprano. She made her debut in Schwerin, Germany, and was quickly signed for her more important debut in Berlin in 1905. In both Berlin and New York she introduced the role of the Marschallin in Strauss's *Der Rosenkavalier*, and this became her most famous role. She also sang the Queen of the Night in Mozart's *The Magic Flute*, Eva in Wagner's

Die Meistersinger von Nürnberg, Violetta in Verdi's *La Traviata*, and Rosina in Rossini's *The Barber of Seville*. Her Susanna was considered definitive, in addition to her later portrayal of the Countess—both in *The Marriage of Figaro*.

The purity of Hempel's sound made up to audiences for her comparative lack of great acting. Her large, lovely voice was in full control, and that is enough of a rarity to please opera-goers. Her acting ability improved as she matured as an artist, particularly in her fine portrayal of the Marschallin. Her versatility was one of her greatest hallmarks, since she could sing a wide variety of roles. After 1919 she retired from opera, but she continued to give concerts for many years after that.

Maria Jeritza (1887–1982)

The great star of the Vienna Opera between the two World Wars, Jeritza premiered many of the Puccini and Strauss operas there, singing the title roles in Vienna's first *Tosca* and *Turandot*. She was born in Czechoslovakia and received most of her vocal training there, but her career was primarily in three cities: Vienna, London, and New York.

Puccini was very fond of Jeritza because of her wonderful acting ability, gorgeous voice, and beautiful figure. She dominated the stage and sang dramatically so that her characters came alive for an audience. Her performances in the title roles of *Tosca* and *Turandot* were considered the best of the period. Richard Strauss also admired her art and wrote the roles of Ariadne in *Ariadne auf Naxos* and the Empress in *Die Frau ohne Schatten* for her. She also sang the major role of Marietta in the premiere of Korngold's *Die Tote Stadt*. Jeritza sang some Wagnerian roles with success, especially Elsa in *Lohengrin*. She was a glamorous figure, regarded as a movie star is today, and she even had a bevy of hysterical fans in several cities. She also wrote a marvelous autobiography, *Sunlight and Song* (1924).

Lotte Lehmann (1888–1976)

One of the great Wagnerian and dramatic sopranos of the early part of this century, Lotte Lehmann was born in Germany but became an American citizen. Her Marschallin in *Der Rosenkavalier* was considered the greatest of her generation of sopranos, and she also succeeded in Wagnerian roles, primarily Elsa (*Lohengrin*), Sieglinde (*Die Walküre*), and Eva (*Die Meistersinger von Nürnberg*). Her dramatic interpretations were usually as successful as her singing.

Richard Strauss was especially fond of Lehmann's artistry, and she originated several roles in his operas. She was the first Composer in *Ariadne auf Naxos*, she created the very difficult role of the Dyer's Wife in *Die Frau ohne Schatten*, and she was the first Christine in *Intermezzo*. She became one of the singers who established the vocal style for Strauss's soprano roles.

Lehmann stopped singing opera after World War II, though she continued as a lieder singer. At the end of her life she settled in California and became a famous voice teacher. She taught extensively there and had some famous pupils, most notably Grace Bumbry.

John McCormack (1884–1943)

Born in Athlone, Ireland, John McCormack was one of the great Irish tenors. He made his operatic debut in Savona, Italy, in 1906 as Fritz in Mascagni's *L'Amico Fritz*. After that, he was engaged to sing at all the major opera companies in England and America. His best roles were Don Ottavio in *Don Giovanni*, Rodolfo in *La Bohème*, Edgardo in *Lucia di Lammermoor*, and the Duke of Mantua in *Rigoletto*. He had all the characteristics of the Irish tenor voice: a light, sweet sound with easy transitions between notes and a taste for sentimentality.

McCormack's acting was always criticized as poor, a view he generally agreed with. He stopped singing opera in 1913 and gave only concerts for the next twenty-five years. He enjoyed not having to act, and audiences generally flocked to his concerts. He also recorded from his operatic repertory, in addition to popular Irish songs.

Lauritz Melchior (1890–1973)

This great Danish tenor dominated Wagnerian heldentenor roles during the 1920s, 1930s, and 1940s and even into the early 1950s. His best roles were certainly his Wagnerian ones of Siegfried, Tristan, Lohengrin, Tannhäuser, and Parsifal. He began as a baritone and then, like so many heldentenors, worked on his high notes so that he could sing the tenor roles. He studied first in his native Denmark and then in Germany, making his heldentenor debut as Tannhäuser in 1918.

Melchior's recordings with Kirsten Flagstad and Helen Traubel reveal a large, bright, accurate, beautiful voice. While his acting was never considered impressive, Melchior's voice overwhelmed audiences around the world, even through thick Wagnerian orchestration. His performances of Wagner's operas began at Bayreuth, and then continued in London and New York. He became an American citizen and taught voice for the last twenty years of his life, primarily in California.

Ezio Pinza (1892–1957)

The great Italian bass of the 1920s, 1930s, and 1940s, Ezio Pinza centered his career in New York and the Metropolitan Opera, but he also sang with great success in all the major opera houses in Europe and South America. He specialized in the Verdi basso roles, but he was also an excellent Don Giovanni in the opera of that title and succeeded even in the title role of *Boris Godunov*, although he sang the role in Italian. By the end of his career, when his voice could no longer sing opera comfortably, Pinza switched to Broadway, where he was a hit in Rodgers and Hammerstein's *South Pacific* in 1949.

Pinza's was a large, beautiful voice and he had an impressive stage presence as well. His comic roles, especially Mozart's Figaro (*The Marriage of Figaro*) and the title role in *Don Giovanni*, succeeded as well as his tragic roles like Fiesco in Verdi's *Simon Boccanegra* and King Marke in *Tristan*. His repertory included almost 100 roles, although he sang primarily in Italian.

Rosa Ponselle (1897–1981)

Born in Connecticut of Neapolitan parents and named Rosa Ponzillo, Rosa Ponselle was the great Verdi soprano of her generation—primarily the 1920s and 1930s. She made her opera debut in 1918 at the Metropolitan Opera as Leonora in *La Forza del Destino*—and she sang there on the advice of Enrico Caruso, who was convinced she was ready for the Met. Ponselle enjoyed a long career, which continued into the 1930s, and her success at the Metropolitan Opera and other opera houses in America and Europe was phenomenal. She succeeded in the great Verdi soprano roles—Leonora (*La Forza del Destino*), Violetta (*La Traviata*), and the title role in *Aïda*—and she rarely ventured outside her repertory, but her interpretations of these roles were considered definitive at the time.

In addition to Verdi's dramatic soprano roles, Ponselle was also a great Norma in the opera of that name, and performed admirably in the soprano leads in *La Vestale* and *La Gioconda*. Fortunately, some of her singing was recorded, with Enrico Caruso, her mentor, among others. She retired from opera in 1937 and moved to Baltimore, where she was active in teaching and coaching.

Friedrich Schorr (1888–1953)

Fritz Schorr, as he was often called, became one of the truly great Wagnerian bass-baritones of the first thirty years of this century. His Wotan was lauded all over the world for the depth of his interpretation if not the sheer beauty of his voice. But his large voice was admirably suited to Wagner, and heavy orchestration was not a problem for him. His greatest successes were in Bayreuth, London, and New York.

Schorr's Wotan was matched by an impressive Hans Sachs in *Die Meistersinger von Nürnberg* and by his performance in *The Flying Dutchman*. He rarely did non-Wagnerian roles and was not impressive in them when he did attempt them. Although born in Hungary and trained in Vienna, Schorr became an American citizen and retired to rural Connecticut, where he taught in his last years.

Ernestine Schumann-Heink (1861–1936)

Born in Czechoslovakia and trained in Germany, Schumann-Heink began her career with Azucena (*Il Trovatore*) in Dresden in 1878. At the turn of the century and into the 1930s, she dominated the mezzo-soprano and contralto roles. She was a great Azucena in Verdi's *Il Trovatore*, and an equally impressive Erda, Fricka, and Waltraute in Wagner's *Ring* cycle. She sang in Bayreuth from 1896 to 1906 and later created Klytämnestra in Strauss's *Elektra* at its Dresden premiere in 1909.

Schumann-Heink recorded extensively and even sang on the radio in the 1930s, and as a result became a public celebrity as well as a great singer. Her popularity, in fact, was partially responsible for saving the Metropolitan Opera in the 1930s when it had great financial difficulties in the Great Depression. Her impressive career budded primarily in Germany, but blossomed in America. She was an American citizen by the end of her long and productive life.

Antonio Scotti (1866–1936)

One of the great Italian baritones, whose career spanned the period from the turn of the century until the 1930s, Antonio Scotti was one of Puccini's favorite baritones, and in fact Puccini wrote several roles with him in mind, primarily the Sheriff in *La Fanciulla del West* and Scarpia in *Tosca*. Although he excelled in serious roles, his comic talents were also considerable. For example, his portrayal of Sir John (*Falstaff*) was considered definitive at the time.

Scotti made his operatic debut in Malta in 1889 and by 1898 he was singing at La Scala. Thereafter he spent most of his career in the major opera houses of Europe and North and South America. Although his career was centered in London and then New York, he toured extensively. His acting ability was in some ways even better than his superb singing. He began a tradition of excellent baritone acting, a tradition continued by Tito Gobbi later in the century. Scotti died where he was born, in his hometown of Naples.

Leo Slezak (1873–1946)

In the first twenty-five years of this century, Slezak was the greatest Otello of all, in addition to handling many of the Wagnerian heldentenor roles. He sang primarily in New York and the major houses in Germany, and in Austria, where he was born. His performances of the title roles in *Lohengrin* and *Tannhäuser* and as Radames (in *Aïda*) were considered the greatest of the period. His acting was impressive, but the size, accuracy, and beauty of his voice were even more so. When he retired in 1926, there were a few dry years before Lauritz Melchior could take over Slezak's roles.

Slezak was also famous for his sense of humor. When he missed his cue in the last act of *Lohengrin* and the swan left without him, he asked the audience, "When's the next swan?" His antics backstage added to the popularity of this excellent heldentenor, who also sang very effectively in Italian roles. His autobiography, appropriately, has a comic title and a comic tone: *Song of Motley, Being the Reminiscences of a Hungry Tenor.*

Luisa Tetrazzini (1871–1940)

One of the great coloraturas, and a contemporary of Amelita Galli-Curci, Tetrazzini made a mediocre debut in Florence in 1890, but by 1910 she was singing in all the major opera houses. She knew her limitations and stayed within her coloratura repertory, but she excelled there as few others have. Her voice was significantly larger than Galli-Curci's, and just as lovely. Her acting was generally weak, although she could be pert in her comic roles. But her acting credibility was hampered by her large figure, which got larger and larger as she matured.

Tetrazzini's great roles were Lucia (*Lucia di Lammermoor*), Rosina (*The Barber of Seville*), Violetta (*La Traviata*), Norina (*Don Pasquale*), and Adina (*The Elixir of Love*). She excelled in coloratura tone and technique and was a fine musician as well. After she retired from operatic singing, she wrote two important books: *My Life in Song* (1921) and *How to Sing* (1925).

LATE TWENTIETH CENTURY: 1945 TO THE PRESENT

Hildegard Behrens (b. 1937)

Behrens is one of the greatest acting singers, and her acting carries a conviction that marks all her performances. She was born in Land Oldenburg, Germany, and studied voice at the Freiburg Music Academy. She was first engaged in 1971 to sing with the Deutsche Opera am Rhein, and was soon invited to sing at other opera houses in Germany. She specializes in the dramatic soprano repertory, roles like the Countess in Mozart's *The Marriage of Figaro*, Fiordiligi in *Così fan Tutte*, Elsa in *Lohengrin*, and Agathe in *Der Freischütz*. She has also succeeded very well with Giorgetta in Puccini's *Il Tabarro*, but she first achieved real stardom for her Leonora in *Fidelio*; in 1975 she sang this role in Zurich and in 1976 she sang the part in London's Covent Garden, and she got raves in both productions. In 1977 she made her debut in the title role of *Salome* at the Salzburg Festival under Herbert von Karajan, and she recorded the role with him as well. Her Isolde (*Tristan und Isolde*) was also captivating for the intensity of her acting, and her Brünn-hildes (*Ring* cycle) took Bayreuth by storm in 1984, again because of her fine acting in addition to the beauty of her voice. There are an honesty, totality, and intensity about her performances, whether in Wagner, Beethoven, Mozart, or Puccini, that have made Behrens famous at opera houses on several continents.

Jussi Björling (1911–1960)

The Swedish tenor Jussi Björling made his operatic debut in 1930 in Stockholm as Don Ottavio in Mozart's *Don Giovanni*. While his debut was not sensational, his voice improved steadily, and he came to dominate the lighter Italian tenor roles in the late 1930s, 1940s, and 1950s. Björling also made some important recordings with Sir Thomas Beecham. In 1937 he sang in Vienna and Chicago, and then his international career began.

Björling excelled especially in the smooth, seamless, flexible control of his tenor voice, particularly in Puccini's roles. His Rodolfo (*La Bohème*), Mario Cavaradossi (*Tosca*), and some of the Verdi roles, especially the Duke of Mantua in *Rigoletto*, were his best, and on records some of them are still remarkable for his elegant, lovely singing. While his acting was never impressive, his voice compensated by its beauty, size, and tasteful projection if not for its drama. He could fill large opera houses like the Met, Covent Garden, and La Scala with a gorgeous tenor sound, a rare feat. When he died Björling's voice was still in excellent condition.

Montserrat Caballé (b. 1933)

The Spanish soprano Caballé has always been a weak actress, yet her performances have succeeded admirably with the public because of her impressive ability to sing very difficult roles beautifully. Her voice, one of the most gorgeous of the post–World War II period, can handle high notes very comfortably, and she has the wonderful ability to sing high notes very softly and with excellent phrasing, a feat requiring great vocal control. Caballé does this easily, and her softly phrased high notes can leave an audience panting.

Her operatic debut occurred in Basel in 1956 as Mimì in Puccini's *La Bohème*, and she was soon singing in Spain, Germany, and Portugal. Her performance of the title role in Donizetti's *Lucrezia Borgia* with the American Opera Society in New York in 1965 and the rave reviews she received in that role first gave her an international reputation. She began in the Italian soprano roles, primarily Mimì (*La Bohème*) and the title role in *Tosca*, but soon extended her range and has sung Strauss very well, primarily the Marschallin (*Der Rosenkavalier*), Ariadne (*Ariadne auf Naxos*), and the title role in *Salome*, which she has recorded with the conductor Erich Leinsdorf. Caballé has sung some Wagner as well, primarily Isolde (*Tristan und Isolde*) and Brünnhilde, although primarily on the concert stage and in recordings. She has also made some fine recordings of Strauss and Schubert lieder.

Maria Callas (1923–1977)

Born in New York City of Greek parents, and with most of her vocal training in Greece, Maria Callas became one of the great sopranos of the post–World War II period. She made her debut in Athens in 1938 as Santuzza in *Cavalleria Rusticana*, and a more important debut after the war in Verona in 1947 in the title role of *La Gioconda*; this second debut began her famous career. By 1951 Callas was a regular diva at La Scala, and although she had begun her Italian career by singing Wagner's Isolde (*Tristan und Isolde*) and Brünnhilde (*Ring* cycle) in addition to the Italian dramatic soprano roles, at La Scala she quickly became famous for her bel canto heroines such as Lucia (*Lucia di Lammermoor*) and the title role of *Anna Bolena*. Despite not being blessed with a particularly beautiful soprano voice, and having a top range that was always a bit insecure, Maria Callas did have dramatic intensity and musical intelligence that made her appearances theatrical as well as vocal events.

Almost single-handedly, Callas revived the bel canto repertory at a time when it had fallen into disrepute and neglect. Her performances of the operas of Rossini, Donizetti, and Bellini, because of her intense approaches to these roles and her intelligent handling of their language, brought the bel canto operas back into the standard repertory. While Lucia or Norma had been thought of as vocal display roles, Callas managed to turn them into credible drama because of her acting talent, fine diction, and her unique ability to make the words and musical phrases dramatically significant rather than just beautiful.

Callas was most famous for her title-role portrayals of *Lucia di*

Lammermoor, *Norma*, and *Tosca*, although she often sang the last of these roles in her vocal decline in the early 1960s. Her off-stage affair with Aristotle Onassis and her famous feuds with her mother and with sopranos like Renata Tebaldi added to her publicity, box office attraction, and her legend. Her career was shorter than it should have been, and her great period was the 1950s and early 1960s, primarily at La Scala in Milan, although she also appeared at London's Covent Garden, Chicago's Lyric Opera, and New York's Metropolitan Opera during this time. She tended to feud with directors and conductors because of her fiery temperament, but also because of her determination to do opera as she wanted it done, with a great conductor and sufficient rehearsals. Hers was the proverbial meteoric career, and luckily the recordings she left allow us to study how she did what she did and to enjoy her performances. The Callas touch made a role memorable and dramatically convincing, if not always exquisitely sung.

Franco Corelli (b. 1923)

With one of the most beautiful tenor voices to come from Italy after World War II, Corelli was born in Ancona. Although he had little education in voice, he was a natural talent, and his singing had a distinctive timbre and a heroic ring. His debut took place in Spoleto in 1951 as Don José in *Carmen*, and he was quickly engaged by the major Italian opera houses. He made a very successful La Scala debut in 1954. His dark, heroic tenor voice excelled in roles such as Manrico in *Il Trovatore*, Mario Cavaradossi in *Tosca*, Dick Johnson in Puccini's *La Fanciulla del West*, and Prince Calaf in *Turandot*. He had success with French opera as well; he was a memorable Roméo in Gounod's version of that famous love story plus an excellent Don José in *Carmen*.

Corelli's acting was rarely impressive since he often seemed tense and unhappy on stage, but his singing generally won the audience. Moreover, he was a tall, handsome stage presence. He certainly destroyed the stereotype of the short, fat Italian tenor, and he had a manly voice to match. His career was shorter than it should have been, and by the early 1970s he no longer sang much in public; his nerves may have been the major reason. Performing was clearly a tremendous strain for him, but luckily his voice was well recorded so we have a good historical record of his greatest roles.

Régine Crespin (b. 1927)

One of the few French singers to achieve international stardom in this century, Crespin ironically enough achieved fame primarily for her German roles. Her interpretations of the soprano roles in Wagner and Strauss made her known around the world. After her promising debut as Elsa (*Lohengrin*) in Mulhouse, France, in 1950, she slowly developed her technique and diction. By 1958 she was singing Kundry at Bayreuth, and then she really became celebrated. Her Sieglinde and Elsa capture the best of her art, for she gave these roles a beautiful sound—yet a big sound—and impressive acting. Her German diction was always good and her ability to sing softly was one of the signatures of her vocal style.

Her Marschallin in Strauss's *Der Rosenkavalier* was perhaps her greatest role, and it was well recorded with the conductor Georg Solti. She gave the part tremendous melancholy, presenting the Marschallin as an essentially depressed person, and the audience responded sympathetically both to the beauty of Crespin's singing and the depth of her interpretation of the role. Toward the end of her career she sang some French roles, primarily Carmen in the opera of that name, and some Offenbach parts, although not with great success. She was successful, however, in the role of the old Abbess in Poulenc's *Les Dialogues des Carmélites*.

Mario Del Monaco (1915–1982)

Mario Del Monaco was the great dramatic tenor in the Italian repertory in the 1940s and 1950s. After a successful debut in Pesaro as Turiddu in *Cavalleria Rusticana* in 1939, he sang with acclaim all over Italy. He was most famous for his highly effective Otello (in Verdi's *Otello*), where he brought dramatic intensity and animal strength to the role and captivated audiences. His was a fearsome Otello, a real man of war who appeared dominant and dangerous from his first note. His "Esultate" in Act I told the audience immediately that he was a man to reckon with—exciting, dangerous, fierce.

His other roles included Dick Johnson in *La Fanciulla del West*, Hagenbach in Catalani's *La Wally*, and various other Puccini roles. In all these roles one sensed in his portrayals an intense dramatic and vocal presence. After his singing career ended, he became a famous teacher; his best-known pupil is the tenor Peter Hofmann. That an Italian tenor teacher could prepare a heldentenor indicates something of Del Monaco's scope and vision.

Plácido Domingo (b. 1941)

Born in Spain and trained in Mexico, Domingo has had an impressive career based on the beauty of his voice, his intelligence, and his dramatic ability. Despite his start as an Italian tenor, singing primarily such parts as Manrico in *Il Trovatore* and Pinkerton in *Madama Butterfly*, he has taken chances and gone beyond his standard roles to attempt other, more difficult parts.

He attempted and succeeded in the difficult dramatic role of Otello (Verdi) at the Metropolitan Opera in 1982, and he has taken on more dramatic tenor roles since, although still singing successful Alfredos (*La Traviata*) and Cavaradossis (*Tosca*). By 1984 he was singing the title role in *Lohengrin* at the Metropolitan Opera very successfully in addition to French roles like Hoffmann in Offenbach's opera *The Tales of Hoffmann* and Aeneas in Berlioz's *Les Troyens*. In the 1980s he also began to conduct, and he got good reviews in that area too. His is one of the great tenor voices of the 1960s, 1970s, and 1980s, and he is a singer with tremendous ambition and range. Not since Jean De Reszke has a tenor done so much so well.

Geraint Evans (b. 1922)

One of the most versatile of baritones, the Welshman Geraint Evans made his debut in London at Covent Garden in 1948 as the Nightwatchman in Wagner's *Die Meistersinger von Nürnberg*, and he quickly rose to sing major roles. His greatest roles include Figaro (*The Marriage of Figaro*), Leporello (*Don Giovanni*), Papageno (*The Magic Flute*), and Beckmesser (*Die Meistersinger von Nürnberg*). He has sung regularly at the summer opera festival at Glyndebourne. He has also sung regularly at Bayreuth, Covent Garden, La Scala, San Francisco, Chicago, and at the Met in New York.

His warm baritone voice has excellent diction and a very wide range, so that he can easily sing bass-baritone and bass roles as well. One of his most memorable parts was certainly the title role in Berg's *Wozzeck*. In London, his operatic home, Evans has created the following roles: Mr. Flint in Britten's *Billy Budd*, Mountjoy in

Britten's *Gloriana*, and Antenor in Walton's *Troilus and Cressida*. Evans has sung at all the major opera houses, and has succeeded in them, and he has been lauded for the depth of his characterizations, in both comedy and tragedy, and the wide range of his repertory.

Mirella Freni (b. 1935)

One of the most beautiful soprano voices to come from Italy since World War II, Mirella Freni is from Modena, as is Pavarotti. She made her debut in Modena in 1955 and soon established herself as a very clever soubrette. She began by specializing in the soubrette roles, especially Adina in *The Elixir of Love*, Susanna in *The Marriage of Figaro*, Zerlina in *Don Giovanni*, and Nannetta in Verdi's *Falstaff*. In 1963, however, she showed herself capable of being a successful Mimì in the famous Zeffirelli/Karajan production of *La Bohème* at La Scala, and the production was filmed and distributed widely. And then Freni became a real diva.

Thanks to her famous collaborations with Herbert von Karajan at the Salzburg Music Festival, she tried and succeeded in the more dramatic Italian soprano roles such as Elisabetta in *Don Carlo* and the title roles in *Aïda*, *Madama Butterfly*, and *Tosca*. The beauty of her voice and her acting ability combined to win tremendous popularity with audiences in both Europe and America. Freni is married to the Bulgarian bass Nicolai Ghiaurov, and they have often appeared together in *Don Carlo*, her Elisabetta to his Philip II.

Nicolai Gedda (b. 1925)

Nicolai Gedda was born in Stockholm, Sweden, to Russian parents and has had an international and very long career after his successful operatic debut in Stockholm in 1952. He first sang French tenor roles, especially in Gounod's *Faust* and Don José (*Carmen*). But he also sang some of the Mozart tenor roles, doing especially well as Don Ottavio in *Don Giovanni*. He sang most successfully at the Met, where in 1958 he created the role of Anatol in Samuel Barber's *Vanessa*.

Gedda performed many Italian roles, such as Edgardo in *Lucia di Lammermoor* and Elvino in *La Sonnambula*. His aristocratic singing style and lovely tenor sound, which could handle high notes very well, made his singing always a pleasure. He also succeeded as Lensky in *Eugene Onegin* and as Gherman in *The Queen of Spades*; his handling of the Tchaikovsky tenor leads, and his expertise in singing Russian, added to his success around the world. His high notes were his glory because he could float them so beautifully, particularly in the light, lyric French and Italian tenor roles.

Nicolai Ghiaurov (b. 1929)

Born in Bulgaria, Nicolai Ghiaurov impressed audiences as a bass singer with a gorgeous voice, wonderful low notes, and formidable acting ability. His career was primarily in Italy, at La Scala, but he appeared all over the world. Ghiaurov studied voice in Moscow, a place famous for producing great bass singers. He made his operatic debut in 1955 in Sofia as Don Basilio in *The Barber of Seville*, and in 1959 made a very successful debut at La Scala. Other successful debuts soon followed: Covent Garden, 1962; Vienna, 1962; Chicago, 1964; and New York's Metropolitan Opera, 1965.

After these debuts he appeared regularly at all these opera houses. His Méphistophélès in Gounod's *Faust* was one of his greatest roles. The next in terms of frequency was certainly his Philip II in Verdi's *Don Carlo*. Ghiaurov has said that he sang the role so often he should be allowed to sleep at the Escorial, the ancient palace of the famous king. He often appeared in operas with his well-known wife, the soprano Mirella Freni.

Tito Gobbi (1915–1984)

One of the great Italian baritones of this century, Gobbi was a real artist, able to sing beautifully yet making a character come alive on stage. Gobbi made his operatic debut in Rome in 1937 as Verdi's Germont in *La Traviata*, but his career did not really take off until after World War II. By the 1950s, he was singing in all the major opera houses. His scope was impressive, for he could work his miracles with both comic and tragic characters. His Iago (*Otello*), Figaro (*The Barber of Seville*), Scarpia (*Tosca*), Gianni Schicchi (*Il Trittico*), and Sir John (*Falstaff*) were considered definitive during the height of his career, from the 1950s to the early 1970s. Gobbi limited himself primarily to the Italian baritone roles, and here he was without equal. The one exception was his excellent portrayal of the title role of Berg's *Wozzeck*. In the Puccini roles, Gobbi's Gianni Schicchi managed to capture that character's shrewdness as well as his buffoonery. His Scarpia was the essence of elegant evil and manipulation, and fortunately he was recorded in the role opposite Maria Callas's powerful Tosca. By the end of his career, when his singing had declined, Gobbi staged operas and also became an effective teacher, giving master classes in Italy and America.

Marilyn Horne (b. 1929)

The greatest coloratura mezzo-soprano of the post–World War II period, Marilyn Horne had tremendous control over a big and gorgeous voice. Her voice always had impressive range, power, and awesome technical control. Her low chest tones could wow an audience, but she could also float a high note beautifully. The color of her voice was always mezzo-soprano or even contralto rather than soprano, and her voice's size could fill the largest opera house easily. Horne's acting ability was also considerable, especially in comic roles like Rosina in Rossini's *The Barber of Seville* or Isabella in his *L'Italiana in Algeri*. Her flair for comedy made even her portrayal of the title role of *Carmen* a comic event, which worked well given the opera's ability to encompass many different interpretations of the title role.

Horne also handled the serious bel canto roles very effectively as well; her Adalgisa to Joan Sutherland's Norma in *Norma* was one of the great operatic events of the 1970s, and they performed these roles together primarily in New York and London. Her portrayals of the title role of Rossini's *Tancredi* and the mezzo part in *Semiramide* were also moving, even though both are trouser roles. She has also sung in some Handel operas, notably *Alcina* and *Rinaldo*. Born in Pennsylvania, she has had an international and long-lived career, from the 1950s through to the 1990s.

Hans Hotter (b. 1909)

The great interpreter of Wagner's bass-baritone roles after World War II, Hotter was a most sought-after Wotan (*Ring* cycle), Friedrich von Telramund (*Lohengrin*), and Dutchman (*The Flying Dutchman*). He made his operatic debut in 1930 in Opava as the Speaker in *The Magic Flute*. Within five years he was engaged by the Munich and Vienna opera companies, but his career was temporarily halted by the war, after which his career blossomed primarily in Vienna, London, New York, and Bayreuth. His collaboration on the *Ring* with Wieland Wagner produced several great cycles in Bayreuth and London. His Wotan was especially effective because of the drama and majesty of his interpretation of the role; he created a real god on stage, and one saw that god age and disintegrate as the *Ring* cycle progressed.

In the non-Wagnerian repertory, Hotter created the Kommandant in Strauss's *Friedenstag* in 1938 and Olivier in Strauss's *Capriccio* in Munich in 1942. In Verdi his Grand Inquisitor in *Don Carlo* was his greatest role, and his portrayal of this part was perhaps the best in the 1960s and 1970s. A great lieder singer as well, Hotter's recordings of Schubert and Schumann lieder succeeded because of the intelligence of his interpretations and the beauty and control of his voice.

Eva Marton (b. 1948)

Of Hungarian descent, Eva Marton is one of the few modern singers who can perform successfully in both the German and Italian repertory. Her Turandot has triumphed in both Europe and America, but her other roles are excellent as well. After beginning with the Hungarian State Opera in Budapest, she quickly began to sing in the German opera houses. There her large voice succeeded in roles such as both Elsa and Ortrud in *Lohengrin*, Elisabeth in *Tannhäuser*, the Empress in Strauss's *Die Frau ohne Schatten*, and Sieglinde and Brünnhilde in the *Ring* cycle. Marton made her Metropolitan debut as Eva in *Die Meistersinger von Nürnberg* and soon was engaged to sing her other major roles, including the title roles in the Italian operas *Turandot* and *La Gioconda*.

Marton's intelligence, acting ability, awesome voice, and flexibility make her an ideal dramatic soprano. That she is one of the few singers who can succeed in German and Italian roles has put her in the category of the greatest singers: Lehmann, Melba, Callas.

Zinka Milanov (1906–1989)

One of the great Verdian sopranos of the world during the 1930s, 1940s, and early 1950s, the Yugoslav soprano Milanov had a long and impressive career singing the title role in *Norma*, Leonora (in both *La Forza del Destino* and *Il Trovatore*), and title roles in *La Gioconda* and *Aïda*, as well as the other dramatic soprano roles of the Italian repertory. She studied voice in her native Yugoslavia and sang in Zagreb from 1928 to 1935. In 1937, however, she sang in the Verdi *Requiem* under Toscanini in Salzburg, which brought her international attention. She made her Met debut in December 1937 and dominated the Italian dramatic soprano roles there until the 1950s.

Milanov was known for her control over her singing, particularly her celestial high notes, which she could sustain beautifully and softly, causing audiences to gasp. Although her acting was never great, her interpretations were vocally dramatic. Her Leonora in *La Forza del Destino* was gorgeous to hear and dramatically affecting, despite her comparative lack of great acting on stage. She retired to New York and taught there.

Sherrill Milnes (b. 1935)

Born in Downers Grove, Illinois, and educated at Northwestern University, Milnes was one of the great Verdi baritones of the post–World War II period. Possessing a naturally lovely baritone voice, he is tall and slim and moves well on stage, which helps his sometimes rudimentary acting.

His Scarpia (*Tosca*) at the Met in 1982 was memorable because for once Scarpia was not an old, ugly man but young and handsome. He has impressed audiences most, however, with his Verdi roles, primarily Iago, the title role in *Rigoletto*, the Count di Luna in *Il Trovatore*, and Posa in *Don Carlo*, all of which he has sung at the Metropolitan Opera, as well as in London and on the Continent. He has rarely touched the German or French repertory but has remained in the Italian baritone roles, where he by and large has succeeded admirably. He has tried comic opera, but he does not have much of a comic flair, and his Figaro in Rossini's *The Barber of Seville* sounds beautiful but is not idiomatic. Toward the end of his singing career, he could still sing well and began to do some conducting too.

Birgit Nilsson (b. 1918)

The Swedish soprano Birgit Nilsson dominated the soprano Wagnerian roles after World War II and was considered *the* Wagnerian soprano of her generation and the heir to Kirsten Flagstad. She made her debut in Stockholm as Agathe in *Die Freischütz* in 1946 and gained international attention as a result of her stellar Elettra in Mozart's *Idomeneo* at Glyndebourne in 1951. In 1954 and 1955 she sang Brünnhilde (*Ring* cycle) and the title role of *Salome* in Munich; thereafter she was a real superstar.

Nilsson became famous for the power and force of her voice, in addition to her ability to sing wonderfully with portamento; her interpretations also impressed with their power and drama. She was best known for the main Wagnerian soprano roles: all three Brünnhildes in the *Ring* operas, Isolde in *Tristan und Isolde*, Elsa in *Lohengrin*, and Elisabeth and Venus in *Tannhäuser*. She also sang Mozart with success, Donna Anna in *Don Giovanni* and Elettra being her best Mozart roles. In the Italian repertory, she was best in the title roles of *Turandot*, *Tosca*, *Aïda*, and Minnie in *La Fanciulla del West*. By the early 1960s, Nilsson had created sensations in Milan, Chicago, London, and New York. She also collaborated in the 1960s with Wieland Wagner at Bayreuth for wonderful productions of the *Ring* operas and *Tristan und Isolde*.

Toward the end of her career, Nilsson sang two Strauss roles with great acclaim: the Dyer's Wife in *Die Frau ohne Schatten* and the title role in *Elektra*. Her career included all the great opera houses, but especially New York's Metropolitan Opera, Milan's La Scala, Munich's Bavarian State Opera, and London's Covent Garden.

Jessye Norman (b. 1945)

Born in Augusta, Georgia, Norman studied voice at Howard University in Washington, D.C. After finding difficulty in starting a career in the United States, Norman went to Germany. In 1968 she won first prize in a voice competition in Munich, after which her career began in earnest. In 1969 she made a very successful debut in Berlin as Wagner's Elisabeth in *Tannhäuser* and became a permanent member of the company. After that triumph, she sang with the conductor Colin Davis at Covent Garden, where she had a series of successes as Mozart's Countess in *The Marriage of Figaro* and in Berlioz's *Les Troyens*. She also sang at the Metropolitan Opera in New York in 1983, singing both Cassandra and Dido in *Les Troyens* in addition to a superb Ariadne in *Ariadne auf Naxos*.

Never birdlike, Norman's voice has an organlike quality because of its size, beauty, and power. Also impressive is her range of roles—from the German, French, and Italian repertories, and all sung with exquisite diction. She has sung both lyric and dramatic soprano roles with equal ease: both Dido and Cassandra, both Aïda and the Countess, both Sieglinde and Elisabeth. Her concerts and recordings have included marvelous interpretations of German and French art songs, particularly by Strauss, Brahms, and Wagner.

Luciano Pavarotti (b. 1935)

Born in Modena, Italy, and with all his musical training in Italy, Pavarotti won a singing contest in Italy in 1961, which launched his career. He made an operatic appearance in Dublin as the Duke of Mantua in *Rigoletto* and came to the attention of the Australian conductor Richard Bonynge and his famous wife, Joan Sutherland. Pavarotti was engaged by them for an Australian tour, and it was during this tour that he became a really fine lyric tenor.

Pavarotti's voice is large, technically secure, and very beautiful. Perhaps the most beautiful Italian tenor voice of the 1960s, 1970s, and 1980s, he quickly became known as the "King of the High C's." After a sensational Metropolitan Opera debut in 1968, he soon became internationally acclaimed. He later sang *La Fille du Régiment* at the Met, and his singing of nine high C's in one aria put him on the cover of *Time* magazine. Soon he came to specialize in the great lyric tenor roles: Nemorino in *The Elixir of Love*, Alfredo in *La Traviata*, Rodolfo in *La Bohème*, Mario Cavaradossi in *Tosca*, Pinkerton in *Madama Butterfly*, the Italian Tenor in *Der Rosenkavalier*, and Ernani in *Ernani*. As he has matured, he has also sung some of the more dramatic tenor roles, particularly Radames in *Aïda* and Prince Calaf in *Turandot*. Although his acting has never been very good, except in comic roles where it could be wonderful, his sweet but large voice and impressive ease with high notes make him a great Italian tenor.

Leontyne Price (b. 1927)

The first black American singer to achieve an international reputation, Leontyne Price was born in Laurel, Mississippi, and studied at the Juilliard School in New York. As *the* Verdi soprano of the 1960s, 1970s, and early 1980s, Price's greatest roles included the title role in *Aïda*, Leonora in both *Il Trovatore* and *La Forze del*

Destino, and Amelia in *Un Ballo in Maschera*. In the non-Verdi soprano roles, she was a wonderful Tosca in the opera of the same name and Liù in *Turandot*, and she sang some German roles as well, achieving success as Strauss's Ariadne (*Ariadne auf Naxos*).

But it was in the Verdi soprano roles that her performances were most successful, because of the opulent beauty of her voice, as well as her superb control of dynamics. There is a rich, smokelike quality to her voice, which luckily has been well recorded on discs. Her acting always remained weak, but the dramatic intensity in her vocal interpretations compensated for this. For a time blacks were barred from operatic careers in America, but Leontyne Price did much to break down the barriers for other black musicians. She retired from opera in 1985 after several wonderful performances of *Aïda* at the Met.

Leonie Rysanek (b. 1926)

Originally from Vienna, the soprano Leonie Rysanek made an unspectacular debut in Innsbruck in 1949, as Agathe in *Der Freischütz*, but when she sang Sieglinde in the *Ring* cycle in Bayreuth in 1951 she received serious attention. Rysanek specialized in the highest dramatic soprano roles, especially the Strauss roles such as Ariadne (*Ariadne auf Naxos*), the title role in *Salome*, the Marschallin in *Der Rosenkavalier*, and the Empress in *Die Frau ohne Schatten*. Some of her Wagnerian roles were also memorable: she succeeded admirably as Senta, Sieglinde, Elsa, Ortrud, and even Kundry.

During the 1950s, Rysanek made important debuts: Vienna in 1954, London in 1955, San Francisco in 1957, and the Metropolitan Opera in 1959 in the very difficult role of Lady Macbeth (*Macbeth*). After these successes, she had an international singing career, marked by great acting in addition to sublime singing. Her Elisabeth in *Tannhäuser* impressed not only for her singing but also for her effective acting: Rysanek knew how to make her voice and body truly dramatic. She was never a soprano eyeing a conductor and waiting for a cue to begin her aria; instead, she always remained in character and as a result made opera into total music theater. The size and beauty of her voice and her comparative lack of vocal problems added to the impact of her performances.

Elisabeth Schwarzkopf (b. 1915)

The German soprano Elisabeth Schwarzkopf studied voice in Berlin and made her debut there in 1938 as a Flower-maiden in Wagner's *Parsifal*. She began as a coloratura, singing roles such as Zerbinetta in Strauss's *Ariadne auf Naxos*, but then became, after World War II, a lyric soprano. She was soon specializing in Mozart and Strauss roles, although she did sing other parts. Her Marschallin in Strauss's *Der Rosenkavalier* resulted in a famous recording and film with the conductor Herbert von Karajan, a performance called by many critics the best ever recorded. This recording captures Schwarzkopf's exquisite, melancholy, and wise Marschallin, and she uses every word, every phrase to make her Marschallin a real person.

While Schwarzkopf's voice was never the most beautiful, her timbre was always distinctive. Her voice was instantly recognizable and never could have been a choral voice. Her Mozart singing was excellent, especially her Fiordiligi in *Così Fan Tutte*, Countess in *The Marriage of Figaro*, and Donna Elvira in *Don Giovanni*. By the 1950s, she was singing at all the major opera houses, especially in Vienna, Milan, and London. After her singing career ended, she continued as an excellent teacher, giving master classes around the world in both opera singing and lieder singing, where she was without peer. Her recordings of Schubert, Strauss, Wolf, and Mahler lieder, primarily with the pianist Gerald Moore, have justifiably been praised by audiences and music critics alike.

Renata Scotto (b. 1934)

Born in Savona, Scotto studied voice in Milan and made her debut there in 1954, singing Violetta in *La Traviata*. Her career is similar in many ways to Maria Callas's, and not only for the fact that they both began as chubby sopranos and then slimmed down to become more attractive. Both sopranos never had particularly beautiful voices, both were plagued with vocal problems like wobbles, and both had difficulties with the highest notes; but both succeeded because of their acting and their ability to make a role vocally and visually dramatic. Both also used excellent diction and colored what they sang to convey dramatic meaning.

Scotto's performance in the title role of *Madama Butterfly* at the Met in 1976 enchanted audiences because of her fine acting. We saw the character change over three acts, and Scotto's telling use of the Italian language made every word meaningful. Her other great roles were Elisabetta in *Don Carlo*, Francesca in Zandonai's *Francesca da Rimini*, and Mimì in *La Bohème*. Her performances in the title roles of *Tosca* and *Lucia di Lammermoor* both impressed more for dramatic than for vocal perfection.

Beverly Sills (b. 1929)

One of the most popular of American divas, Beverly Sills was born in New York City and sang with the New York City Opera for years, never receiving much attention. Her career became international, however, with her famous performance as Cleopatra, along with Norman Treigle as Caesar, in the New York City Opera's production of Handel's *Giulio Cesare* (1966). The rave notices she received for that role made her an international diva. What characterized her performances were her outstanding acting ability and her way of making diction count for dramatic effect. In addition, she impressed audiences with her amazing skill with difficult coloratura passages.

Sills's Lucia (*Lucia di Lammermoor*) also succeeded not just for beautiful sound, although her voice certainly was beautiful, but for her wonderful vocal technique and impressive acting ability. Her singing of the famous flute obbligato passages in the mad scene evoked a demented creature haunted by an inner voice and made credible a woman who has truly gone insane and just committed murder. Her Lucia was performed at the Met and elsewhere, and her performances in London and Milan added to her reputation. Her roles in the three Donizetti operas set in Tudor England— *Roberto Devereux*, *Maria Stuarda*, and *Anna Bolena*—made the most of Donizetti's acting and vocal demands.

Sills also excelled in the French repertory, achieving fame for her interpretations of Massenet's *Manon* and *Thaïs* as well as singing all three soprano roles in Offenbach's *The Tales of Hoffmann*. After her singing career ended, she moved easily into operatic management and became the head of the New York City Opera, where she succeeded in running the theater innovatively. Her lively appearances on television have made her a media presence. In fact, Beverly Sills became synonymous with "opera" to millions of Americans in the 1970s, 1980s, and 1990s.

Joan Sutherland (b. 1926)

Born in Australia, Dame Joan Sutherland has had one of the most beautiful voices and one of the longest careers of the twentieth century. She began as a dramatic soprano, but her husband, the conductor Richard Bonynge, convinced her she was really a coloratura. Her voice was naturally very large and had a spiritual, ethereal sound, and Bonynge trained it for greater agility, control, and numerous technical feats such as the trill, the portamento, and the diminuendo.

The result of all this training was a big, ethereal voice with all the technical expertise and control possible. The only thing that was lacking was clarity, for her diction always tended to be mushy. But what impressed audiences was to have such a large voice of Wagnerian proportions with all this agility, flexibility, and a lovely tone. Sutherland's first major success as a dramatic coloratura came during her famous performance in the title role of *Lucia di Lammermoor* at Covent Garden in 1959, which won her international acclaim. Her Norma, in the opera of the same name, with Marilyn Horne as Adalgisa, created a sensation in London, Vienna, and New York. She has also worked to revive lesser-known works for the coloratura bel canto repertory, especially Rossini's *Semiramide*, Donizetti's *La Fille du Régiment* and *Anna Bolena*, and two early Handel operas: *Alcina* and *Rodelinda*.

Renata Tebaldi (b. 1922)

Tebaldi was born in Pesaro, studied voice in Parma, and made her debut in Rovigo in 1944 as Elena in Boito's *Mefistofele*. But she first gained national attention in Italy when Toscanini picked her for the reopening of La Scala in 1946. By 1955, she had made debuts in London, Chicago, San Francisco, and the Met in New York, and from then until her retirement in the early 1970s, she sang around the world.

Tebaldi's acting was rarely very good and her stage movements did not inspire, but her voice was gorgeous and large, and it remained gorgeous consistently from the top to the bottom of her vocal range; hence the ravishing beauty of her singing won her wide praise. In fact, Maria Callas's dramatic approach to singing was quite opposed to Tebaldi's, and their fans had many heated arguments about the sopranos' respective qualities. But the two rarely sang the same roles. Tebaldi was not a coloratura soprano but a lyric and spinto soprano, and her greatest roles were Mimì in *La Bohème*, the title roles in *Tosca, Madama Butterfly, Adriana Le-couvreur*, and *Aïda*, and Elisabetta in *Don Carlo*. These she sang with ravishing tone if not with dramatic intent. She also recorded extensively. Since her retirement, her large, gorgeous Italian voice has never been duplicated.

Richard Tucker (1913–1975)

Born and educated in New York, Richard Tucker was a famous tenor of the 1950s, 1960s, and early 1970s. His voice was large and beautiful, which compensated for his comparative lack of acting ability in most of his roles. He specialized in the Italian and oc-casionally French tenor roles, and by and large he did only those parts. He was an excellent Manrico (*Il Trovatore*), Alfredo (*La Traviata*), Rodolfo (*La Bohème*), and Enzo (*La Gioconda*).

Tucker made his operatic debut at the Met in New York in 1945 in the role of Enzo in *La Gioconda*, a role that would become one of his most popular. In 1949 he was picked by Toscanini to sing Radames in an important performance of *Aïda*, and this was when Tucker's career became international. Most of his performances were in New York, London, and several theaters in Italy, primarily the Arena in Verona. But his greatest successes were in New York and other American cities, though his occasional appearances in Europe succeeded as well. He has left many recordings of his im-portant roles. An American singer with American training, Tucker helped to continue the tradition of fine American singing.

Jon Vickers (b. 1926)

Born and trained in Canada, Jon Vickers has had an international career as a dramatic tenor, primarily in the Wagnerian heldentenor roles. He made his debut as Don José in *Carmen* at the Stratford Festival in 1956, and the following year he was singing at Covent Garden. His Tristan, Siegmund, and Parsifal were considered the best of his time—the 1960s, 1970s, and even 1980s. He also achieved acclaim as Florestan in Beethoven's *Fidelio*. Among his non-German roles, he succeeded especially as Canio in *Pagliacci*, in the title role in Benjamin Britten's *Peter Grimes*, and as Radames in *Aïda*. Vickers had a big, clear voice that easily filled the largest opera houses. In addition, his timbre was lovely and his diction was good. What added to his genius was his dramatic talent, his ability to immerse himself in a role and communicate that character to the audience. His performance in the title role of *Peter Grimes* was particularly moving, especially in that character's mad scene in the last act of the opera. A great acting singer, with intelligence and intensity, Vickers made his indelible mark on many of the post–World War II tenor roles. Fortunately, most of his roles have been recorded.

Wolfgang Windgassen (1914–1974)

One of the great heldentenors of the post–World War II period, Windgassen centered his career in his native Germany, although he did sing at all the major opera houses around the world. He made his debut in Pforzheim in 1941 as Alvaro in Verdi's *La Forza del Destino*, but his career did not blossom until after World War II. In 1951, at the first Bayreuth festival after the war, he sang the title role in *Parsifal* and soon became a regular tenor there, appearing often in Wieland Wagner's productions.

Windgassen's voice was never as beautiful or as large as some heldentenors, but the intelligence and intensity of his interpretations created splendid performances. What nature did not give him, he created, and the result succeeded, particularly in small opera houses such as Bayreuth. In Bayreuth, Stuttgart, and London's Covent Garden especially, his interpretations of the title roles of *Tannhäuser*, *Lohengrin*, and *Parsifal*, and Walther (*Die Meistersinger von Nürnberg*), Tristan (*Tristan und Isolde*), and Siegfried (*Ring* cycle) succeeded. In the non-Wagnerian roles, his Otello (Verdi) was much admired. At the end of his career Windgassen taught voice in Germany.

Eight

The Standard Repertory: The Fifty Most-Often-Performed Operas

Without music life would be a mistake.

—Friedrich Nietzsche

The standard repertory, the list of works considered the greatest and the most popular, changes constantly. A hundred years ago the standard repertory would have certainly included works by Meyerbeer, especially *Le Prophète* and *Les Huguenots*, operas now performed quite rarely. On the other hand, fifty years ago Verdi's *Don Carlo* would certainly not have been considered part of the standard repertory, though now it certainly is.

Moreover, what the standard repertory includes depends to an extent on who puts the list together. While some contemporary critics would include Britten's *Peter Grimes*, others would not; some critics would include Puccini's *Manon Lescaut*, but others would not. Puccini's *Manon Lescaut* would definitely be considered standard repertory in Italy, but not in Germany, just as Weber's *Der Freischütz* is standard repertory in Germany, but not in Italy. And in France Charpentier's *Louise* is standard repertory, but nowhere else.

The following, then, represents this critic's attempt to list the standard repertory operas in America, despite the fact that many operas fall into a gray area. On the other hand, there are black-and-white areas as well, since all music critics would include Puccini's big three, *La Bohème*, *Madama Butterfly*, and *Tosca*, and Verdi's *Aïda*, *Don Carlo*, and *Otello* in the repertory these days. So, trying to be as fair as possible, I will in this chapter list and discuss one version of the standard repertory. The operas that follow are the backbone of operatic production around the world, although most opera houses like to vary their seasons with some obscure and rare works as well. Still, most opera companies spend most of their energies and resources to produce the repertory operas.

Books on the subject generally discuss the standard repertory operas in terms of musical phrases, major arias, and musical style, complete with musical illustrations quoted from the opera's score. Plot summaries are also generally provided in the typical guides, but since such plot summaries are contained in most opera programs and record notes, I will do little plot summarizing. Since most readers cannot read music and so are completely befuddled by printed musical notations, I will instead analyze these operas in terms of dramatic and thematic conflicts, with only passing references to the music, and only insofar as the music reinforces the dramatic conflicts in the works. I will not quote the music, although I will refer to it in a nontechnical way. Music, the great glory of opera, is not its only glory; therefore, to approach the standard repertory through theater, theme, and characterization is eminently valid. I will list the works by composer so that the development of the composer and the evolution of operatic style will be a part of the discussion of these operatic classics. Understanding the standard repertory operas and why they are considered great will improve the reader's awareness of this basis of operatic appreciation.

The fifty operas of the standard repertory can be best understood in terms of their periods and styles. To facilitate that understanding, let us look at them first in terms of their historical periods, and then individually.

THE STANDARD REPERTORY

EIGHTEENTH CENTURY

Gluck, Christoph Willibald (1714–1787)
Orfeo ed Euridice (1762)

Mozart, Wolfgang Amadeus (1756–1791)
The Abduction from the Seraglio (1782)
The Marriage of Figaro (1786)
Don Giovanni (1787)
Così Fan Tutte (1790)
The Magic Flute (1791)

NINETEENTH CENTURY

Beethoven, Ludwig van (1770–1827)
Fidelio (1805)

Rossini, Gioacchino Antonio (1792–1868)
L'Italiana in Algeri (1813)
The Barber of Seville (1816)

Bellini, Vincenzo (1801–1835)
Norma (1831)

Donizetti, Gaetano (1797–1848)
The Elixir of Love (1832)
Lucia di Lammermoor (1835)
Don Pasquale (1843)

Wagner, Richard (1813–1883)
The Flying Dutchman (1843)
Tannhäuser (1845)
Lohengrin (1850)
Tristan und Isolde (1865)
Die Meistersinger von Nürnberg (1868)
The *Ring* Cycle (1876)
Das Rheingold
Die Walküre
Siegfried
Götterdämmerung
Parsifal (1882)

Verdi, Giuseppe (1813–1901)
Rigoletto (1851)
Il Trovatore (1853)
La Traviata (1853)
La Forza del Destino (1862)
Don Carlo (1867)
Aïda (1871)
Otello (1887)
Falstaff (1893)

Gounod, Charles François (1818 – 1893)
Faust (1859)

Moussorgsky, Modest (1839 – 1881)
Boris Godunov (1874)

Bizet, Georges (1838 – 1875)
Carmen (1875)

Tchaikovsky, Peter Ilyich (1840 – 1893)
Eugene Onegin (1879)

Mascagni, Pietro (1863 – 1945)
Cavalleria Rusticana (1890)

Leoncavallo, Ruggiero (1858 – 1919)
Pagliacci (1892)

TWENTIETH CENTURY

Puccini, Giacomo (1858 – 1924)
Manon Lescaut (1893)
La Bohème (1896)
Tosca (1900)
Madama Butterfly (1904)
Turandot (1926)

Debussy, Claude (1862 – 1918)
Pelléas et Mélisande (1902)

Strauss, Richard (1864 – 1949)
Salome (1905)
Elektra (1909)

Der Rosenkavalier (1911)

Ariadne auf Naxos (1912)

Berg, Alban (1885 – 1935)

Wozzeck (1925)

Lulu (1937)

Britten, Benjamin (1913 – 1976)

Peter Grimes (1945)

EIGHTEENTH CENTURY

Gluck, Christoph Willibald (1714 – 1787)

Orfeo ed Euridice/Orpheus and Euridice (1762)

Gluck's most famous opera, *Orfeo ed Euridice*, was originally written in Italian by the famous librettist Ranieri di Calzabigi for the Vienna Opera, although the work was later translated into French for Paris and a highly successful second premiere there. It has become most often performed in Italian rather than French and is considered the earliest of the standard repertory operas, although Monteverdi's Orpheus opera, *La Favola d'Orfeo* (1607), competes with Gluck's work for this title.

But Gluck's is certainly more often performed, and I think it's the better opera. Given the typical opera seria of the eighteenth century, Gluck's *Orfeo* is clearly a reform opera that avoids the vocal fireworks of the castrati and instead creates the calm and somber tone of classical tragedy. Although this opera is not a tragedy and does have a happy ending, its mood and tone are consistently elegiac and tragic.

Gluck tried very hard to avoid the aria/recitative pattern in this opera, and often he succeeds, though the most famous piece from the opera is Orfeo's moving lament "Che farò senza Euridice," and audiences always wait for this aria. The opera also includes long choral and ballet sequences and much static drama.

The enjoyment of this opera requires an awareness of the simple story from Greek legend about the love of Orfeo and Euridice. Orfeo can be sung by a mezzo-soprano, although the role was originally written for a castrato, and the opera has been altered so that the part can be played by a tenor or baritone. But the real eighteenth-century style of the piece is best experienced with a mezzo-soprano in the role of Orfeo, despite the loss of dramatic realism.

A good production of *Orfeo ed Euridice* should include the elegiac tone, controlled singing from chorus and soloists, and a dramatic style characterized by classic restraint. This classic restraint is very difficult to create because it demands intensity yet control. But only control, both vocal and dramatic, will create the eighteenth-century elegiac style, reminiscent of ancient Greek tragedy, that Gluck was trying to re-create. Greek art, the wellspring of opera, regularly influences composers as a model. Greece, which produced the first recognizable operatic performances, inspired many subsequent composers to create opera in the Greek ideal.

Mozart, Wolfgang Amadeus (1756–1791)
The Abduction from the Seraglio/Die Entführung aus dem Serail (1782)

This opera was the result of a commission from the Austrian Emperor Josef II, who wanted to encourage national opera in German rather than the standard operatic language of the time in Vienna, Italian. *The Abduction* was the result, and it succeeded because of its use of Italian musical forms with a German text. The piece is a singspiel, a light, popular German opera with spoken dialogue rather than the recitative customary for opera at the time, with a clever text by Gottlieb Stephanie based on Christoph Friedrich Bretzner's comic play.

This opera contrasts European culture—the Europeans are Spanish although they sing in German—with Turkish culture; and the Turkish marches and Turkish musical effects, achieved primarily with the triangle, characterize this work as unique among Mozart's operas. Mozart also used the device of parallel characterization, a device that became increasingly popular in the operas of the nineteenth century, for purposes of contrast and sometimes comedy as well. Constanze and Belmonte are the noble lovers; Constanze is imprisoned in the seraglio of the Turkish ruler Selim Pasha. Blonde and Pedrillo, the common, lower-class lovers, are comic and cynical where the other pair is serious and idealistic. A conflict of the cultures appears as well, since Turkish culture, often dismissed as barbaric by the Europeans of the period, has an eloquent and humane representative in the Pasha Selim, perhaps the most interesting character in the opera, although he only speaks and never sings. Pasha Selim has a humanity and grandeur that culminate in his allowing the Europeans to leave his country since he cannot persuade Constanze to stay with him. The opera ends with the European characters singing their praises for the generous and noble Pasha.

The Marriage of Figaro/Le Nozze di Figaro (1786)

Mozart's greatest social comedy, *The Marriage of Figaro* reflects the revolutionary implications of the Beaumarchais play that is its source. Lorenzo Da Ponte's great libretto gives clear motivation to the characters, presents clever dramatic situations, provides much comedy, and maintains the balance of comedy and pathos that Mozart was so fond of—"gray comedy," as it is often called. The opera was the first product of a very successful collaboration that produced the three great Italian operas of Mozart's middle period.

The Marriage of Figaro, based on an infamous revolutionary play of the same title by Pierre-Augustin de Beaumarchais, reflects many of the social conflicts of the eighteenth century. Did a nobleman have the right to seduce any peasant woman who crossed his path? Traditionally, the lord had the right to sleep with any peasant woman on his manor before she married—the legendary *droit du seigneur*. But was this really honest or moral? These are some of the conflicts and questions in the play, and in Mozart's opera as well. The characterizations present us with each of the major social classes of the period: the swaggering Count Almaviva, who has lost interest in his wife; the neglected Countess, who yearns for the love her husband used to show her; the wily servant Figaro, determined to outsmart his lecherous lord; his fiancée, the soubrette Susanna, who wants to be loyal to her lady but outsmart her lecherous lord; and the page Cherubino, an adolescent boy who is totally a victim of his puberty.

Musically, the opera is a series of arias (or other musical numbers) and recitatives, a typically Italian operatic comedy of the eighteenth century in terms of form. But the orchestration fascinates the symphonist, and the musical numbers, especially the famous finale to Act II, indicate Mozart's genius for melody that is appropriate both for character and dramatic situation.

Don Giovanni (1787)

Don Giovanni has frequently been called the greatest opera ever composed because of its clever mixture of comedy and tragedy in the typically Mozartian fashion. Lorenzo Da Ponte's libretto is not as neat and contained as that of *Figaro* or of *Così Fan Tutte*, the opera to follow and their last collaboration. But here librettist and composer take big chances and produce an opera that is comic, tragic, and profound. In its two long acts, *Don Giovanni* questions the nature of God, Catholicism, male sexuality, male/female relationships, and the justice of the social class system in eighteenth-century Europe.

Here, too, we have a servant who is tired of obeying a master, as in *Figaro*. Leporello in this opera, like Figaro in *The Marriage of Figaro*, sings of how sick he is of serving and how he would like to do what he wants with his life, and curses the fact that given his background he must serve someone if he wants to eat. The Don himself fascinates since his character can be played in many different ways. Is he simply lecherous in his determination to seduce as many skirts as possible? Or does he move from woman to woman because he is incapable of real intimacy and love with any woman? Or is he simply a bored cynic and misogynist who wants to prove how weak and lecherous women really are behind their prim and puritan facades? And how Catholic are the other characters, who criticize the Don and claim to be loyal Catholics, yet who also vow revenge on him?

The women in the opera demand special notice because of their complexity and especially their sexual availability. Donna Anna decides to avenge her father's murder, yet clearly loves the Don still; Donna Elvira will follow the Don anywhere, despite his dreadful treatment of her; Zerlina is perfectly willing to leave her fiancé Masetto for the Don; and hundreds of other women find him irresistible as well. The musical numbers make the most of the comic situations in the opera: the Don's drinking song, "Finch' han dal vino"; the seduction duet, "Là ci darem la mano"; and Leporello's wonderful catalogue aria listing the thousands of the Don's sexual conquests all create much comedy. Yet during the opera, the Don never succeeds in his attempts at seduction—a clever bit of irony. But the serious numbers impress as well: Donna Anna's "Or sai chi l'onore," Don Ottavio's two beautiful arias, and the Don's own determination to defend his lifestyle even in the face of a gaping hell under him.

Così Fan Tutte/They All Do It (1790)

Così Fan Tutte has been called the most perfect product of the spirit of the Rococo, and there is indeed a wonderful perfection, symmetry, and cynicism about this intimate work. Two men decide to test the fidelity of their fiancées, with sad results, and reunion of the original lovers or union with their new-found lovers is left to the director to decide; Mozart and Da Ponte imply that it doesn't much matter.

The conflict between the cynical old bachelor, Don Alfonso, and the naive young lovers, Guglielmo and Ferrando, creates a wonderful dramatic contrast that sustains the entire opera. This is balanced by the cynical maid Despina (like the bachelor Don Alfonso) in opposition to the idealistic sisters, the noble Fiordiligi and the more venal and pliable Dorabella. The symmetry of this work captures the spirit of the Rococo: two sisters, two male lovers, two cynics, and two dramatic reversals.

Some critics of the opera, including Beethoven, have been repelled by its very cynicism. Some commentators have argued that cynicism and skepticism have no place in the greatest works of art, but *Così Fan Tutte* clearly stands as a refutation of this argument, for it is pretty difficult to dispute that this is a great opera. It did, however, languish for a time and was not produced often until after World War II, when productions in Germany and Glyndebourne, England, returned *Così Fan Tutte* to the standard repertory.

The Magic Flute/Die Zauberflöte (1791)

This, Mozart's final opera, brings the German singspiel to its most perfect embodiment. Taking a light, popular play with spoken dialogue and transforming it from a text by Emanuel Schikaneder,

Mozart turned this childlike fairy-tale plot into one of the most profound works. What dazzles us about this opera is its scope—including, as it does, religion, philosophy, love, comedy, a suicide attempt, and slapstick all in one great work. Once again, we have the distinctly Mozartian form of gray comedy, which includes a silly bird-catcher who attempts suicide, a powerful woman who vows revenge, and the battle of the sexes. A Rococo obsession with symmetry is apparent in this work as well: two pairs of lovers, Tamino/Pamina and Papageno/Papagena; two forces of power, one for good (Sarastro) and one for evil (the Queen of the Night); and the male versus the female principles. Based on Mozart and his librettist Schikaneder's belief in the brotherhood of the Masons, the opera presents Free Masonry as the hope for a universal brotherhood to transcend the class system of eighteenth-century Europe.

Yet this work presents a class system as well as a value system. The noble Tamino seeks goodness and truth, while the lower-class Papageno seeks food, drink, and a pretty young wife. The noble Tamino endures the tests of fire and water to attain enlightenment, while the cowardly Papageno has to be dragged through these tests by the scruff of the neck. All of us, of course, are both Tamino and Papageno, and Mozart seeks a unity for this duality that would provide human beings with intellectual fulfillment and sexual satisfaction. Sarastro's nobility must conquer the vindictive hysteria of the Queen of the Night so that the new age of enlightenment can begin. Mozart's triumph is to unite such profound ideals in a childlike, fairy-tale opera.

NINETEENTH CENTURY

The nineteenth century has provided the standard repertory with more operas than any other, and gave birth to the two operatic giants Verdi and Wagner. These two composers have given more operas to the standard repertory than all others, and their operas, with all their complexity of plot and characterization and the grandeur and dramatic intensity of their music, have provided the art form with classic models of greatness.

Beethoven, Ludwig van (1770 – 1827)
Fidelio (1805)

Fidelio takes the singspiel form and brings it to heights of expressiveness beyond itself. As a result, this opera, to a text by Josef Sonnleithner, although flawed, is a musically wonderful work. Act I begins with the typical situation of a singspiel, that popular comic form of German folk opera, which features a love triangle, but in this case the triangle occurs among the employees of a prison. The situation is further complicated by the fact that one of the characters in the love triangle, the boy Fidelio, is actually a woman in disguise. She is looking for her husband, Florestan, who has been imprisoned there for political reasons by the tyrant Don Pizarro.

The conflicts in the opera require an expansion of the comic singspiel form, and Beethoven provides the music for this, if not always the drama. Truth and justice conflict with power and repression in this mighty opera. The power of the faithful woman and the force of conjugal love sustain the two acts. Leonora, in disguise as the boy Fidelio, risks her life to save her husband. Like many bachelors, Beethoven idealized women and conjugal love, as he does in this opera.

What begins as a silly and improbable love story becomes by the end a cantata to the power of love and freedom. The most dramatic scene in the opera is certainly the first scene in the second act, when Don Pizarro arrives to murder Florestan, but Leonora manages to save him. The rescue story, that innovation of Romantic theater in the nineteenth century, propels the opera to its greatest dramatic tension. The action halts in the last scene, however, allowing Beethoven's sublime choral finale to provide ample musical compensation for the loss of drama.

Rossini, Gioacchino Antonio (1792 – 1868)
L'Italiana in Algeri/The Italian Girl in Algiers (1813)

This opera, with a text by Anelli, is the most often performed of all Rossini's operas after *The Barber of Seville* and is similar to that later work in many ways. Both use a two-act structure and both involve the conflict of a determined and intelligent young woman, here named Isabella, and a pompous and silly old man, in this case the Algerian Mustafà. The comedy in this opera centers in part on the conflicts between Italian and Islamic culture, as in Mozart's *The Abduction from the Seraglio*. But while the Mozart opera has a more philosophical theme, concerning European versus Islamic culture and values, Rossini's opera relies on more purely comic situations and effects.

Isabella, the Italian girl, who has come to Algiers to find her lover, Lindoro, who has been captured and enslaved by the Algerians, typifies the Rossinian woman—strong-willed, independent, and possessed of a wonderful voice and tremendous vocal agility. The bel canto soprano or mezzo-soprano par excellence excels in these roles, but she must possess a sense of comedy as well as technical vocal prowess.

Rossini's situations are quite comic here, complete with a rescue attempt in the last act to fool the old and tyrannical Mustafà. The chorus of eunuchs who open the opera cleverly establish the tone of the work, as they sing of their fear of their master, Mustafà. But in the middle of the act, when Isabella appears and sings her bravura aria, we know that she will win this particular battle, a fact made even more apparent when she finally gets to meet her rival, Mustafà. Their comic duet establishes their characters immediately. She sings "Che musa" (What a face) while he sings "Che pezza" (What a piece). She finds him silly, but he finds her irresistible, and that is the essence of their conflict. That she wins is a foregone conclusion, but how she wins and why she does ignite the comedy of the piece.

The Barber of Seville/Il Barbiere di Siviglia (1816)

The Italian comic opera form of the early nineteenth century reached divine embodiment in Rossini's most famous and most frequently performed opera, *The Barber of Seville*, with a witty text by Cesare Sterbini. While the German singspiel form used spoken dialogue, the Italian comic form of the eighteenth century used harpsichord-accompanied recitative between musical numbers, especially the famous bravura arias; and this form also typifies the Italian operatic comedy of the early nineteenth century. Dramatically, the sources of the plot come from Beaumarchais's comedy, commedia dell'arte, and the Roman comedy of Plautus and Terence. The story involves the age-old tale of an old man pursuing a lovely young lady, who of course much prefers her young lover.

The drama provides Rossini and his librettist Sterbini with great opportunities for bravura arias. Each major character gets one, and they are all vocally marvelous and dramatically comic. The most famous is Figaro's "Largo al factotum" with its clever "Figaro, Figaro" refrain. Rosina's "Una voce poco fa" perfectly characterizes her soubrette quality and determination to outsmart her amorous old suitor. Don Basilio's famous "La Calunnia" aria sings the praises of calumny as an effective way to get rid of an enemy. The orchestration adds to the fun of these showy arias, providing the death stroke in the calumny aria and the bird song for Rosina.

The character types generate much of the comedy, especially in the case of Dr. Bartolo and Don Basilio, the two old cronies who resist the determination of the young lovers to marry each other. Their bravura arias—Dr. Bartolo's "A un dottor della mia sorte" and Don Basilio's "La Calunnia"—not only characterize these people, their sense of importance, and their approaches to conflicts, but also delight audiences. If these arias are sung well, they should bring down the house.

The opera's characters resemble commedia dell'arte types—the dashing young suitor, Lindoro; the lovely young maiden, Rosina; the nasty old professor, Don Basilio; the foolish and pompous old man, Dr. Bartolo. The music, especially the ingenious use of the orchestra, adds to the pleasures of this opera. In his time Rossini was called "the young Mozart" because of his subtle and clever orchestration. The fast tempi and comic use of the woodwinds add to the rhythm and richness of the orchestral texture.

Sterbini's comic genius includes clever use of the recitatives as well as the arias. Sterbini often followed an aria with clever dialogue to comment ironically on the aria. After Rosina's wonderful "Una voce poco fa" and the thunderous applause that should follow it, Rosina's next line is "Sì, sì, io vincero"—"Yes, yes, I'll win." After Don Basilio's tour de force in "La Calunnia" in which he recommends calumny as the best way to deal with the youthful intruder, Dr. Bartolo's response is an abrupt "No!"—which adds to the comedy of the situation. The text and music unite to create the great classic early-nineteenth-century opera buffa that is *The Barber of Seville*.

Bellini, Vincenzo (1801–1835)
Norma (1831)

Using a text by Felice Romani, Bellini wrote this opera's title role for the soprano Giuditta Pasta, known for her dramatic intensity and vocal beauty. The plot is based on Roman history, when the Roman proconsul Pollione rules Gaul, with the consequent hatred of the native people for their foreign ruler. The love interest, with the Roman Pollione taking as a lover first the Druid priestess Norma, and then another priestess, Adalgisa, emphasizes the conflict of the two cultures. The plot makes for some sublime duets between the two women, as well as some impressive arias for all three of the soloists.

The story of the opera reminds us of that of *Medea*, since the high priestess Norma, who has had two children despite her vow of chastity, considers killing them in their sleep to get revenge on their faithless father. As this situation indicates, the opera clearly echoes several famous aspects of Greek tragedy, and its main character, Norma, recalls the nobility and vengefulness of Medea, Electra, and Antigone. Norma has sublime music to sing, notably her wonderful aria in Act I, "Casta diva,"—sung to the chaste goddess, the moon, as Norma cuts the sacred mistletoe on the holy oak tree in a Druid religious rite. The calm beauty and religious fervor of this aria present us with the public Norma, the chaste virgin who has dedicated her life to her religion and her people.

In the next scene we see the passionate woman Norma, in love with the man who is supposed to be her people's enemy, the Roman proconsul. Several modern productions of this opera have suggested a revolutionary subtext to the plot. The Druids under the yoke of Rome are really to be understood as they were understood by nineteenth-century Italian audiences, that is, as the Italian people under the yoke of Austria. Representation of the Druid desire for freedom from foreign oppression, like the suffering of Jews under Babylonian control in Verdi's *Nabucco*, was a way of getting around the strict Austrian censorship in nineteenth-century Italy. Such an interpretation of the plot is certainly defensible. Audiences of the time would surely have responded this way to the suffering of the Druids and the sublime suffering of their religious leader, Norma.

Donizetti, Gaetano (1797–1848)

The Elixir of Love/L'Elisir d'Amore (1832)

Donizetti's early comedy, *The Elixir of Love*, uses a libretto by Felice Romani and follows the Rossinian tradition of Italian comic opera. The situation involves the conflict of the wily basso buffo, Dr. Dulcamara, and the apparently naive peasants, Nemorino and Adina. It is Nemorino who sings the famous aria "Una furtiva lagrima," that marvelous piece about a young boy in love, which, if sung properly, should stop the show. Beyond this famous aria, the opera involves the peasant boy's determination to win his girlfriend, and he succeeds despite the trickery of the basso buffo.

The elixir that Nemorino hopes will make his beloved love him in return, which he buys from the clever trickster Dr. Dulcamara, really contains only wine. The broad comedy and occasional pathos of this situation unite to create an entertaining musical and theatrical evening. The conflict of the seemingly naive peasant and the cynical city trickster provides much of the comedy in this opera. But the not-so-naive country boy wins his beloved and love is triumphant in the end.

Lucia di Lammermoor (1835)

Of all the bel canto composers (Rossini, Bellini, and Donizetti), Gaetano Donizetti had the best dramatic instinct, especially for serious drama. His operas, particularly his famous trilogy on English Tudor history—*Anna Bolena, Maria Stuarda*, and *Roberto Devereux*—contain intensely dramatic scenes. But his most famous opera, *Lucia di Lammermoor*, set to a libretto by Salvatore Cammarano, is based on a famous novel by Sir Walter Scott, *The Bride of Lammermoor*. The plot portrays the tribal feuds of the Scottish chiefs and the suffering of their children as a result of these bloody feuds. Similar to Shakespeare's *Romeo and Juliet*, the plot involves the love of the daughter of one family, Lucia, for Edgardo, the son of her family's sworn enemies.

What captivates most audiences is the character and singing prowess of the soprano in the role of Lucia. One of the most difficult of coloratura roles, Lucia demands tremendous agility and vocal flexibility along with dramatic intensity. There are several ways of approaching this role, and each can be successful with audiences. The role of Lucia can be sung beautifully, especially the famous and very difficult mad scene in the third act, and the drama can be largely ignored. If the singing is powerful and beautiful, most of the audience will love this approach for its vocal splendor. For the soprano without a particularly gorgeous voice, the dramatic aspects of the role can be emphasized, and the mad scene can be done not as a vocal tour de force but as a theatrical event. Lucia can be portrayed as a weak person pushed too far who goes insane and commits murder—or as a vengeful and determined woman who succumbs to insanity. While the opera is not a verismo work, its dramatic content is potent, and a successful soprano can make the role of Lucia very convincing.

Approaches to production can vary in this opera as well. *Lucia* can be staged in a Scottish never-never land, with the fairy-tale aspects of the opera emphasized. Or the dramatic, realistic aspects can be stressed through the portrayal of a less picturesque Scotland on stage, a Scotland full of murderous vengefulness, an ugly and war-scarred land. Against such possible backgrounds, the role of Lucia should dominate and fascinate.

Don Pasquale (1843)

Don Pasquale, written to a text by Giacomo Ruffini, is the second of Donizetti's comedies that remains in the standard repertory. The plot is similar to that of Rossini's *The Barber of Seville*, involving as it does the classic conflict of a lecherous old suitor, in this case Don Pasquale, and Norina, a lovely young widow. Here too the source of the comedy begins with the determination of the beautiful but also clever young girl to outsmart her wealthy suitor and marry the man she wants, Ernesto.

The opera has dramatic conflict and excitement despite its conventional plot. The famous slap that Norina gives Don Pasquale, her recognition that she really has gone too far, and her subsequent contrition, add to the complexity of the characters and situations. While Donizetti is known for his unsubtle use of the orchestra, he is also famous for his clever use of drama and voice.

Wagner, Richard (1813–1883)

Wagner is one of the great revolutionaries in opera, and all of his mature works have remained in the standard repertory. For most of his life, Wagner said he hated opera and instead wanted to produce "music drama," that Wagnerian blend of music and drama that avoids recitative and aria and instead tries to create melos, the eternal melody that is both dramatic and beautiful. The late Wagnerian operas (*Tristan und Isolde*, the *Ring* cycle, and *Parsifal*) achieve a style akin to that of the Italian arioso, or the halfway point between recitative and aria that is both melodic and suitable for the dramatic situations and characters. To help achieve this end, Wagner used leitmotivs, or "leading melodies," to help present the main characters and ideas in his music dramas.

Wagner could control his dramaturgy more than most composers because of his wonderful ability to write his own librettos, unlike most opera composers, who have to work in collaboration with one or in some cases several other people to produce an opera. His aim, "to unify Shakespeare with Beethoven," demanded the creation of a new form of opera that he felt was the Greek ideal for tragedy, a form that uniquely unified music, literature, and drama—the *Gesamtkunstwerk*, or "combined art work."

The Flying Dutchman/Der Fliegende Holländer (1843)

The first of Wagner's operas to become part of the standard repertory, this opera reflects much of Wagner's early interest in the folk operas of Carl Maria von Weber, especially his then very popular *Der Freischütz* (1821). The concept of the common people and how they treat the outsider is central to *The Flying Dutchman*, as in Weber's opera. Two kinds of music dominate Wagner's opera: the light, cheerful folksy dance music of the people in this Norwegian town counterpointed with the brooding, obsessive, undulating music for Vanderdecken, the cursed Dutchman, and Senta, the woman attracted to him. The music of these two tells us immediately that they are isolated from other people in the town, obsessed, attracted to each other, and consequently doomed. Indeed they die together, though the curse on the Dutchman is lifted by Senta's sacrificial death. Redemption through love, that recurrent Wagner theme, first occurs in this earliest of his mature operas.

What complicates the plot is Senta's other lover, the huntsman Erik, who tries to persuade her to marry him instead of running off with the peculiar Dutchman. The conflict between the landsman, Erik, and the seaman, Vanderdecken, begins a contrast that will recur frequently in Wagner and that uses the symbolism of water. Water represents that great unknown, uncontrollable, natural, and dangerous element that normal people are afraid of, repelled by, and avoid, but to which some souls are attracted, even if this fascination will result in their deaths, as it generally does. There are many ways of interpreting this symbolism in the opera. In one view, the Dutchman is the misunderstood outsider who needs love and someone who will be faithful to him. Another possible interpretation sees the Dutchman as the misunderstood artist who wants to be part of the community of normal human beings, but who never can be, and who will in fact kill those who try to help him, as happens in this opera. But is this death really the proverbial blessing in disguise for Senta, who has been redeemed and removed from a silly, superficial society and a loveless family?

The opera, one of Wagner's earliest, includes several set musical numbers. The Dutchman's famous monologue, close to a formal aria, in fact, "Die Frist ist um," presents the loneliness of this man of the sea, according to myth doomed to wander the seas with his crew and who can land only once every seven years to try to find a faithful woman whose love will free him from his curse. Senta's famous ballad, in the next scene of the opera, presents her as a sympathetic woman who has heard of the Dutchman's curse and vows to help him if she can. Bored with her suitors, especially the landlubber Erik, Senta is attracted to the strange Dutchman. Despite the efforts of Erik to stop her, she follows the Dutchman to her death. The opera, in many ways, confronts a reality in many people's lives: What Freud would call the life force versus the death wish. Since Wagner so often presents this theme in his operas, they frequently repel people who do not want to see this conflict between the life force and the death wish in themselves.

Tannhäuser (1845)

The dramatic and musical conflicts in this opera, as in most of Wagner's operas, occur on many levels and generate many themes and subplots. Here the conflict involves the pagan goddess Venus, who, of course, represents all the sexual pleasures of the whorehouse—a kind of sexual abandon and variety that the medieval minstrel Tannhäuser wallows in during the first scene of the opera. He has left humanity for the grotto of Venus, complete with her nymphs and satyrs, yet he is unhappy there, and he escapes at the end of scene one.

The second act introduces Elisabeth, the saintly woman who is the heiress to the throne of Thuringia and is in love with Tannhäuser, wanting in fact to marry him. She represents the sexuality of marriage and society, complete with its religious and social commitments and the repression all that represents. Tannhäuser loves her, but ultimately rejects her by the end of the second act because of his scandalous performance in the hall of the minstrels. During the contest there, in which the minstrels compete to create a song on the theme of love, Tannhäuser defends the pagan sensuality of Venus, and only Elisabeth comes to his aid and suggests that the Pope in Rome will forgive him for such a sin.

In the third act Tannhäuser has taken his famous pilgrimage to Rome to seek forgiveness for the horrible sin of living with Venus. As Tannhäuser describes the scene in his Rome monologue, when he asked the Pope for forgiveness of that sin, the pontiff was so horrified by such a grave sin that he said Tannhäuser would be forgiven only when the Pope's old staff sprouted green leaves again. Tannhäuser relates the hopeless story and dies convinced that he will never be forgiven, but other pilgrims come in with a staff that has green leaves on it. Tannhäuser has been forgiven, despite the Pope, and is redeemed. The concept of redemption and forgiveness possible for all sinners, no matter what the sin and no matter what the official representatives of the Church say, becomes the wonderful and hopeful moral of this medieval legend. Here, too, Wagner creates mythic drama, here Christian medieval myth, rather than realistic drama. And here, too, Wagner presents us with Tannhäuser as man in conflict with concepts of the feminine. When he is with the voluptuous Venus, he yearns for the virtuous Elisabeth, and when he is faced with commitment to Elisabeth, he yearns for the freedom and abandon of Venus.

Lohengrin (1850)

The most popular of Wagner's operas, certainly the most often performed, *Lohengrin* begins with silvery, celestial music for the knight of the Grail, Lohengrin, and his descent to earth to find a woman who will believe in him. Like the Dutchman, Lohengrin is a strange and attractive creature who needs human love, and he helps Elsa in the first act when she is falsely accused of murdering her brother. She promises to love Lohengrin and not ask his identity in return for his help in the tournament to prove her innocence against her false accuser, Friedrich von Telramund, and his wife, Ortrud.

Friedrich and Ortrud, worshippers of pagan gods, fight throughout the opera for the defeat of the heavenly Lohengrin. This conflict lends itself to several possible interpretations. Is Lohengrin the artist common humanity can never understand? Is he the outsider the community always suspects? Is he the savior of humanity, the person humanity always uses but fears and finally rejects? Complexity and conflict occur on many levels in this opera, and these conflicts involve some of Wagner's most fascinating characters. Elsa, the young innocent, contrasts wonderfully with the evil but noble Ortrud, that worshipper of pagan gods and goddesses. Neither she nor Friedrich is a two-dimensional villain. Friedrich is concerned with his honor, as is Lohengrin with his own. Friedrich is like Macbeth, also under the influence of a powerful and evil woman, but himself a noble man.

And Elsa seems so foolish to use her own wedding night, in Act III, to ask the fatal question of Lohengrin. She decides she must know his identity, even if it will kill her. Her desire to know is so human, yet she renounces her own vow never to ask this question. By the end of the opera Lohengrin must return to the knights of the Grail, and humanity must do without the help of its celestial warrior. Can man and the divine ever meet? The opera suggests they cannot.

Tristan und Isolde (1865)

This opera influenced the development of modern music more than any other, for here Wagner created a system of musical structures that completely ignores the standard diatonic key system that formed the basis for Western music since the Renaissance. His use of chromaticism to provide an undulating sound for the music so that it seems to float gently from note to note was considered lunatic by many music critics at the time. There were no set musical pieces in the opera, and it seemed like a formless mess to many contemporary critics, especially the conservative ones like Eduard Hanslick. But there is much form in *Tristan und Isolde*, though an experimental and original one uniquely suited to the subject matter of this opera.

Each act begins with an off-stage musical sound: the sailor's a cappella song in Act I, the hunting horns in Act II, and the shepherd's pipe in Act III. And each act ends with Tristan attempting suicide: in Act I, by drinking the potion that he thinks is poison but that is really a love potion; in Act II, by dropping his own sword and allowing himself to be wounded by Melot; in Act III, by ripping off his bandages and causing his wounds to bleed again, which finally succeeds in killing him.

Tristan und Isolde argues for the rejection of life, including a conception of life as inevitably frustrating and doomed to failure. Wagner had been reading Schopenhauer's gloomy philosophy and was involved with a futile love affair with Mathilde von Wesendonck at the time; he was undoubtedly suicidal during this unhappy and very frustrating period of his life, and the opera presents a hopeless view of life and the dim possibilities for love. Just as Tristan and Isolde are trapped by the love potion into a love affair that is adulterous and dooms them to suffering and social ostracism, so they come to see that only in death can their love be fulfilled, or at least their misery ended. The opera closes with Tristan dead and Isolde singing the "Liebestod," a dream vision in which she imagines Tristan alive and floating in water and clouds. She sings that to join him would be the greatest bliss: She, too, wishes for the death that alone can bring them happiness.

Such a suicide- and death-ridden opera contains some of the most gorgeous and sexual music ever written, especially the sensual

"Liebesnacht" love music in Act II, which comes to jarring frustration rather than climax with the entrance of Isolde's husband King Marke, who catches them in their adulterous embrace. This frustration continues in Tristan's long monologue at the beginning of Act III, serving as a structural balance for Isolde's monologue at the beginning of Act I. While Isolde's monologue is full of anger and hatred, Tristan's in Act III is one of the most beautifully painful in all opera; although in the night he cherishes his love, in the blazing light of day he curses the love potion and yearns for Isolde to bring him the only relief that can help him in his tortured and hopeless situation, death. The whole opera floats on the sounds of water, the first act actually taking place on a ship, and the water symbolism suggests both life and death by drowning.

Die Meistersinger von Nürnberg/The Mastersingers of Nuremberg (1868)

That the same composer who wrote *Tristan* could also have created the comedy *Die Meistersinger von Nürnberg* indicates the enormous range of Wagner's genius. Here we have a social comedy with many thematic conflicts: the artist versus society, the arts versus the crafts, the demands of the old versus the desires of the young for the new. But here the result is not the hopeless frustration of *Tristan* but the happy conclusion of *Die Meistersinger*, with social acceptance, marriage, and the artist welcomed, revered, and indeed loved by society.

The artist is indeed welcomed into society but not, however, without a struggle. The nature of artistic creation is scrutinized by the guild of the mastersingers, who defend the old rules of song and poetry. This conflicts, however, with the young genius Walther von Stolzing and his formless, emotional love song. The social classes are in conflict here as well: the mastersingers as self-satisfied bourgeoisie versus the pride of the aristocratic young artist—*Stolzing* itself means "pride" in German. The characters David and Magdalene are stout representatives of the lower classes, the apprentices and servants. The classes are unified in song by the end of the opera, with all conflicts happily resolved.

The most interesting character in the work is certainly Hans Sachs, the cobbler-poet who represents both the working classes and the bourgeois mastersingers, of whose guild he is a member. Although he is a member of the old order, he immediately recognizes the genius of the new artist Walther. He finds the lovely young Eva beautiful and desirable, and Eva is attracted to him as well as to the handsome young knight Walther. In one of the most moving passages of the opera, in the third act, Sachs tells Eva that he knows the sad story of Tristan and Isolde and does not want to become a King Marke to her Isolde; while he sings this the orchestra plays the sad, yearning, frustrating music from *Tristan und Isolde*. And unlike that death-directed opera, this one ends with a happy community praising "heilige Deutsche Kunst"—or "holy German art"—not a call for German nationalism, but an appreciation of the glories of "holy German art," which will endure even if the German nation turns to dust.

The *Ring* Cycle: *Der Ring des Nibelungen*/*The Ring of the Nibelungs* (1876)

Perhaps the greatest operatic work ever composed, this tetralogy (*Das Rheingold, Die Walküre, Siegfried*, and *Götterdämmerung*) creates a mythic world encompassing both tragedy and comedy. A universe in itself, the mighty *Ring* cycle deserves study for its richness of characters, situations, themes, and the development of its peoples and ideas.

In this mythic world exist first of all the gods—Wotan, Fricka, Freia, Donner, and Froh; there are also creatures who serve the world of the gods—the Valkyries, especially Brünnhilde and Waltraute, their mother Erda, and the Rhinemaidens. While the gods are creatures of the air and the Rhinemaidens live in water, underground are the Nibelung dwarves, including Alberich and his brother Mime. The creatures who live on the earth are the human beings, the Wälsungs, primarily the brother and sister Siegmund and Sieglinde and their son Siegfried. In the midst of this complex world is the Rhinegold, innocently sitting in the Rhine and adding beauty to the river while the Rhinemaidens swim around it, both praising and guarding it. But the person who makes the gold into a ring and renounces love will have power over this entire complex world of gods, dwarves, and people. When the dwarf Alberich, one of the Nibelungs, steals the gold, renouncing love, he then has such

power. This occurs in the first scene of the first opera of the tetralogy, *Das Rheingold,* and the rest of the four operas follow the
struggles of different creatures in Wagner's universe for possession
of this powerful golden ring, with the curse of a loveless life attached
to it.

In the process we see the corruption of various characters and
their changing situations as the moral and political issues connected
with the powerful ring affect their lives and those around them.
Wotan, the god who originally coveted the gold and stole it from
Alberich, appears in three of the four operas and changes from an
arrogant young god into an older, wiser god who desires the end
of the conflict and his own death. His daughter Brünnhilde begins
as a warrior-maiden, a Valkyrie, who gradually sees the grief of
her father Wotan and the despair of Siegmund when told that he
will have to leave his sister and lover Sieglinde when ordered to
Valhalla. Brünnhilde becomes the humanized, all-wise woman at
the end of this vast tetralogy who sings the famous immolation
scene, hoping that by her death and the sacrifice of her husband
Siegfried, the world will be purged of this evil ring.

Siegried begins as an innocent though sometimes cruel adolescent,
yet becomes a helpless and naive victim of the ring's power. He is
accused of treacheries that he is unaware of having committed,
thereby presenting the audience with the suffering innocent who
will be the scapegoat for all the evil plotting around him. His murder
will ultimately cause the return of the ring to the Rhine and its
rightful owners, the Rhinemaidens. Only when in the Rhine, giving
off beautiful reflected light to the river's flowing waters, does the
Rhinegold provide any goodness for the universe. Human beings
and the other creatures of this world can now begin again with
hope.

The plot, characters, and dramatic situations are complex in this
magnificent work that lends itself to many moral, political, philosophical, and ecological interpretations. The conflict of love and
power, one of the recurrent themes in Western literature, finds
operatic embodiment in the *Ring* cycle. To enter the world of Wagner's *Ring* cycle is to enter a uniquely fascinating place, and that
fascination will repay study with enjoyment.

Parsifal (1882)

Wagner's final opera is his most subtle and religious, although religious only in the Wagnerian sense and certainly not aligned with any orthodox religion. This opera, like *Siegfried* in the *Ring* cycle, concerns the young innocent, the pure fool, Parsifal. Unlike Siegfried, however, this mythic hero learns through his suffering and becomes a wise and forgiving adult by the end of the opera. As leader of the brotherhood of the Grail, Parsifal provides the redemption and consolation that all humanity seeks. Rather like Tamino in Mozart's *The Magic Flute*, Parsifal must go through a series of tests before he is admitted into the circle of the enlightened.

He must also struggle with the evil magician Klingsor and his agent, Kundry, the eternal temptress who incorporates all the evil women in history. This proto-woman is both mother and whore, and her change from the evil agent of Klingsor into the forgiven and penitent woman parallels the changes in Parsifal. The suffering Amfortas, dying from a festering wound that will not heal, finds healing only at the end and in the hands of the former fool, Parsifal. The opera also includes the wise old man, Gurnemanz, who cannot act but only advises and comments on the action; he is in fact like the chorus in Greek tragedy, interpreting the drama on stage for the audience.

This most static of Wagner's operas demands much patience, but that patience is rewarded with exquisite music, interesting ideas, and a unique sense of timelessness that this opera can create. Water symbolism, which appeared in *The Flying Dutchman, Tristan*, and the *Ring* cycle, appears here as well as a source of purification for the evils of the world and as a balm for suffering humanity. *Parsifal* tries to console humanity for the suffering in life, a suffering that can, however, end in redemption. But the redemption Wagner offers springs from the world of art: as if the religion of art is all that can help humanity.

Verdi, Giuseppe (1813–1901)

The greatest composer of Italian operas, Verdi passed through several phases of artistic development and in the process added many operas to the standard repertory. Unlike his great contemporary, Wagner, Verdi was essentially conservative in his approach to opera. Although he had changed opera by the end of his career, he began in the bel canto tradition and moved toward a closer union of drama, words, and music by the end of his composing career. He worked primarily within the traditions of Italian opera and the theater of his own time. While Wagner was attracted to myth, Verdi's heart was always with the real, and his characters have a human dimension unique to opera.

Rigoletto (1851)

Within three very productive years, Verdi wrote three operas that are part of the mainstay of the standard repertory: *Rigoletto, Il Trovatore,* and *La Traviata.* Indeed, some opera companies could survive staging just these three works. *Rigoletto,* with a text by Francesco Maria Piave, is an opera dominated by duets, and some of the most famous duets in all opera occur in this work: Rigoletto and Sparafucile, Rigoletto and Gilda, Gilda and the Duke. The opera also contains two of Verdi's best arias: the Duke's "La donna è mobile" and Gilda's "Caro nome."

Based on the radical Victor Hugo's *Le Roi s'amuse*, the plot concerns the lecherous Duke of Mantua and his decadent, venal court. In the first act, the court jester, the hunchback Rigoletto, teases Count Monterone when he laments that his daughter has become the latest victim of the Duke's lechery. Monterone, in his fury, curses the jester, and that curse falls first on Rigoletto's daughter Gilda, who is abducted by the courtiers at the end of the first act. Gilda, in her innocence and naiveté, believes that the Duke really loves her. This opera contains one of the dramatic relationships that Verdi is most famous for, the intense love of a father and daughter.

The hunchback Rigoletto fascinates audiences because of his hatred of the unjust political system he himself is a part of and indeed abets. By the end of the opera, he has learned all the horror of this evil aristocracy as his daughter dies after offering her own life for the Duke's. Rigoletto and Gilda's final duet is one of the most beautiful Verdi ever wrote. While the dramaturgy contains the sudden reversals and twists of fate that are exciting in the melodramatic tradition of nineteenth-century theater, though often difficult for modern audiences to accept, the music is sublimely written for the voice. Although Wagner's concerns were often orchestral, Verdi created some of the most gorgeous and dramatic vocal music ever written for opera, and in *Rigoletto* soprano, tenor, baritone, and bass all have superb roles.

Il Trovatore/The Troubadour (1853)

The plot of this very popular Verdi opera, with a text by Salvatore Cammarano, concerns a gypsy's obsessive desire for revenge. Azucena's mother has died on the pyre for witchcraft, and Azucena has grabbed the wrong child to throw on that same pyre. The switch of babies, so often used in nineteenth-century melodrama, occurs here too. But the vengeful old witch, Azucena, is balanced with the pure and ethereal Leonora, who only wants to be with the man she loves, the troubadour Manrico. He is, however, mortal enemies with another vengeful character, Leonora's suitor, the Count di Luna.

The complex and incredible plot means that a successful performance of this opera is primarily a vocal feast. With the right singers the audience will enjoy one vocal delight after another—primarily Manrico's cabaletta "Di quella pira," Azucena's "Stride la vampa," Leonora's "Tacea la notte," and the Count di Luna's "Il balen." The ever-popular Anvil Chorus in the second act and the exciting finale make this an enjoyable opera for vocal if not credible dramatic effects. Verdi's mature style requires that this opera must be carefully sung, and he has provided the singers with wonderful melodies and strong situations that will ensure an audience's attention.

La Traviata/The Lost One (1853)

Based on *La Dame aux Camélias* by Alexandre Dumas and set to a text by Francesco Maria Piave, *La Traviata* tells the popular story of the courtesan who falls in love with the young innocent and then renounces him for the sake of his family's reputation. Although she dies of tuberculosis at the end of the opera, she dies in his arms. The plot is melodramatic, but the dramaturgy realizes the potential of the story's fascinating characters. The personality of Violetta Valery dominates the action; she begins as a sickly but cynical courtesan who decides to enjoy what she can of life, and that enjoyment demands the money she can so easily earn with her body.

But her attachment to the loving, sentimental but naive young Al-fredo Germont affects her with real love for the first time in her young and mercenary life.

Verdi's ability to use the traditional forms of bel canto opera for telling dramatic effect is what makes the story such a musical and dramatic success. Verdi employs the traditional form of slow aria and lively cabaletta for Violetta: "Ah, fors' è lui," a slow, thoughtful aria, followed by her sudden and cynical reversal in the cabaletta "Sempre libera," in which she determines to avoid all emotional attachments and seek only freedom and wealth.

The part of Violetta demands three different soprano voices. In the first act, coloratura flexibility and agility characterize the vocal line, but the opera requires a spinto soprano in the second act and a dramatic soprano for the death scene in the last act. Few sopranos can do all this convincingly, and part of the pleasure of seeing and hearing *La Traviata* involves evaluating how the soprano singing the lead role gets through all the acts of this difficult opera. Can she reflect all the changing conflicts and complexity of the character, showing the changes as well as the enduring qualities in Violetta's personality?

The roles of Alfredo and his strict, Victorian father, the elder Giorgio Germont, also require first-class singing. While these parts lack the complexity of the main role, Alfredo especially needs a wide range of vocal and emotional colors, from intense, boyish love to despair when that love is rejected, to hatred and revenge, to, finally, understanding, forgiveness, and tragic grief over the death of Violetta.

La Forza del Destino/The Force of Destiny (1862)

To a libretto by Francesco Maria Piave and based on a Spanish play by Angel de Saavedra, this opera also concerns a father/daugh-ter relationship. In the first scene of the opera a daughter's love affair causes the accidental death of her father, the Marquis of Calatrava. The rest of the opera shows the result of that transgres-sion, the force of that destiny. Leonora, the daughter, perfectly embodies the Verdi soprano—sweet, essentially innocent, and too delicate for the conflicts and forces of life around her. She is sur-rounded by a passionate lover (Don Alvaro) and a vengeful brother (Don Carlo), and these violent men doom her to suffering and death.

The hard, driven nature of much of the music reflects the fate that is pursuing these characters.

The tenor loves Leonora, while the baritone, her brother, seeks revenge for his father's death. His desire for revenge ultimately causes the death of two characters. The rigidity of the men and the delicacy of the heroine create tragedy, but *La Forza del Destino* contains something quite unusual for Verdi's tragic operas, comic relief. Fra Melitone, an old monk, adds comedy to a tragic situation, and the clergy is presented sympathetically in this opera, something unusual for the generally anti-clerical and anti-religious Verdi. Verdi was an agnostic for most of his life, although his *Quatro Pezzi Sacri* written at the end of his life suggests that he became somewhat religious toward the end, as Wagner's final work, *Parsifal*, suggests the same of him.

Don Carlo (1867)

Don Carlo, certainly Verdi's most ambitious opera, replete with complex ideas and characters, is based on a play by Friedrich von Schiller. Originally composed for the Paris Opéra in French to a libretto by François Joseph Méry and Camille du Locle, the opera was commissioned by the Paris Opéra and was composed in the style of the French grand opera. *Don Carlo* characterizes and perfects that form better than any French opera of the period. But the opera is more often performed in Verdi's revised four-act version to an Italian libretto by Antonio Ghislanzoni. The conflicts center on Church and State in the sixteenth-century Spain of the Inquisition. In addition, the rights of the individual are presented in opposition to the demands of the state, a basic tension in the opera.

The opera opens with the French Elizabeth of Valois (Elisabetta) on her way to marry the heir of Spain, Don Carlo. She loves him, and they sing a wonderful duet together, but because of the wars between the two countries and the bloodshed that has occurred, she is ordered by her father to marry instead Don Carlo's father, the King, Philip II. From here on, she and Don Carlo become trapped in a *Tristan und Isolde*–like situation. The theme of incest complicates the impossibility of their love. If tragedy involves seeing how people perform in an impossible situation, certainly this opera is great tragedy. The frustrated and conflicted Don Carlo also sympathizes with the cause of the Flemish people, encouraged by his great friend Rodrigo, the Marquis of Posa, who reminds Carlo and the King of the suffering of Flanders under the harsh yoke of Spanish rule.

Don Carlo does not have the simple, one-dimensional characters found in much nineteenth-century melodrama. King Philip emerges as a suffering, lonely man in his famous aria "Ella giammai m'amo" (She never loved me). He has come to realize that his wife never loved him, that he is a lonely old man waiting for his tomb in the Escorial. He finds relief from the loneliness in the arms of the Princess Eboli, his mistress, who, alas, secretly loves his son, Don Carlo. This opera shows the tragedy of an old man's seeing all the love he desires going to his son and the younger generation. The Oedipal conflict between father and son in part propels this opera and its characters to heights of tragedy and grandeur.

One of the greatest scenes of the opera occurs when the Grand Inquisitor has an ugly confrontation with the King over the powers of the Church in Spain. Verdi's proverbial suspicion of the Church propels the intensity of the scene. Ultimately, the Church orders the murder of Posa, and Church and State destroy the love of Elisabetta and Don Carlo. But Don Carlo does not die at the end; instead, he is saved by his grandfather (or the ghost of his grandfather) and namesake, Charles V.

In this opera Verdi uses his theory of the *parola scenica*, or the dramatic word. Some of the most dramatic music in the opera accompanies words and phrases like Posa's "La pace è dei sepolcri!" (the peace of the tomb) and the Grand Inquisitor's mighty "Forse" (maybe), indicating how dramatically Verdi could use language and dramatic situations in his greatest operas.

Aïda (1871)

Aïda, certainly the most popular Verdi opera, was also written in the style of French grand opera, but composed to an Italian libretto by Antonio Ghislanzoni. The opera was commissioned by the Khedive of Egypt and was first performed in Cairo on Christmas Eve 1871, though the premiere had been delayed because of the Franco-Prussian War. This opera uses the grand scenes and triumphal marches that typify French grand opera in the nineteenth century. In addition, the plot, based on an old opera seria story, involves the conflicting demands of personal affections versus the demands of the state. Aïda, an Ethiopian princess, enslaved and in captivity, appears in the music of the overture as a spiritual presence. Her fragility and spiritual qualities are immediately characterized, and, by implication, as with most Verdi sopranos, her goodness and innocence are soon to be tested by the conflicts around her, which will ultimately claim her life.

Radames, the Egyptian general and the man Aïda loves, is also loved by the Princess of Egypt, Amneris, who arranges for her father to give her in marriage to Radames after his glorious victory over the Ethiopians. The rivalry between the two women for the same man complicates the plot and influences the music. Princess Amneris, the fiery and powerful daughter of the Pharaoh, ultimately loses Radames because of his love for her slave Aïda.

In the famous Nile scene in Act III, Aïda is forced by her father Amonasro, the King of Ethiopia, to trick Radames into betraying the hiding places of the Egyptian forces so that Amonasro can stage a surprise attack on them. Amneris and the high priest, Ramfis, catch Radames giving away state secrets. Verdi's anti-clericalism is apparent in the final act, especially the judgment scene, when the state is willing to forgive the great hero Radames, but the priests demand his death. They sentence him to be buried alive under the high altar of the temple of the god he offended, Vulcan. While awaiting his death in a crypt under the temple, Radames finds Aïda and together they die while Amneris prays in the temple above them for peace for their souls—and hers. In many ways *Aïda* is an old-fashioned opera with a series of set musical numbers, but the quality of the music justifies the form.

Otello (1887)

Verdi's interest in Shakespeare began with his earlier operatic version of *Macbeth* (1847) and continued with the two great master-pieces of his old age, *Otello* and *Falstaff*. *Otello*, often called the greatest of operatic tragedies, simplified Shakespeare's complex plot with a libretto written by the poet and composer Arrigo Boito, and to this brilliant libretto Verdi wrote some of his greatest music. The opera is uncharacteristic in the Verdi canon because it does not contain the set musical numbers for which Verdi is so famous.

Instead, this opera is more dramatic and revolutionary. It was accused of being Wagnerian at the time, and in some ways it is, but basically it is Italian with a more dramatic and unified approach.

In this opera, Verdi provides a powerful musical dimension for the nobility of Otello, his military mentality, and his neurotic jealousy. Desdemona, sweet and pure, has celestial music to match, while Iago has a snakelike, meandering sound for his music. The drama on stage intensifies from the opening storm scene in Act I to the murder of Desdemona and subsequent suicide of Otello in the final act. Verdi's characters and tragic drama come alive in this thoroughly integrated composition of music and theater. And Verdi's use of the orchestra reflects a new subtlety and refinement, from *Otello*'s opening storm scene to the somber sounds of the final suicide of the main character.

Falstaff (1893)

With a clever libretto by Arrigo Boito based on Shakespeare's *Merry Wives of Windsor, Falstaff* is perhaps the greatest Italian comic opera ever composed. It took Verdi a long time to write—five years, which for him was very slow work indeed—but he refused to be rushed and he wrote his final work with leisurely enjoyment, savoring especially the rascally old knight, Sir John. Once again, this work was revolutionary for a Verdi opera. *Falstaff*, an ensemble opera, needs the unified efforts of a well-trained cast and a very good conductor. There are few arias or musical set pieces, and those that exist are quite short; for example, the bewitching and lovely duet for the young lovers Fenton and Nannetta—"Bocca baciata non perde ventura, anzi renuove come fa la luna." This duettino lasts just a few minutes, but it is sublime.

Old Sir John Falstaff dominates the opera, rather like Hans Sachs in Wagner's great comedy, *Die Meistersinger*, and in both works the composer is presenting images of himself. Verdi, in his correspondence, indicates how much he identified with the "vecchio John" of the opera. But this old John Falstaff had to be taught humility: In the second and third acts of the opera, the community, especially Alice Ford, Mistress Page, and the wonderfully comic Dame Quickly, chastise his pride and vanity—the first time dumping him with some dirty laundry into the Thames, the second time teasing him and publicly exposing him in Windsor Park in the final scene of the opera. The wonderful fugue that ends the opera, "Tutto nel mundo è burla" (Everything in the world is a joke), brings together all the characters, plus the chorus, for a brilliantly comic and musically complex finale. What a marvelous final work Giuseppe Verdi gave the world!

Gounod, Charles François (1818–1893)
Faust (1859)

Based on the first part of Goethe's famous poetical drama, and with a libretto by Jules Barbier and Michel Carré, *Faust*, like *Carmen*, began as an opéra comique with spoken dialogue. After it became so popular, Gounod orchestrated the spoken text and made the work an opera. The opera demands an impressive production, especially in the famous *Walpurgisnacht* scene in Act V, with a wonderful ballet for devils and temptresses. But the opera's attraction really owes very little to Goethe, since the philosophical content and religious meanings are by and large removed in *Faust* and only Goethe's plot remains. What keeps the opera in the standard repertory is its music, especially the melodies for the principal roles.

The opera's vocal numbers impress by their variety and melodious beauty. Marguerite's famous "Jewel Song" captures the naiveté of this character and her consequent susceptibility to Faust. The most bravura character is surely Méphistophélès, and a good bass has several impressive and difficult musical numbers with which to impress an audience, especially "Le veau d'or" and "O nuit, étends sur eux ton ombre." Faust's own famous arias include "Salut! O mon dernier matin" and "Salut! demeure chaste et pure." *Faust*'s numerous arias and their beauty sustain interest in this dramatically unconvincing work.

Moussorgsky, Modest (1839–1881)
Boris Godunov (1874)

Boris Godunov is the most popular of Russian operas in the West, as in Russia itself. Moussorgsky's opera was a failure when it was first staged, but it was subsequently reorchestrated by that dazzling composer for the orchestra, Rimsky-Korsakov. In his version, the opera became famous worldwide and provided an impressive role for a great acting bass singer and much work for the chorus as well, for essentially this opera concerns the people of Russia, and the chorus often dominates the stage. But, more recently, the original Moussorgsky version, in his rather than Rimsky-Korsakov's orchestration, has been staged with great success. Given the desire for authenticity in our time, the original version may eventually supplant the Rimsky-Korsakov version in most opera houses.

In either case, the opera is based on a famous play by Alexander Pushkin about the particularly brutal Czar Boris. Much like Shakespeare's Macbeth, Boris is often cruel and he even kills a young boy (who is heir to the throne) to get the throne, but Boris himself never gets much happiness from his great desire to be Czar of all the Russias. His tormented guilt and insecurity once he is Czar lead to his death. The opera includes many interesting smaller roles, especially the ambitious Polish princess Marina, the jolly hostess in the inn scene, and the various monks who use religion to seek personal happiness or even political power despite the poverty around them. The combination of religion and political power ignite the forces behind the pretender to Boris's throne.

The complexity of Russian society itself is presented on stage, from the suffering people, with the pathetic Fool as their spokesman, who hopes for a just government, through the Russian aristocracy to the Czar himself. Throughout the suffering the people endure at the hands of both the Russian Orthodox Church's leaders and the various czars who seize power, the chorus remains, bewailing its fate as victim of these hostile and self-serving forces.

Bizet, Georges (1838–1875)

Carmen (1875)

With its wonderful text by Henri Meilhac and Ludovic Halévy, Carmen remains the most popular of French operas because of the legendary attraction of its title role. Carmen can be played many ways and has attracted mezzo-sopranos and sopranos with great voices and an ability to act convincingly. Some have played Carmen as the primordial temptress and vamp who loves to seduce men. Others have portrayed her as essentially childlike and innocent, with no awareness that the fleeting nature of her love devastates other people. Some singers have presented her as political, the product of a poverty-ridden environment and an angry spokesperson for her oppressed people. She has even been portrayed as a suicidal personality, attracted to Don José because he seems dangerous and is likely to kill her. One portly mezzo-soprano played her as a mother figure who was becoming bored with all the boyish men who flocked to her.

Don José, also complex, has been portrayed in diverse ways as well. Some tenors have played him as essentially a naïf who should have remained faithful to the country girl, Micaëla, who loved him, and who remained always a country boy confused by the complexities of city life and city people. More recently Don José has been played as a man with a triggerlike temper who gives up too much for Carmen ever to allow her to leave him. He can also be played as a dangerous, homicidal person eager to end his own and another person's unhappy lives.

In many ways the opera presents opposing views of love. For Carmen love is like a gypsy boy, as she sings in her famous entrance aria, always changeable, to be enjoyed but not detained. For Don José love is an eternal truth; once he loves someone he gives (and demands) fidelity, something Carmen would never be able to endure or even ask of another. How Carmen and Don José will be portrayed is always central to the audience's curiosity when this dramatic opera is staged.

Another complication for the production of *Carmen* involves which version to use. Bizet wrote the opera as an opéra comique, which means the original version has spoken dialogue with musical numbers. But the work became so popular that it was transferred to the Paris Opéra, where continuous music was the rule, so the Opéra commissioned the New Orleans–born Ernest Guiraud to compose music for the spoken dialogue based on Bizet's style or using music Bizet wrote for other compositions. This Guiraud version has been performed more frequently in the twentieth century, though the opéra comique version remains in use as well. Certainly the opéra comique version is more theatrical, while the through-composed version is more musically satisfying.

Carmen has an eternal quality because of its basis in the male-versus-female conflict and its tragic ending, and because of Bizet's music. There have been ballet versions, film versions, spoken-theater versions, even mime versions of this fascinating story by Prosper Mérimée. With wonderful roles for mezzo-soprano (or, raised a key or two, for soprano) and tenor, and a good role (Escamillo) for the baritone as well, this work continues to delight and fascinate operatic audiences.

Tchaikovsky, Peter Ilyich (1840–1893)
Eugene Onegin (1879)

Another opera in the Russian repertory, *Eugene Onegin*'s source is the famous poem by Alexander Pushkin about a very strange character indeed. The complexity of Eugene Onegin captivates most opera-goers: An isolated, gloomy figure, Onegin attracts women yet is repelled by them. Is he looking for his conception of the perfect woman? Or is he simply incapable of intimate relations with women? Is he a sadist who enjoys attracting women and then swiftly rejecting them? Is he a victim of fate, since he does not realize he loves a woman until she has ceased loving him? Is his pride a symptom of his extreme shyness or merely a way of rejecting people before they have a chance to reject him? Or is he a homosexual in a society that does not tolerate homosexuality? Combinations of these theories, plus several more, may help explain his character, but never completely. The role demands a baritone who can sing beautifully yet still act well enough to make this character interesting, mysterious, and sympathetic to the audience.

While Onegin becomes more lonely, isolated, and desperate as the opera progresses, his great love, Tatiana, changes from an impulsive, loving girl to a mature, cautious woman who has gotten over her infatuation with Onegin and has married instead a stable, older man, Prince Gremin. In the first act she impulsively writes a love letter to a man she barely knows, Onegin, while in the last act she is a married woman who rejects that same man who now desperately wants her. She has married and will remain true to her vow, but does she still love Onegin? Once one has loved a person, the opera suggests, one never stops loving. The opera raises many interesting questions about the nature of people and the nature of love, especially unrequited love.

Eugene Onegin includes some lovely dance pieces for the two ball scenes in the opera—something one would surely expect from the greatest composer for ballet. The opera also contains several gorgeous arias, especially one for Vladimir Lenski, who is Onegin's best friend in Act I and later is killed in a duel with him. The relationship between the men, as fraught with conflict as that between the other characters, creates another dramatic confrontation on the theme of the complexity of human relationships.

Mascagni, Pietro (1863–1945)
Cavalleria Rusticana/Rustic Chivalry (1890)

The most famous of the early verismo operas, this opera in fact made Italian verismo a staple of the operatic stage. Based on a famous Sicilian tale by Giovanni Verga and with a libretto by Guido Menasci and Giovanni Targioni-Tozzetti, the plot dramatizes a broken love affair, the Sicilian obsession with personal honor, and its consequent demand for revenge. Clearly influenced by French naturalism, especially by the novels of Zola, this story involves basic passions of people caught in a primitive and very poor society: rural Sicily. The rustic chivalry of the title refers to the rural Sicilian's code of honor and defense of one's word of honor. When the tenor, Turiddu, reneges on his promise to marry Santuzza and has an affair with another woman, Santuzza tells the husband of the woman Turiddu is having an affair with, which results in a knife duel between the two men and the death of Turiddu. The very names of the characters and their situation, plus the dialect of Italian they speak, created a new kind of opera.

Structurally conservative, the opera includes set musical numbers and even the obligatory drinking song for Italian operas of the nineteenth century, but the dramaturgy of the opera revolutionized the art form. Gone are the kings and queens and the figures of Greek and Roman mythology, and instead a new kind of verisimilitude dominates the operatic stage. While Verdi's characters in *La Traviata* are not royalty, they are mostly wealthy and sophisticated, but Mascagni's characters are very poor. Unlike Bizet's *Carmen*, which also involves sexual infidelity and revenge, *Cavalleria Rusticana* immediately became popular on European stages for the intensity of its emotions and the beauty of its music.

One of the contradictions that adds to the dramatic conflict is the pretty melodies used for such ugly and intense emotions, although the opera, especially in the final duet between Turridu and Santuzza, does include some ugly sounds.

The language of this work changed the way opera was viewed by a generation of opera-goers. Written primarily in the Sicilian dialect rather than proper Italian and set in one of the poorest sections of Italy, *Cavalleria Rusticana* captures the desperate poverty and intense loves and hatreds of these people.

Leoncavallo, Ruggiero (1858–1919)
Pagliacci/The Clowns (1892)

The other half of the classic verismo bill of *Cav* and *Pag*, this opera works on the play-within-a-play principle that Pirandello was to use so successfully in the spoken theater. The libretto, by the composer himself, was suggested by a newspaper article reporting a murder in a roving band of players, the crime taking place during an actual performance. The opera is set in another very poor section of Italy, Calabria, and involves a group of wandering commedia dell'arte actors and actresses. Nedda, the wife of the head of the company, Canio, is having an affair with a village man, Silvio. Canio suspects that Nedda is not being faithful to him, and when, during the commedia dell'arte performance (that is itself a story of sexual infidelity), he gets positive proof, he loses control despite the presence of an audience, and he kills Nedda and her lover.

The plot of the older husband trying to keep the affections of his young wife is one of the classic commedia dell'arte situations. That here the plot becomes tragic adds an ugly irony. Although theatrically innovative, *Pagliacci* also includes several set arias that have become famous. The most famous, "Vesti la giubba," is Canio's lament that although his personal life is falling apart he must still put on his costume and makeup and entertain the paying customers. Caruso recorded the aria several times and that, plus his powerful stage renditions of the role, made it popular and consequently attractive to other tenors who could master the role's high tessitura and its theatrical demands.

Nedda's love for Silvio results in a harmonious duet for the lovers. But they are interrupted by Tonio, one of the nastier clowns in the troupe. Tonio, a hunchback, desires Nedda's love, and when it is rejected, he reports her affair with Silvio to the vindictive and desperate Canio. Nedda's desire for a normal life among stable people and away from the wandering theatrical troupe, a natural wish, destroys the one relationship that Canio wants in life. He achieves truly tragic depths of despair in his grief over the loss of his beloved wife.

TWENTIETH CENTURY

Some critics think of twentieth-century opera as only the atonal music of Schoenberg, Berg, and Webern, but while these Austrians were being wildly experimental with some success, the more conservative Puccini and Strauss continued to fill theaters with the luscious melodies that operatic audiences preferred to the excruciating harmonics of the Austrian experimenters. Certainly in the twentieth century a divergence between the modernists and the anti-modernists or post-modernists developed a split that had rarely occurred before in music. In terms of the standard repertory, by and large the modernists lost.

In the discussion of twentieth-century operas, we will begin with the 1890s, which is a slight departure from chronology but generally allowed in operatic history.

Puccini, Giacomo (1858–1924)

Manon Lescaut (1893)

The first of Puccini's big successes, *Manon Lescaut* (which had been introduced on the operatic stage in a version by Auber) contains some of the most beautiful melodies he ever wrote, including the famous love music between Manon Lescaut and Des Grieux. Also, Puccini uses here the leitmotiv technique he learned primarily from Wagner. The opera is constructed along leitmotiv patterns, although it also includes the arias and duets that made Italian opera so famous.

The libretto was the work of many hands; in fact, the libretto was not credited to any librettist because so many people worked on it. Even in his first major success, Puccini indicated the difficulties he would have with his librettists, and the difficulties they would have with him. How often he envied Wagner's ability to write his own librettos and not have to deal with librettists, although, given the many demands he placed on writers, Puccini was often accused of writing his own librettos anyway.

Despite the fact that so many writers worked on this libretto (among them Ruggiero Leoncavallo, Marco Praga, Domenico Oliva, Giuseppe Giacosa, Giulio Ricordi, and Luigi Illica), the result is still quality, thanks especially to the main role. Manon Lescaut captures the essence of the archetypal whore. Her interests in attracting men and getting their money involve her with both the dashing young Des Grieux and the elder Geronte, the man who supports her in luxury in the second act. Ultimately, she rejects Geronte's money for love and runs off with Des Grieux, but not before trying to steal as much of Geronte's jewelry as possible. In fact, it is this very theft that causes her to delay her departure and results in her getting caught by the police.

As punishment, Manon is deported to Louisiana, where Des Grieux follows her and where she dies of exposure. Her terrible end has been fated from the beginning. There is a fatalistic quality about the entire opera, especially the first and last acts. In Act I the young student's machinations to get Manon Lescaut and Des Grieux to meet each other indicate a force of fate at work, a force that will ultimately kill Manon. The second act contains the opera's most famous aria, "In quelle trine morbide," in which Manon sees in her curtained bed the symbol of her new rich life and the death of her real love. The third act's famous embarkation scene graphically presents the grief and horror of European poverty and emigration in the eighteenth century. In the opera's final act we witness Manon's terrible ending in one of Puccini's shortest but most intense and effective acts.

La Bohème/The Bohemian (1896)

This is the first of what are called the big three, or the most popular of Puccini's operas, the other two being *Tosca* and *Madama Butterfly*. Giuseppe Giacosa and Luigi Illica wrote the wonderful libretto, which is based on Henri Murger's novel *Scènes de la vie de Bohème*. This pair also wrote the librettos for the other two most popular of Puccini's operas; their genius lay in producing the most strikingly natural and conversational of texts for these most real of characters. Nevertheless, *La Bohème* was not an immediate success, but it quickly became one as it was produced on various opera stages in Europe and America. Puccini often traveled around Europe and even to America to ensure that his operas were properly staged and sung, and, of course, his involvement always added to the publicity that the production received.

At the core of *La Bohème* are two mighty realities: love and poverty. Puccini himself experienced terrible poverty, especially during his student days in Milan; thus the lives of poor students and artists of *La Bohème* are realistically conveyed. Poverty causes the death of Mimì, whose tuberculosis would have been cured if she had had the money for medical treatment. The love of Rodolfo and Mimì, therefore, is doomed from the beginning because of their poverty.

Puccini was fond of the technique of parallel characterization, and he uses it effectively in this opera. The gentle, lyrical love of Rodolfo and Mimì contrasts throughout with the turbulent, angry, bickering love of Marcello and Musetta, who has the most famous aria in the opera, her wonderful waltz in the second act. The parallel characterization of these two couples is used by Puccini to present two kinds of love: the fulfilling and supporting as opposed to the hate-ridden and spiteful. Both loves prosper in their different ways and despite the obstacles life creates for them. The characterization suggests the varying natures of people and their varying needs for love.

The opera showcases Puccini's genius for the gorgeous, memorable melody, especially in the arias in the first act: Rodolfo's "Che gelida manina" and Mimì's "Mi chiamano Mimì." If sung properly, these arias should stop the show because of their unique and haunting beauty, and also because they personify their singers' characters so well. A wonderful arietta in the last act, Colline's "Vecchia zimarra, senti," is his sad and silly lament to his coat as he is about to pawn it for some medicine for the dying Mimì. Colline's arietta captures the misery of poverty in the opera and the hopelessness of the Bohemians' situation. The arietta suggests the revolutionary nature of Colline's thinking, that capitalism destroys the poor people it has also created, but the song suggests comedy as well.

Tosca (1900)

Very different from *La Bohème* is the violent drama in Puccini's great success, *Tosca*. Based on a very popular play Victorien Sardou wrote as a vehicle for Sarah Bernhardt, *Tosca* is a thriller with great situations, characters, and philosophical and religious ideas. The libretto by Luigi Illica and Giuseppe Giacosa shortens and tightens the drama in the play.

Thematically, the core of the opera is the conflict between Tosca's belief in God and the Catholic Church and Mario Cavaradossi's agnosticism, perhaps atheism. Between these two ideological poles moves the powerful Baron Scarpia, who outwardly expresses a strong belief in God and the Church but in actuality is a hypocrite who uses his powers as Rome's chief of police to destroy the rebellion against the old regime in any way expedient, and who uses his political power to force women to go to bed with him. Tosca wants to save the life of her lover, Mario, who is a political prisoner, while Scarpia wants Mario dead and Tosca in his bed. Tosca's killing of Scarpia in the second act indicates the desperation of her situation, and her hope that God will forgive her.

That murder is preceded by her famous aria, "Vissi d'arte," which is at the philosophical core of the opera. She says that she has lived for art and love, and tried to do good in the world, and she asks God why he is putting her in such a horrible situation. Her prayer includes that most profound question: Why does God allow the suffering of the innocent? Her only response is Scarpia's renewed demands for her favors in exchange for the life of Cavaradossi.

In the last act, Mario sings his final aria, "E lucevan le stelle"; his final thoughts before he dies are of the beauty of Tosca's body and the intensity of his love for her. Tosca thinks she has outsmarted Scarpia and that this execution will only be a sham, but she is sadly mistaken. The bullets are real and Mario is killed; Tosca's final words and suicide in the opera suggest that she does not want to continue living in a world where Mario's philosophy of life prevails.

Madama Butterfly (1904)

The suffering of the innocent also concerns Puccini's next great opera, although Butterfly was a resounding flop when it was first staged at La Scala on February 17, 1904. The source for the opera was a play by David Belasco, put into libretto form for Puccini by the duo of Giuseppe Giacosa and Luigi Illica, but despite their former successes with Puccini, Butterfly's premiere was one of the noisiest failures in the history of Italian opera. Puccini wisely withdrew the work, revised it, and tried again at a smaller theater in Brescia with Toscanini conducting, where it succeeded, and succeeded over and over again at opera houses all over Europe.

In Madama Butterfly, as in La Bohème, we have an essentially innocent heroine, Cio-Cio-San, and the horrible consequences of her naiveté. It is usually dangerous to be naive in a Puccini opera, for the naive and innocent soon learn that the world uses their very innocence to destroy them. Puccini's view of life suggests that power and force control events and that one must be crafty in response, but, alas, Cio-Cio-San believes Benjamin Franklin Pinkerton when he promises to be faithful to her.

The opera also attacks American imperialism, personified by the tenor Pinkerton. The "Yankee vagabondo," as he calls himself in his first aria, Pinkerton symbolizes the imperialist mentality of superiority to the natives in poorer countries, and he tries to make the most advantageous deal he can to get all the wealth and pleasure possible. But he is also a handsome young man who does not anticipate the horrible consequences of his actions, though his actions cause him to grieve by the end of the opera.

The naive native and the wily, amoral imperialist conflict in this opera with predictable results. Butterfly has rejected her own culture and religion to marry what she thinks is a superior being from a superior civilization. She also thinks that the imperialist represents progress and a better way of life. Ultimately, she traps herself by rejecting the cultural and religious ties of Japan that would have helped her. That naiveté is painfully captured in "Un bel dì," her aria in Act II when she proclaims her belief that her American husband will return to her and their son. When Pinkerton returns it is to introduce his American wife and ask for his son to bring back to his own, superior country. The role of Butterfly, very difficult because of its vocal and dramatic demands, begins as a 15-year-old girl and ends as a mature woman determined to defend her honor by suicide since she cannot defend and keep her child.

Turandot (1926)

Puccini's final opera, which he unfortunately did not live to complete, *Turandot* presents us with the composer at his most ambitious and epic. Based on a famous play by Carlo Gozzi and to a text by Giuseppe Adami and Renato Simoni, this fairy-tale opera contrasts the fierce hatred, mixed with neurotic love, of Princess Turandot with the passive, generous love of Liù. Although their conflict ends with the inevitable death of Liù, her death is life-giving, for from her sacrifices Turandot learns not only to love, but to love the man who so desperately wants her, Calaf.

There are Freudian overtones in this opera as well, for the intense hatred that Turandot feels toward men in the first act is clearly obsessive, neurotic, and mixed with love. Calaf, the noble but disguised prince who defies her, answers her riddles, and ultimately wins her, is obsessed as well. Once he sees her face he will even defy death to have her, and this is exactly what he must do, for if he fails to answer her riddles he will be beheaded. Allegorically, the opera connects hatred with love, and death with love as well, certainly Freudian themes.

Vocally, the role of Turandot has more difficulties than any other soprano role in the Puccini canon. The part demands a Wagnerian soprano who can also act. Liù's role, on the other hand, needs the lyricism and pretty sound we associate with Puccini heroines like Mimì or Butterfly. Calaf requires a heroic tenor whose voice will carry over the power of the large orchestra.

A unique aspect of this Puccini opera is its use of the chorus. Singing of their reactions to the actions of the heroic characters, they are on stage for most of the opera. Of course, their lives are affected by those actions; they are the common people looking always for the good leader, rather like the chorus in *Boris Godunov*. This was perhaps Puccini's comment on the Italian people after World War I, desperately looking for a leader, though all they got was Mussolini. Ping, Pang, and Pong—the three masque figures—come from the commedia dell'arte figures in Gozzi's play. They, along with the chorus, speak for the suffering of the common people under the tyrannical and bloody reign of Turandot. Although Puccini did not live to complete the opera's final scene, Franco Alfano produced a stageable version of this most ambitious and philosophical of Puccini's works.

Debussy, Claude (1862–1918)
Pelléas et Mélisande (1902)

Based on a play by Maurice Maeterlinck, *Pelléas et Mélisande* typifies many of the strengths of French operatic theory. The text must always be audible and the music must complement the drama on stage, rather than call attention to itself, a concept similar to Wagner's theories of music drama, and Debussy was indeed a devout Wagnerian as a young composer. By the time he composed this opera, however, he claimed to be an anti-Wagnerian, but Wagnerian elements remained.

The plot is similar to that of Wagner's *Tristan und Isolde*, involving an adulterous, fated love affair, although the effect of the opera is hardly Wagnerian. The rivalry of brothers complicates the plot as well, since both men love the same woman, even though one is already married to her. There is a delicacy and mystery about these characters, especially Mélisande, who dies in childbirth at the end of the opera.

A mysterious, insinuating quality also resonates in the music, in addition to its famous delicacy. The music extensively employs the chromaticism that *Tristan* is so famous for, and the undulating, liquid sound of the orchestra characterizes both works. Ultimately, Mélisande fascinates most because of the mystery of her being. She seems impulsive and childlike, yet she knows that she loves the forbidden Pelléas and she makes herself available to him. She should be young, thin, and move gracefully, since her music suggests this.

The opera progresses through impressions and insinuations—very unlike the mighty force of Wagner's *Tristan*. Also in contrast to the characters in Wagner's *Tristan*, who curse their destiny and the doomed nature of their adulterous love affair, Pelléas and Mélisande are like two lambs—innocent and childlike victims who accept their fates quietly. Their catastrophe affects us because of their very lack of emotionalism; their grief moves us deeply by its understatement.

Strauss, Richard (1864–1949)
Salome (1905)

Salome, Strauss's first operatic success, is also his first mature work. Using a play of the same title by Oscar Wilde and a German translation of it by Hedwig Lachmann, *Salome* personifies the decadent school of the arts that blossomed in Europe at the turn of the century. What is decadence? Puritans would argue that it was excessive sexuality and lack of discipline that caused the fall of Rome, but rampant sexuality has certainly occurred in all periods in history. A more accurate definition of decadence is the obsessive interest in death, especially when mixed with sex and love, that grew from the exceedingly popular *Tristan und Isolde* at the end of the nineteenth century. An obsessive interest in death combined with sexual love certainly occurs in *Salome*.

As in the Bible story, Salome falls madly in love with the prophet Jokanaan (John), who rejects her as an evil harlot, daughter of the wicked Herodias and step-daughter of Herod. She then performs her famous dance of the seven veils for Herod, who had promised to give her anything if she danced for him. After her dance, she casually requests the head of John on a silver platter. Herod, who respects this man and his new religion, tries to dissuade her but cannot. The opera ends with Salome's wonderful and grotesque monologue to the severed head, which revolts even Herod sufficiently to order his guards to crush her beneath their shields; the audience hears her dying screams in the orchestra.

Expressionistic in character, the opera presents extremes of goodness and corruption. Salome changes, as the one act of the opera progresses, from a determined little girl to a mature and passionate woman. The role demands a Wagnerian soprano who can act convincingly and has a good figure as well—a rare combination.

Elektra (1909)

Based on the famous tragedy by Sophocles, *Elektra*'s libretto was written by Hugo von Hofmannsthal, beginning one of the most productive collaborations in opera. Strauss and Hofmannsthal together created six operas, three of which are now in the standard repertory. *Elektra* is an expressionistic drama in Hofmannsthal's hands, including the Freudian basis of expressionistic theater and with a suitably expressionistic sound provided by Strauss. Based on the primordial conflict of mother and daughter, the opera concerns Elektra's determination to get revenge for the murder of her father, Agamemnon, at the hands of Klytämnestra, her mother, and her mother's lover, Aegisth. The opera uses the classic five-part form from Greek tragedy, presenting five confrontations between the major characters.

Structurally, Strauss employs the Wagnerian technique of the leitmotiv, the opera itself beginning with the striking Agamemnon motif, which also ends the opera after Elektra's death. This is musically and dramatically appropriate, for the murdered father's ghostly presence dominates the opera and its action. Agamemnon's two daughters, Elektra and Chrysothemis, personify the two kinds of women in the work: the appeasing, practical Chrysothemis versus the rigid, idealistic, even obsessive Elektra, who will not waver in her determination to do what she feels is just. Hofmannsthal's libretto provides wonderful language and intense dramatic conflicts for these fascinating characters, who interact and finally cause the deaths of both mother and daughter. The opera reflects the distorted, ugly side of family life, with most of the love gone: Only the hatreds and resentments remain.

Der Rosenkavalier/The Knight of the Rose (1911)

This opera's libretto, also by Hugo von Hofmannsthal, reflects both his and Strauss's interest in Mozart, for the plot resembles that of *The Marriage of Figaro*. Here, as in *Figaro*, the most interesting character is a sad older woman abandoned by her husband—she is called the Marschallin. But unlike the languishing Countess in *Figaro*, the Marschallin has had a series of young lovers, the current one being the sixteen-year-old Octavian; like Cherubino in *Figaro*, this is a trouser role sung by a mezzo-soprano. The Marschallin loves her young Octavian but predicts in Act I that he will soon leave her for a younger woman. Octavian becomes furious at the very suggestion and argues vehemently that he will always, always be true to her.

In the very next act, occurring on the following day, Octavian falls madly in love with Sophie, although he has been sent to announce the betrothal of the Marschallin's cousin Baron Ochs to Sophie. Octavian and Sophie are allowed to marry by the end of Act III, after much comedy and the overcoming of many obstacles, primarily from the oafish Baron Ochs, the Marschallin's rustic and lecherous cousin.

The contrast between the Marschallin and Baron Ochs reflects the primary theme in the opera: How does one face the sad reality of growing old? The contrast is heightened by the fact that both cousins desire the same person: Octavian, a young boy who disguises himself as a young maid in the first act, and whom the Baron finds irresistible as the maid Mariandel. These sexual shenanigans add to the comedy of the opera.

While Baron Ochs makes an ass of himself in his hot pursuit of Mariandel, the Marschallin sadly accepts the inevitable and makes it easier for Octavian to leave her for the younger Sophie. The

Marschallin is certainly the most sympathetic and interesting of the characters because of her wisdom in accepting the loss of youth and the loss of love, because of her loneliness, and because of her sadness over the loss of Octavian. Her famous monologue at the end of the first act presents us with a fascinating woman who knows what she has to face and wishes for a way out, which does not exist, except in death. The sad nature of this gray comedy stamps its drama as Mozartian.

Ariadne auf Naxos/Ariadne on Naxos (1912)

This opera is another happy product of the fruitful collaboration of Strauss with the poet and playwright Hugo von Hofmannsthal. Like *Elektra*, *Ariadne* also revolves around the conflict between two types of women; in this case the rigid, noble, idealistic Ariadne and the practical, if not cynical, Zerbinetta. While Zerbinetta moves happily from man to man, the noble Ariadne is ready to kill herself when her great love, Theseus, abandons her on the island of Naxos. Zerbinetta advises her to cheer up and grab the next man who comes by, who happens to be the god Bacchus, who hears her lament and approaches her island.

The comedy of the opera also reflects the comic realities of producing opera in the eighteenth century, when the story is set. The first act is called "the prologue" and the second act is called "the opera," for during the first act we are in the home of the wealthiest man in Vienna where the evening's entertainment is being rehearsed while the guests are dining. When the dinner runs late, the master of the house orders the two parts of the evening's entertainment, a new opera seria called *Ariadne auf Naxos* and an Italian commedia dell'arte troupe, to run their shows together so that both can end at precisely midnight in time for the most important part of the evening's festivities, the fireworks. Amid the general horror, especially the horror of the young composer of the opera seria, the first act ends. In the second act we see what the two troupes have come up with. The act begins with the three nymphs grieving for the abandoned Ariadne, who herself appears bewailing her fate; she then sings her long and tragic monologue, "Es gibt ein Reich," about the kingdom of death that now awaits her since the man she loves has abandoned her.

Suddenly a group of clowns appears, the commedia dell'arte

troupe, to try to cheer Ariadne up, to her tragic horror. The comedy is heightened when Zerbinetta herself appears to sing her wonderful "Grossmächtige Prinzessin." In this tour de force, Zerbinetta attempts to help Ariadne and presents her own cynical view of life as a series of affairs with men. "How could God expect women to be faithful, when he created so many men?" she asks. Ariadne rejects Zerbinetta's cynical advice and awaits her death, instead only to be confronted with the god Bacchus, who finds her and falls in love with her. Zerbinetta appears briefly at the end to assert that Ariadne's actions prove Zerbinetta's own view correct; Ariadne has found a new man. This opera, perhaps the most sophisticated operatic comedy ever written, delights by its ingenuity of form and ideas.

Berg, Alban (1885–1935)
Wozzeck (1925)

One of the few operas of the atonal Viennese school to establish itself in the standard repertory, *Wozzeck* uses the composer's version of a famous play by Georg Büchner. It is an intensely political play and an intensely political opera, as the center of the action, Wozzeck, is exploited by his society as well as by his faithless lover, Marie. The horror of his situation becomes more and more grotesque, until finally he murders her and commits suicide. The final scene, one of the most gruesome in all opera, shows a group of children playing, one of them the son of Wozzeck and Marie. He's playing on his hobbyhorse when another group of children runs toward him, saying, "Your mother is dead!" But the young boy understands nothing, continues playing on his horse, and hums, "Hip, hop, hip, hop."

The characters in the opera are not complex or particularly interesting, but the horror of the life of the lower classes and the bleakness of their situation capture our sympathy. In spite of their efforts to make a living and get some happiness in life, society eliminates their choices, grinds them down, and appears to drive them to homicide and/or suicide.

The music of this opera sounds grotesque and eerie to most listeners the first few times they hear it, but with repeated listenings its modernist beauty becomes apparent. The orchestration is especially fascinating in the music that bridges the fifteen short scenes of the opera. Marie's famous prayer scene with her child captures her fears of the afterlife, her fears of her lover Wozzeck, and the hopelessness of her situation. Using traditional forms like passacaglias and fugues, Berg creates a modernist drama without the classical conception of tragedy, for there is no tragic hero here, only horror and pathos.

Lulu (1937)

Berg himself wrote the text for *Lulu,* basing it on two plays by Frank Wedekind: *Erdgeist* and *Die Büchse der Pandora.* Unfortunately, Berg did not live to complete this, his second opera, but it was finished in the 1970s by the Czech musicologist Friedrich Cerha. Berg's widow wanted the work to remain unfinished despite the extensive notes and sketches Berg left for the incomplete last act when he died in 1935. The complete *Lulu,* which was first staged in Paris in 1979, has since been performed successfully at many other opera houses.

Lulu's music is even more atonal than *Wozzeck*'s, in part to suggest the ugliness and grotesqueness of the Expressionist plays by Frank Wedekind upon which it is based. Unlike *Wozzeck,* in *Lulu* we have very complex and fascinating characters, especially the title role of Lulu herself. She attracts men who sometimes kill each other to get to her, yet she never seems particularly interested in them. There are many ways to interpret the role: She is a nymphomaniac who loves to control men; she is really a lesbian who hates men and wants to torture them; she is essentially an innocent, unaware of her own sexual attraction and power over men; or she is a suicidal personality attracted to men who are dangerous. By the end of the opera, Lulu is murdered by Jack the Ripper when she is reduced to prostitution in London. She dies there with one of her great loves, the Countess Geschwitz.

The strange, nocturnal, neurotic world of *Lulu* attempts to reach the unconscious levels of the primordial woman, or the primordial person. Both maternal and seductive, yet finally rejecting, Lulu is the primordial temptress who loses interest once she has the man she has been enticing. A great acting singer can do wonderful things with this role, especially now that we have a working version of the complete opera. Though hardly tuneful, *Lulu* presents us with a view of humanity that is frighteningly persuasive and theatrically effective.

Britten, Benjamin (1913–1976)
Peter Grimes (1945)

With a text by Montagu Slater, *Peter Grimes* is based on George Crabbe's poem "The Borough." One of the few operas composed since World War II that so far has found a niche in the standard repertory, *Peter Grimes*'s music sounds very conservative compared to that of *Wozzeck* or *Lulu*, which may be one of the reasons for its comparative popularity with audiences. It is famous for its sea interludes, with the rushing, ebbing and flowing sounds that characterize the sea, as well as the nature of the relationships in this English seaside city, called The Borough.

Dramatically, the character of Peter Grimes dominates the action. A loner who is viewed with suspicion by the town, Peter Grimes has been accused of being responsible for the death of a young boy who had been apprenticed to him, though the court concludes the death is accidental. Moreover, he has indirectly been responsible for the death of another young boy. The townspeople finally form a posse to lynch him, and he is ultimately driven to commit suicide by drowning himself in the sea that has musically dominated the opera.

The opera's meaning may be analyzed in several ways: Is it the story of how humanity drives out and hounds to death the outsider, the person who does not fit into the community? Or is the opera about the struggles of the isolated, and the isolated person's difficult attempts to get along with his fellow man? Is the opera about the homosexual, whose sexual orientation makes him repellent to other people in the community? Obviously, there can be no single answer to the questions *Peter Grimes* poses.

In any case, the conflict between the individual and the demands of society, a recurrent theme in drama, finds a successful embodiment in this opera. By the end of the work, with the townspeople noticing a boat sinking offshore and not much caring, our sympathy with Peter and his suicide is complete. The scene before, his gripping mad scene sung without any orchestral accompaniment, prepares the audience for Peter's suicide. The sea that has given him a livelihood now gives him a grave and perhaps some peace at last. Water, then, becomes the final reality, that totality that includes the sources of both life and death. The opera suggests a modern version of Wagner's *The Flying Dutchman* with its recurrent use of water as a theatrical and musical symbol. Britten's musical style in this opera manages to be both melodious and dramatically integrated without being brainlessly tuneful.

CONCLUSION

These then are the generally accepted operas of the standard repertory. In twenty years the list will undoubtedly be somewhat different, and were another writer drawing up the list today the operas would also be slightly different. Nevertheless, these fifty works have achieved the greatness of inclusion into that group of operas most often performed by opera houses around the world.

Conclusion:

An Ancient Art Eternally Renewing Itself

There are many barriers to appreciating opera, but many rewards are also there for those who will attempt to understand it. "Opera" generally means a long performance in a foreign language, but beneath this complex and mysterious exterior lies one of the great artistic wonders of the world. I have been suggesting a six-part approach to opera: If you understand something about these six elements, then opera will cease to be a snobbish mystery to you and instead become a real pleasure. These six elements—the history of opera, operatic language, operatic production, opera's conducting tradition, opera's vocal tradition, and the standard repertory —are what complicate opera, but these same elements are the very ones that add so much pleasure to the art form. Only complex works of art, like complex people, remain interesting over a long period. People become opera fans because of their awareness of these six elements, and I hope that this book has given you a glimpse into the regular opera-goer's understanding and enjoyment of the art form.

For some people opera is an elegant night on the town; for others it is a religious experience. Between these extremes lies an educated appreciation of an art form that can bring to your life enjoyment, beauty, and fulfillment.

Sources

Chapter One

Davenport, Marcia. *Mozart*. New York: Avon Books, 1979.

FitzLyon, April. *Lorenzo Da Ponte*. New York: Riverrun Press, 1982.

Grout, Donald Jay. *A Short History of Opera*. New York: Columbia University Press, 1965.

Heriot, Angus. *The Castrati in Opera*. New York: Da Capo, 1975.

Knudsen, Vern O., and Cyril M. Harris. *Acoustical Designing in Architecture*. New York: Acoustical Society of America, 1978.

Kupferberg, Herbert. *Opera*. New York: Newsweek Books, 1975.

Landon, H. C. Robbins, and Donald Mitchell, eds. *The Mozart Companion*. New York: Norton, 1969.

Norwich, John Julius. *A History of Venice*. New York: Alfred A. Knopf, 1982.

Rosenthal, Harold, and John Warrack. *The Concise Oxford Dictionary of Opera*. London: Oxford University Press, 1974.

Sadie, Stanley, ed. *The New Grove Dictionary of Music and Musicians*. London: Macmillan, 1980.

Wechsberg, Joseph. *The Opera*. New York: Macmillan, 1972.

Chapter Two

Brockett, Oscar G. *History of the Theatre*. Boston: Allyn and Bacon, 1977.

Budden, Julian. *The Operas of Verdi*. New York: Oxford University Press, 1981.

DiGaetani, John Louis, ed. *Penetrating Wagner's Ring: An Anthology*. New York: Da Capo, 1983.

Grout, Donald Jay. *A Short History of Opera*. New York: Columbia University Press, 1965.

Kimball, David R. *Verdi in the Age of Italian Romanticism*. Cambridge: Cambridge University Press, 1981.

Kupferberg, Herbert. *Opera*. New York: Newsweek Books, 1975.

Macgowan, Kenneth, and William Melnitz. *The Living Stage*. Englewood Cliffs, N.J.: Prentice-Hall, 1955.

Martin, George. *The Companion to Twentieth Century Opera*. New York: Dodd, Mead, 1984.

Mordden, Ethan. *Opera in the Twentieth Century*. New York: Oxford University Press, 1978.

Rosenthal, Harold, and John Warrack. *The Concise Oxford Dictionary of Opera*. London: Oxford University Press, 1974.

Sadie, Stanley, ed. *The New Grove Dictionary of Music and Musicians*. London: Macmillan, 1980.

Walker, Frank. *The Man Verdi*. New York: Alfred A. Knopf, 1962.

Wechsberg, Joseph. *The Opera*. New York: Macmillan, 1972.

Chapter Three

Appelman, Dudley Ralph. *The Science of Vocal Pedagogy: Theory and Application*. Bloomington, Indiana: Indiana University Press, 1967.

Ardoin, John. *The Callas Legacy: A Biography of a Career*. New York: Charles Scribner's Sons, 1982.

Bunch, Meribeth. *Dynamics of the Singing Voice*. New York: Springer-Verlag, 1982.

Coffin, Berton. *The Sounds of Singing: Vocal Techniques*. Boulder, Colorado: Milton Press, 1975.

Fields, Victor Alexander. *The Singer's Glossary*. Boston: The Boston Music Co., 1952.

Hines, Jerome. *Great Singers on Great Singing*. Garden City, New York: Doubleday, 1982.

Kloiber, Rudolf. *Handbuch der Oper*. Kassel: Bärenreiter Verlag, 1973.

Knapp, J. Merrill. *The Magic of Opera*. New York: Da Capo Press, 1984.

Martin, George. *The Opera Companion*. New York: Dodd, Mead, 1982.

Pleasants, Henry. *The Great Singers*. New York: Simon and Schuster, 1981.

Rosenthal, Harold, and John Warrack. *The Concise Oxford Dictionary of Opera*. London: Oxford University Press, 1974.

Rushmore, Robert. *The Singing Voice*. New York: Dodd, Mead, 1971.

Chapter Four

Brockett, Oscar. *History of the Theatre*. Boston: Allyn and Bacon, 1982.

Brockway, Wallace, and Herbert Weinstock. *The Opera: A History of Its Creation and Performance, 1600–1941*. New York: Simon and Schuster, 1941.

Eaton, Quaintance. *Opera Production I and II: A Handbook*. Minneapolis: University of Minnesota Press, 1974.

Gartenberg, Egon. *Mahler: The Man and His Music*. New York: Schirmer Books, 1978.

Haskell, Arnold. *Diaghileff: His Artistic and Private Life*. New York: Simon and Schuster, 1935.

Heriot, Angus. *The Castrati in Opera*. New York: Da Capo, 1975.

Maynard, Olga. *Enjoying Opera*. New York: Charles Scribner's Sons, 1966.

Nagler, A. M. *Misdirection: Opera Production in the Twentieth Century*. Hamden, Conn.: Archon Press, 1981.

Orrey, Leslie. *A Concise History of Opera*. London: Thames and Hudson, 1972.

Osborne, Charles. *The World Theatre of Wagner*. New York: Macmillan, 1982.

"Stage Design," *The New Grove Dictionary of Music and Musicians*. Edited by Stanley Sadie. London: Macmillan, 1980.

Strauss, Richard, and Hugo von Hofmannsthal. *The Correspondence Between Richard Strauss and Hugo von Hofmannsthal*. Edited by Franz and Alice Strauss. Translated by Hanns Hammelmann and Ewald Osers. Cambridge: Cambridge University Press, 1961.

Witsen, Leo Van. *Costuming for Opera: Who Wears What and Why*. Bloomington: Indiana University Press, 1981.

Chapter Five

Bauer, Oswald Georg. *Richard Wagner: The Stage Designs and Productions from the Premieres to the Present*, New York: Rizzoli, 1982.

Brockway, Wallace, and Herbert Weinstock. *The Opera: A History of Its Creation and Performance, 1600–1941*. New York: Simon and Schuster, 1941.

Burian, Jarka. *Svoboda: Wagner*. Middletown, Conn.: Wesleyan University Press, 1983.

DiGaetani, John Louis, ed. *Penetrating Wagner's Ring: An Anthology*. New York: Da Capo, 1983.

Drummond, John D. *Opera in Perspective*. Minneapolis: University of Minnesota Press, 1980.

Eaton, Quaintance. *Opera Production I and II: A Handbook*. Minneapolis: University of Minnesota Press, 1974.

Fuchs, Peter Paul. *The Music Theater of Walter Felsenstein*. New York: Norton, 1975.

Hartmann, Rudolf. *Richard Strauss: The Staging of His Operas and Ballets*. Translated by Graham Davies. New York: Oxford University Press, 1981.

————, ed. *Opera*. Translated by Arnold J. Pomerans. Hong Kong: Chartwell Books, 1976.

Lindenberger, Herbert. *Opera: The Extravagant Art*. Ithaca: Cornell University Press, 1984.

Martin, George. *The Companion to Twentieth Century Opera*. New York: Dodd, Mead, 1984.

Mayer, Hans. *Richard Wagner in Bayreuth, 1876–1976*. Translated by Jack Zipes. New York: Rizzoli, 1976.

Mayer, Martin. *The Met: One Hundred Years of Grand Opera*. New York: Simon and Schuster, 1983.

Nagler, A. M. *Misdirection: Opera Production in the Twentieth Century*. Hamden, Conn.: Archon Press, 1981.

Osborne, Charles. *The World Theatre of Wagner*. New York: Macmillan, 1982.

Porges, Heinrich. *Wagner Rehearsing the 'Ring'—An Eye-Witness Account of the Stage Rehearsals for the First Bayreuth Festival*. Translated by Robert L. Jacobs. Cambridge: Cambridge University Press, 1983.

Robinson, Paul. *Opera and Ideas*. New York: Harper & Row, 1985.

Rosenthal, Jean, and Lael Wertenbaker. *The Magic of Light*. Boston: Little, Brown, 1972.

Skelton, Geoffrey. *Wagner at Bayreuth: Experiment and Tradition*. London: Barrie and Rockliff, 1965.

Sokol, Martin L. *The New York City Opera, An American Adventure*. New York: Macmillan, 1981.

Wagner, Wieland, ed. *Richard Wagner und das Neue Bayreuth.* Munich: Paul List Verlag, 1962.

Chapter Six

Bamberger, Carl, ed. *The Conductor's Art.* New York: McGraw-Hill, 1965.

Carse, Adam. *The Orchestra from Beethoven to Berlioz.* Cambridge: Cambridge University Press, 1948.

Finn, William J. *The Conductor Raises His Baton.* New York: Harper and Brothers, 1944.

Garretson, Robert L. *Conducting Choral Music.* Boston: Allyn and Bacon, 1970.

Goldbeck, Frederick. *The Perfect Conductor.* New York: Pellegrini and Cudahy, 1951.

Green, Elizabeth A. *The Modern Conductor.* Englewood Cliffs, N.J.: Prentice-Hall, 1969.

Grosbayne, Benjamin. *Techniques of Modern Orchestral Conducting.* Cambridge, Mass.: Harvard University Press, 1973.

Hartmann, Rudolf. *Richard Strauss: The Staging of His Operas and Ballets.* Translated by Graham Davies. New York: Oxford University Press, 1981.

Rudolf, Max. *The Grammar of Conducting: A Practical Study of Modern Baton Technique.* New York: G. Schirmer, 1950.

Schonberg, Harold C. *The Great Conductors.* New York: Simon and Schuster, 1967.

Singher, Martial. *An Interpretive Guide to Operatic Arias.* University Park: The Pennsylvania State University Press, 1983.

Westrup, Jack. "Conducting," in *The New Grove Dictionary of Music and Musicians.* Edited by Stanley Sadie. New York: Macmillan, 1980.

Chapter Seven

Ardoin, John. *The Callas Legacy: A Biography of a Career.* New York: Charles Scribner's Sons, 1982.

Heriot, Angus. *The Castrati in Opera.* New York: Da Capo, 1975.

Jackson, Stanley. *Caruso.* New York: Stein and Day, 1972.

Jefferson, Alan. *The Glory of Opera.* New York: Exeter, 1983.

Pleasants, Henry. *The Great Singers*. New York: Simon and Schuster, 1981.

Reed, Vernon William. "The Development and Use of the Tenor Voice, 1600 to the Present." Ph.D. dissertation, Teachers College, Columbia University, 1983.

Rosenthal, Harold, and John Warrack. *The Concise Oxford Dictionary of Opera*. London: Oxford University Press, 1974.

Rushmore, Robert. *The Singing Voice*. New York: Dodd, Mead, 1971.

Sadie, Stanley, ed. *The New Grove Dictionary of Music and Musicians*. London: Macmillan, 1980.

Schonberg, Harold C. *The Glorious Ones: Classical Music's Legendary Performers*. New York: Times Books, 1985.

Slonimsky, Nicholas, ed. *Baker's Biographical Dictionary of Musicians*. New York: Schirmer, 1984.

Tuggle, Robert. *The Golden Age of Opera*. New York: Holt, Rinehart & Winston, 1983.

Chapter Eight

Deathridge, John, and Carl Dahlhaus. *The New Grove Wagner*. New York: W. W. Norton, 1984.

Greenfield, Howard. *Puccini, A Biography*. New York: G. P. Putnam's Sons, 1980.

Martin, George. *The Opera Companion*. New York: Dodd, Mead, 1982.

Rosenthal, Harold, and John Warrack. *The Concise Oxford Dictionary of Opera*. London: Oxford University Press, 1974.

Simon, Henry W. *100 Great Operas and Their Stories*. Garden City, N.Y.: Doubleday, 1960.

Smith, Patrick J. *The Tenth Muse: A Historical Study of the Opera Libretto*. New York: Alfred A. Knopf, 1970.

Toye, Francis. *Giuseppe Verdi: His Life and Work*. New York: Alfred A. Knopf, 1931.

Walker, Frank. *The Man Verdi*. New York: Alfred A. Knopf, 1962.

For Further Reading:

A Bibliography

Ardoin, John. *The Callas Legacy: A Biography of a Career*. New York: Charles Scribner's Sons, 1982.

Bamberger, Carl, ed. *The Conductor's Art*. New York: McGraw-Hill, 1965.

Bauer, Oswald Georg. *Richard Wagner: The Stage Designs and Productions from the Premieres to the Present*. New York: Rizzoli, 1982.

Brockett, Oscar. *History of the Theatre*. Boston: Allyn and Bacon, 1982.

Brockway, Wallace, and Herbert Weinstock. *The Opera: A History of Its Creation and Performance, 1600–1941*. New York: Simon and Schuster, 1941.

Camner, James. *How to Enjoy Opera*. Garden City, N.Y.: Doubleday, 1981.

Carner, Mosco. *Puccini, A Critical Biography*. New York: Alfred A. Knopf, 1959.

Chancellor, John. *Wagner*. London: Granada Press, 1980.

Dent, Edward J. *The Rise of Romantic Opera*. Cambridge: Cambridge University Press, 1976.

DiGaetani, John Louis. *Richard Wagner and the Modern British Novel*. Rutherford, N.J.: Fairleigh Dickinson University Press, 1978.

———, ed. *Penetrating Wagner's Ring: An Anthology*. New York: Da Capo Press, 1983.

———, *Puccini the Thinker*. New York: Peter Lang Press, 1986.

Eaton, Quaintance. *Opera Production I and II: A Handbook*. Minneapolis: University of Minnesota Press, 1974.

Gammond, Peter. *The Illustrated Encyclopedia of Recorded Opera.* New York: Harmony Books, 1979.

Grout, Donald Jay. *A Short History of Opera.* New York: Columbia University Press, 1965.

Hartmann, Rudolf. *Richard Strauss: The Staging of His Operas and Ballets.* Translated by Graham Davies. New York: Oxford University Press, 1981.

———, ed. *Opera.* Translated by Arnold J. Pomerans. Hong Kong: Chartwell Books, 1976.

Heriot, Angus. *The Castrati in Opera.* New York: Da Capo, 1975.

Jackson, Stanley. *Caruso.* New York: Stein and Day, 1972.

Jefferson, Alan. *The Glory of Opera.* New York: Exeter, 1983.

Knapp, J. Merrill. *The Magic of Opera.* New York: Da Capo, 1984.

Landon, H. C. Robbins, and Donald Mitchell, eds. *The Mozart Companion.* New York: Norton, 1969.

Martin, George. *The Companion to Twentieth Century Opera.* New York: Dodd, Mead, 1984.

———. *The Opera Companion.* New York: Dodd, Mead, 1982.

Mayer, Martin. *The Met: One Hundred Years of Grand Opera.* New York: Simon and Schuster, 1983.

Mitchell, Ronald E. *Opera: Dead or Alive.* Madison: University of Wisconsin Press, 1972.

Mordden, Ethan. *Opera in the Twentieth Century.* New York: Oxford University Press, 1978.

Orrey, Leslie. *A Concise History of Opera.* London: Thames and Hudson, 1972.

Pleasants, Henry. *The Great Singers.* New York: Simon and Schuster, 1981.

Robinson, Paul. *Opera and Ideas.* New York: Harper & Row, 1985.

Rosenthal, Harold, and John Warrack. *The Concise Oxford Dictionary of Opera.* London: Oxford University Press, 1974.

Rushmore, Robert. *The Singing Voice.* New York: Dodd, Mead, 1977.

Sadie, Stanley, ed. *The New Grove Dictionary of Music and Musicians.* London: Macmillan, 1980.

Schmidgall, Gary. *Literature as Opera*. New York: Oxford University Press, 1977.

Schonberg, Harold C. *The Glorious Ones: Classical Music's Legendary Performers*. New York: Times Books, 1985.

———. *The Great Conductors*. New York: Simon and Schuster, 1967.

Skelton, Geoffrey. *Wagner at Bayreuth: Experiment and Tradition*. London: Barrie and Rockliff, 1965.

Smith, Patrick J. *The Tenth Muse: A Historical Study of the Opera Libretto*. New York: Alfred A. Knopf, 1970.

Sokol, Martin L. *The New York City Opera, An American Adventure*. New York: Macmillan, 1981.

Walker, Frank. *The Man Verdi*. New York: Alfred A. Knopf, 1962.

Weaver, William, and Martin Chusid, eds. *The Verdi Companion*. New York: Norton, 1979.

Wechsberg, Joseph. *The Opera*. New York: Macmillan, 1972.

Witsen, Leo Van. *Costuming for Opera: Who Wears What and Why*. Bloomington: Indiana University Press, 1981.

A Glossary of Terms

A cappella (It., in the chapel)   This began as a type of choral music written without orchestral or organ accompaniment; in other words, just the choral voices singing. A cappella is very difficult for a singer because an orchestra or accompanying instrument will help keep him or her on pitch. However, the effect can be exquisitely beautiful. Lovely examples of a cappella singing occur during the pilgrim's chorus in Wagner's *Tannhäuser* or the mad scene in the last act of Britten's *Peter Grimes*.

Adagio (It., slow)   Slow singing or orchestral playing; this is a direction for tempo.

Agility   Great singers must have vocal agility, the ability to move nimbly from note to note. Coloratura singing in Mozart and the bel canto composers especially demands vocal agility.

Allegro (It., fast)   Quick, lively tempo for voice or orchestra or both.

Andante (It., slow)   A direction for voice or orchestra or both, indicating a moderate tempo.

Aria (It., air)   A song, generally for solo voice, which is sometimes a part of the action of the opera and sometimes stops the action of the opera. In seventeenth- and eighteenth-century opera, there were many different types of arias, but now the term is used generally; "Un bel dì" from Puccini's *Madama Butterfly* and "Ritorna vincitor" from Verdi's *Aïda* are examples of arias.

Arietta (It., little aria)   A short, rather simple aria, not as complex and splashy as a full aria. "Vecchia zimara, senti" from *La Bohème* beautifully exemplifies the arietta.

Arioso (It., aria-like)   A musical effect somewhere between an aria and a recitativo. Gluck and Wagner's operas contain many examples. The action does not stop for an arioso, but the music is more melodic and more interesting than for standard recitative, and instead of harpsichord accompaniment (as with standard eighteenth-century recitative), full orchestral accompaniment is used.

Attack   The moment a singer begins a particular note. The singer should start the note decisively and clearly rather than vaguely —that is, right on pitch rather than sliding up to the proper pitch.

Ballad opera   An English form of operetta with popular folk songs interspersed with spoken dialogue. This kind of opera was popular in London in the eighteenth century, and in New York as well. The most famous ballad opera is John Gay's *The Beggar's Opera* (1728), which was among other things a parody of Handelian opera seria. Gay's work became popular in this century as Kurt Weill and Bertolt Brecht's *The Threepenny Opera*, which premiered in Berlin in 1928 and was based on Gay's ballad opera.

Barcarolle   A song or aria in a lilting rhythm that is supposed to be what Venetian gondoliers sing, though they don't, actually. The most famous operatic barcarolle occurs in the second act of Jacques Offenbach's *The Tales of Hoffmann,* "Belle nuit, ô nuit d'amour."

Baton (F., stick)   A short stick used by the conductor to lead an orchestra and soloists.

Bel canto (It., beautiful singing)   A school of singing and operatic composition that flourished in Italy in the eighteenth and early nineteenth centuries. The great bel canto composers were Rossini, Donizetti, and Bellini, and some musicologists argue that their music remains the most suitable for beautiful voices and fine singing. Bel canto singers today specialize in the operas of those composers, such as *Lucia di Lammermoor, Tancredi, The Barber of Seville,* and *Norma.* The bel canto singer excels at a beautiful sound, a well-controlled trill, and technical facility and agility so that the singing has dazzling yet effortless technique and a beautiful tone.

Bravura aria (It., skillful or courageous aria)   A bravura aria is designed to stop the show with audience applause. A bravura aria is composed to showcase a singer's range and agility. Some of the great bravura arias are the "Largo al factotum" from

Rossini's *The Barber of Seville*, "Una voce poco fa" from the same opera, and "La donna è mobile" from Verdi's *Rigoletto*.

Break See *passaggio*.

Brindisi (It., a toast) A drinking song. Nineteenth-century Italian operas often contain a brindisi. The most famous occurs in the first act of Verdi's *La Traviata*, "Libiamo." Verdi wrote a much more dramatic one for Iago in the first act of his *Otello*, with the refrain "Beva, beva, beva con me."

Buffo (It., comic) A comic role, used especially in the form basso buffo, or a bass singer who specializes in the many comic roles for that voice in Italian opera, for example Taddeo in Rossini's *L'Italiana in Algeri* or Don Basilio and Dr. Bartolo in *The Barber of Seville*.

Cabaletta (It., horselike or trotting) A short, fast aria that follows a slow one. The traditional slow aria in nineteenth-century Italian opera is often followed by the cabaletta to provide a dramatic contrast and change of tempo. Verdi also often uses this to indicate a change of heart, as in Violetta's cabaletta "Sempre libera" after her slow, thoughtful aria "Ah fors' è lui" in *La Traviata*.

Cadenza A passage for voice or instrument, or both, intended for musical display. Sometimes cadenzas are written in the score by the composer, but often they are only generally indicated. The composer in these situations wants the singer or instrumentalist to improvise whatever brilliant display he or she can, as long as it remains in the style of the piece.

Canon A musical form of repetition of the same music in harmonic variations.

Cantata (It., something sung) An eighteenth-century form, this is a piece written for singers with small orchestra. Bach remains the most famous composer of cantatas, and a portion of a cantata is being sung offstage during the second act of Puccini's *Tosca*.

Castrato (It., castrated; plural, *castrati*) A castrated male singer who sang in the female vocal range. In the seventeenth and eighteenth centuries, the greatest and most popular singers were usually castrati. The operation was done on impoverished boys with vocal ability in the hope that their voices would raise them and their families out of poverty.

Cavatina   A very short, often dramatic aria. While the regular aria is frequently long, the cavatina is short and often quite moving. A fine example of a cavatina is the Countess's "Porgi amor" from Mozart's *The Marriage of Figaro*.

Chamber opera   A short opera that uses a small orchestra and only a few soloists. Examples of chamber operas include Mozart's *The Impresario*, Strauss's *Capriccio*, and Britten's *Curlew River*.

Claque (F.)   People hired to applaud a particular singer or a particular opera. This custom started at the Paris Opéra in the early nineteenth century so the audience would know where to applaud and not interrupt the performance in the wrong places, but the claque eventually became a way for singers or composers to pay to ensure success with an audience. Though claques have fallen into disfavor, they still exist in some opera houses.

Coda (It., tail)   A final selection of a piece of music, generally to bring it to a suitable conclusion.

Coloratura   The most florid and technically difficult kind of singing, coloratura can apply to any of the vocal ranges. Today, however, coloratura generally refers to sopranos specializing in roles such as the Queen of the Night in Mozart's *The Magic Flute*, Lucia in Donizetti's *Lucia di Lammermoor*, and Rosina in Rossini's *The Barber of Seville*.

Comprimario, comprimaria (It., with the lead, male and female forms, respectively)   A singer or a role that is a small solo part but does not require a particularly beautiful voice or much endurance. All opera houses have comprimario singers, generally technically very gifted and with good acting ability, but not the kind of beautiful voices or forceful dramatic presences that will generate star quality. Comprimario roles include the doctor and Annina in *La Traviata*, Ines in *Il Trovatore*, and Goro in *Madama Butterfly*.

Con brio (It., with spirit)   A direction to singers or orchestra, from the composer, to play a particular passage in a lively way.

Countertenor   A very high tenor voice, sounding to most ears like a soprano. The countertenor rarely appears in opera, though the role of Oberon in Britten's *A Midsummer Night's Dream* is written for the countertenor. The countertenor can also be a falsettist, a tenor using only the top extreme of his voice. The sound of both countertenor and falsettist has a freakish but spiritual quality that often succeeds in the church music of the seventeenth and eighteenth centuries.

Crescendo (It., growing)   A gradual increase in volume, generally used in opera as a marking in an orchestral score or for singers.

Da capo (It., from the head)   This refers to a repetition of a particular passage of music. The da capo aria, for example, involves a repetition at the end of an earlier part of the music. In Italian musical practice, "da capo" at a rehearsal indicates that the conductor wants a piece of music repeated, or as we would say, "Take it from the top."

Diaphragm   The major inspiratory muscle under the stomach where most singers start their breathing for purposes of singing.

Diction   The ability of a singer to project the sounds of the language being sung. A good singer should be able to sing so that the words are intelligible to the audience.

Diminuendo (It., diminishing)   The opposite of a crescendo; a gradual decrease in volume, both for soloists and orchestra.

Diva (It., goddess)   An accolade used to describe the most popular soprano in a particular opera house. Fans often claim the title of "diva" for their favorite soprano.

Encore (F., again)   A demand by an audience for a repetition of a particular piece of music or for more singing or playing in general. Thus, a particularly successful recital will include several encores to satisfy the demands by the audience—often made by yelling "encore" during the applause.

Entr'acte (F., between the acts)   Music written for between the acts of an opera, especially before the second act. The entr'actes in Bizet's *Carmen* are especially famous.

Fach (G., drawer)   A system of vocal categories used in German-speaking countries. German opera houses cast singers according to their fach, or vocal category. The Fächer (plural) for women are: Soubrette, Lyrischer Koloratur Sopran, Lyrischer Sopran, Dramatischer Koloratur Sopran, Jugendlich-dramatischer Sopran, Dramatischer Sopran, Hochdramatischer Sopran, Lyrischer Mezzosopran, Dramatischer Mezzosopran, and Alt. The fach categories for males are: Spieltenor, Lyrischer Tenor, Italienischer Tenor, Jugendlicher Heldentenor, Heldentenor, Lyrischer Bariton, Kavalierbariton, Charakterbariton, Heldenbariton, Bassbariton, Bass-buffo, and Seriöser Bass.

Fioritura (It., flowering)   These are embellishments singers sometimes add to a vocal part. Many such ornaments were written into the score by the composer, but most are added by singers themselves, either because of tradition or because the conductor expects them to improvise. Fioritura characterizes much Baroque vocal music.

Flat   Below the note or pitch indicated. Flat singing is always wrong and generally an irritation to the audience.

Forte, fortissimo (It., strong and most strong, respectively)   This is a direction a composer writes in a score about volume, and the more fortissimos written, the louder the music should be sung or played. The composer indicates this in a score as f = loud, ff = very loud, and so forth.

Fugue   A term from eighteenth-century music, made most famous by Bach. The fugue involves the repetition and development through variations of a particular musical theme or melody. The most famous fugue in opera is the finale of Verdi's *Falstaff*, "Tutte nel mundo è burla."

Glissando   See *slide*.

Grand opera   Technically, this term applies only to a particular kind of nineteenth-century French opera. Meyerbeer and Auber were the major proponents of this form of opera whose center was the Paris Opéra. Grand opera was designed for very large forces—large orchestra, large chorus, a large number of soloists, and very lavish scenery. The scene designers were often the most important persons in this enterprise, since grand opera was designed to impress with its size. Famous French grand operas include Meyerbeer's *Le Prophète* and *Les Huguenots* and Auber's *La Muette de Portici*. Less exactly, "grand opera" can refer to operas that are lavishly staged.

Green room   A room used by performers after an opera in which to receive congratulations. Originally, theaters had rooms especially for these receptions, but now this is more often done in a singer's dressing room.

Head voice   A term used by singers to describe the voice that seems to be produced from the head (as opposed to the chest). The term "head voice" is generally used most by sopranos and tenors, the highest voices, and is really a metaphor. Technically, the singer uses the crycothyroid muscle for producing the head voice.

Impresario (It., manager)   A person who manages a ballet or opera company, generally one away from a permanent opera house, that is, a traveling company.

Instrumentation   The instruments used in a particular piece of music. In most cases, the composer decides on the instruments used while he is composing the score, although some composers have employed other people to choose the instruments for their music. Instrumentation remains a major concern for opera singers, since the blending of instruments with voices is important for them and for the quality of their performances.

Intendant (G., manager)   The director and manager of a German opera house, or of a particular company within a theater.

Intermezzo (It., in the middle)   A piece of music written for the middle of an act, usually indicating the passage of time. Famous intermezzos in opera occur in Mascagni's *Cavalleria Rusticana* and in Wagner's *Götterdämmerung* (Siegfried's Rhine Journey).

Key   The tonal system of scales devised by European composers to control and describe musical sounds. There are two basic key systems: diatonic and chromatic. The diatonic is the standard one for Western music, with notes a step up or down and centered from middle C to high C. The chromatic scale uses a half-step tonal system between the notes to give a more undulating effect. Wagner's *Tristan and Isolde* (1865) contains the most famous early use of the chromatic key system in opera, used much more frequently for twentieth-century music, especially by composers such as Berg, Schoenberg, and Debussy.

Largo (It., broad)   A musical direction to play or sing a passage slowly, broadly, and grandly.

Larynx   This is the voice box, the bodily organ that produces vocal sound.

Legato (It., tied or connected)   A musical direction to sing a series of notes so that they are connected and move smoothly from one note to the other. Legato is the opposite of staccato (q.v.).

Leitmotiv (or leitmotif—G., leading motive)   A term connected with Wagnerian opera, though the term itself was never used by Wagner. The leitmotiv is the use of a musical motive or tune to represent characters or ideas on the operatic stage. The leitmotiv helps an audience to connect characters or ideas with a particular musical theme. The technique actually goes back to the beginning of Italian opera in the late Renaissance. Monteverdi used leitmotivs, but Wagner used them in a much more elaborate and subtle way, especially in his *Ring* cycle.

Libretto (It., little book)   The text of an opera; the words sung on stage.

Lied (G., song; plural, lieder)   Lieder music is written most frequently for solo voice and piano, primarily by Schubert, Schumann, Brahms, Mahler, Strauss, and Wolf. Lieder singers are usually, though not always, opera singers, and lieder singing is much more intimate in scale than operatic singing.

Maestro (It., master)   A great musician; generally a conductor, composer, or very famous performer receives the accolade of maestro.

Melodrama   In England and America, this term refers to a variety of nineteenth-century theater characterized by heroes and villains, sensational theatrical and scenic effects, and exciting but incredible turns of events. Melodrama came into popularity in the nineteenth century, and so some operas of that period have melodramatic plots, especially those by Verdi; in fact, some of them were based on popular melodramas of the time.

Melodrame (F.)   When a character speaks (not sings) on stage while music is playing. Movies often use a musical background while actors and actresses are speaking. Beethoven's *Fidelio* uses this technique, along with Bizet's *Carmen* in its original opéra comique version (with spoken dialogue).

Melodramma (It., music drama)   An Italian word describing much nineteenth-century operatic composition. The term suggests an attempt to write dramatic music for opera, as in the operas of Verdi, rather than merely tuneful music.

Mezza voce (It., half voice)   Using the voice without much volume, or only half the volume usually required. This can be a notation in a score, or what singers sometimes do at rehearsals to save their voices for the performance.

Mise-en-scène (F., placing in the scene)   The staging of a work, a term often used in opera to describe direction and sets. Americans would also say the "production" of an opera.

Morbidezza (It., gentleness or delicacy)   This notation in an operatic score indicates that a musical passage should be played delicately, gently, and not morbidly. Sweet, delicate music is what the composer wants when he uses this mark, like the music for Verdi's Desdemona in *Otello* or Puccini's heroine in *Madama Butterfly*.

Music drama   Wagner made this term famous because that is how he referred to his own works. He said he hated "opera," which he called the most corrupt of art forms, but his "music dramas" were quite different. While the "opera" contained a series of musical numbers, the music drama was a synthesis of music and drama, and the music served only dramatic ends. While some critics argue that this is exactly the synthesis achieved in Wagner's operas, other critics disagree and insist that the late Verdi operas, especially *Otello* and *Falstaff*, are better music dramas than any of Wagner's works. The term "music drama" itself is now rarely used, and even Wagner's works are usually called operas.

Number   A song or aria, performed solo, by several singers, or by a chorus in an operatic work. The numbers contain the most musical, tuneful portions of a work, as opposed to the recitatives.

Obbligato (It., obligatory)   The use of a solo instrument, generally in connection with a solo voice. Some of the famous obbligatos in opera include the flute obbligato in Lucia's mad scene in *Lucia di Lammermoor*, the trumpet obbligato for Rinaldo's final aria in Handel's *Rinaldo*, and the violin obbligato for Violetta in the last act of *La Traviata*.

On pitch   Singing that remains on pitch is accurate singing that produces each note exactly as written in the score and on the correct frequency. A professional singer should be able to sing on pitch, a technical requirement for correct singing.

Opera buffa (It., comic opera)   A comic opera meant to make an audience laugh. Some of the great Italian comic operas include Rossini's *The Barber of Seville*, Donizetti's *Don Pasquale*, Verdi's *Falstaff*, and Puccini's *Gianni Schicchi*.

Opéra comique (F., an opera written for the Opéra Comique Theater in Paris)   Originally, the term referred to works with spoken dialogue and musical numbers—for example, the original version of Bizet's *Carmen*. Then the term was used for realistic French operas rather than romantic and heroic ones—for example, Massenet's *Manon* and Thomas's *Mignon* exemplify opéra comique.

Opera seria (It., serious opera)   Opera seria, as opposed to opera buffa, was serious opera with no comic relief. The term opera seria is connected with opera composition in the seventeenth and eighteenth centuries and was a very artificial art form usually performed with castrato singers. Among the great opera serias are Handel's *Rinaldo*, Mozart's *Idomeneo*, and Rossini's *Tancredi*.

Operetta (It., little opera)   Operetta usually has lighter music than opera buffa, and is usually by a non-Italian composer. Vienna is most famous for operetta, with examples such as Strauss's *Die Fledermaus*, Lehár's *Die Lustige Witwe*, and Strauss's *Eine Nacht in Venedig*. Gilbert and Sullivan's most famous operattas include *The Mikado*, *The Pirates of Penzance*, and *H.M.S. Pinafore*.

Opus (L., work)   The number given to a composition of a particular composer. Thus, opus numbers represent the sequential numbering of a composer's works in order of composition. Sometimes these numbers are edited by a musicologist and the numbering system used is ascribed to that particular scholar, the most famous example being Köchel, the German musicologist responsible for the numbering of Mozart's works.

Oratorio   A religious composition for soloists, chorus, and orchestra, an oratorio is characteristically a large, solemn musical work. Examples of famous oratorios include Handel's *Messiah* and Mendelssohn's *Elijah*. Opera composers occasionally wrote oratorios, most notably Handel after the vogue for Italian opera faded in London in the eighteenth century.

Orchestration   Writing for an orchestra, including the composer's choice of musical instruments to accompany the singers in an opera. Some composers are notorious for unimaginative orchestration in their operas, especially Donizetti, while others are noted for a very subtle use of the orchestra, especially Wagner and Puccini.

Overture   A short piece of orchestral music, generally about ten minutes long, played before the opera begins. The overture began as a way of getting the audience's attention, allowing time for latecomers to be seated, and setting the mood of the opera. A good overture should capture the audience's attention and prepare them for the opera to follow. Rossini succeeded especially in creating lively, dramatic overtures, and those of his comic operas remain very famous.

Passaggio (It., passage)   The section of the voice between a singer's natural vocal registers. Singers often work on their voices so that they can move easily from note to note and from register to register.

Patter song   The term is generally connected with the operettas of Gilbert and Sullivan, and these songs are solo tour de force pieces that generate comedy by testing a singer's ability to sing complicated words very quickly. "I am the very model of a modern Major General" from *The Pirates of Penzance* is a clever example of a patter song. An Italian example of a patter song is Figaro's famous bravura aria "Largo al factotum" from Rossini's *The Barber of Seville*.

Perfect pitch   The ability to tell exactly what note is being sung or played. Very few singers or listeners have perfect pitch, although many claim to.

Piano, pianissimo (It., soft and very soft, respectively)   This is a composer's direction to singers and orchestras about his desire for low volume. These terms are often subjective since a piano by Mozart is a bit different from a piano by Debussy, yet *p* or *pp* (piano, pianissimo, etc.) indications in a score are often ignored by some conductors who cannot control their orchestras. Too many Wagnerian performances have sounded bombastic because most of the pianos in the score were ignored by conductor and orchestra.

Pizzicato (It., plucked)   A notation that a stringed instrument be plucked rather than played with a bow. The effect is lively, staccato, and rather startling.

Placement   This is where singers feel that their singing voices come from, often behind the teeth or in the sinuses. Placement involves adjusting the vocal resonators to secure the best quality of tone. Some singers use the same placement for all their notes, while others vary placement for different notes.

Portamento (It., carrying)   A way of connecting two notes smoothly and roundly rather than abruptly. Portamento involves singing from one note to another by means of a continuous gliding tone that passes through all intervening pitches. Portamento is a stylish way of moving from one note to another, although if it is used too often it can become mannered.

Prelude   An orchestral introduction to an entire opera or to an act of an opera, the prelude is very similar to an overture except it can come before an act in addition to coming before an entire opera. Also, the prelude is generally more serious than an overture and tries to establish the mood and theme of an opera more precisely.

Presto, prestissimo (It., fast and very fast, respectively) A composer's direction on tempo, presto generally means a particular aria or section of an opera should be sung and played in a quick, lively way.

Prima donna (It., the first lady) Historically, this term means the first soprano, or the greatest soprano, of a particular opera company. Now it also means any great female singer, although still generally a soprano. Members of the audience often employ this term for a singer they consider especially great.

Probe (G., testing) This is the German word for an operatic rehearsal, and the dress rehearsal is called either the *Kostümprobe* or the *Generalprobe*.

Projection Transmitting the voice from the stage to the audience. Proper projection demands volume and clarity in a singer's voice so that the voice fills the auditorium and reaches even the farthest members of the audience.

Recitative (It., *recitativo*) In seventeenth-, eighteenth-, and early nineteenth-century opera, recitative is music written for soloists between set musical numbers. Recitativo secco, the most common, is the voice accompanied by only a harpsichord, while the more interesting recitativo accompagnato includes the voice and the orchestra. Recitatives are often underrated musically and dramatically, but great artists can make the recitatives come alive, creating dramatic intensity. Mozart, Rossini, and Bellini were especially subtle in their use of recitatives.

Register This is a classification for parts of the singing voice, the two most common being "head register" and "chest register." These terms are metaphors to describe where the voice seems to be coming from. Actually, registers describe a singer using different sets of muscles in his vocal apparatus.

Rehearsal The preparation before the public sees a performance. Rehearsals are done in several ways for opera: with just the soloists and the conductor and his or her assistant, with just the conductor and the orchestra, with the chorus and the conductor or the choral director, and with the conductor and the entire cast and orchestra. Opera also uses technical and lighting rehearsals;

the dress rehearsal includes this last category, with the entire cast on stage and in costume.

Répétiteur (F., repeater)   The person who trains a singer in a particular role, the répétiteur often repeats the part and takes the singer through the role with a piano so that the singer knows it very well. Good répétiteurs are very much appreciated by singers and extremely useful in any opera house since they do the work of both singing teachers and dramatic coaches.

Ring   Also called the voice's forward placement, or the ping of the voice. The ring explains an operatic voice's carrying power and its ability to project easily into a large auditorium. The voice's ring is the reason why opera singers do not need microphones, since the voice's ring provides both focus and projection of the tone.

Ritornello (It., the little return)   The closing of an aria or other musical number with a short orchestral passage that serves to end the piece with a forceful musical flourish.

Rubato (It., robbed)   Varying the time values of a piece of music so that certain notes are held longer than indicated in the score. Rubato can be used to sustain a high note or vary a melody during its repetition. If not abused, rubato can be very effective.

Scales   The placing of all the notes in patterns that correspond to the major and minor keys, scales are often used by singers to practice their voices. Practicing scales, while dreary to listen to, gives singers control, accuracy of pitch, and agility.

Scena (It., scene)   The actions of a character on stage during one particular operatic scene. Thus, Radames's scena in the first act of *Aïda* includes an aria, "Celeste Aïda," and some singing with the high priest. Also, the scena refers to the part of an act set in one location and occurring on one theatrical set. Verdi became famous for organizing his operas by scene, as opposed to Wagner, who more often organized by act.

Scoop   Generally an error in singing, a scoop occurs when a singer glides up to a high note from below. The scoop can also, however, be a style of singing, especially in Italy.

Score   Musical notations on sheet music, generally printed; there are several types of operatic scores. The most complete is the orchestral score, which includes every note for each singer and all the instruments in the orchestra. The vocal score, or piano score, includes just the vocal parts and a piano reduction representing the orchestra.

Sharp   Slightly above pitch. While singing flat is always wrong, singing a bit sharp can give the voice a cutting edge for greater brilliance and allows it to cut through an orchestra more easily. Some Wagnerian sopranos and coloratura sopranos sometimes sing a bit sharp to give their voices these qualities. Singing sharp, however, can easily become an annoyance and must be done sparingly and carefully.

Singspiel (G., a singing play)   A German opera with spoken dialogue and musical numbers. The most famous singspiels are Beethoven's *Fidelio* and Mozart's *The Magic Flute*. Singspiels were originally a popular form of entertainment in Germany and Austria for the working people, and were presented in their native tongue rather than the Italian of the more aristocratic court operas.

Slide (It., glissando)   An error when a singer falls just below the pitch of a note, and as a result is singing flat.

Solo (It., alone)   A section of an opera written for just one singer or one instrument; the most popular kind of solo has traditionally been the singer's aria.

Soubrette (F., a female servant)   A kind of operatic role for a soprano, generally that of a clever maid. These characters are generally portrayed as very pretty, very coquettish, very clever, and able to sing high, very difficult arias. Mozart's soubrette roles include Susanna in *The Marriage of Figaro*, Despina in *Così Fan Tutte*, and Blondchen in *The Abduction from the Seraglio*.

Squillo (It., ring)   See *Ring*.

Staccato (It., detached)   A musical notation to indicate that each note should be sounded quickly and separately—as opposed to legato, where the notes are tied together. The staccato effect is generally lively and abrupt.

Stagione (It., season)   This is a way of organizing an opera company around particular singers and productions—as opposed to the repertory system whereby the same singers are used as an ensemble in all the operas presented during a run of performances.

Stretto (It., stressed)   The composer uses a stretto, a musical notation, to indicate the stressing of a particular note or passage in the score, and it is generally used in opera for dramatic effect, as in the emphasis on a particularly important note or word.

Tempo (It., time)   This is an indication of the rate of speed of a particular passage in an opera—fast or slow or many shades in between. Composers try to indicate tempos (It. plural, *tempi*) in the score, but these are often only rough approximations. The conductor must establish the tempo, at a speed the composer wanted and the performers can handle.

Tessitura (It., texture)   The vocal demands (or texture) of a particular role, whether the vocal range of the role is high or low for a voice category, or somewhere in between. Thus, the tessitura for Elsa in *Lohengrin* is higher than the tessitura for Ortrud. By extension, tessitura has also come to mean the compass of a particular voice or where most of its tones lie.

Timbre   The distinctive vocal sound of a particular voice; in operatic singing, timbre is the distinctive resonance quality and character of tone that a particular singer can produce. All great voices have a unique timbre, while choral voices generally blend more easily because they do not have distinctive timbres.

Transposition   Shifting a piece of music into a key different from the one indicated by the composer. Transposition occurs so that a particular role is more suited to a particular singer's vocal abilities. Thus, the title role in *Carmen*, though written for a mezzo-soprano, is occasionally transposed up a key or two so a soprano can sing it comfortably. Or the role of Lucia in *Lucia di Lammermoor*, a very high soprano role, may be transposed down a key or two so a soprano who does not have all the high notes in the role can still sing it. Most composers, as practical men of the theater, have allowed some transposition for particular singers who could not otherwise sing a particular role.

Tremolo (It., trembling)   An irregular and uncontrollable unsteadiness or faulty trembling of the pitch caused by interfering tensions, muscular weakness, and a singer's inability to maintain a stable adjustment of the throat during singing. Usually a tremolo varies more than a half tone off pitch, and should not be confused with a vibrato, which always varies within a half tone interval.

Trill The rapid alternation of two distinct notes, one in quick succession to another; the trill is a vocal ornament often used in eighteenth- and nineteenth-century singing, especially in the operas of the bel canto school. The trill should be fully controlled and can really excite an audience when it is properly performed.

Verismo (It., realism) Verismo began as a violent, naturalistic form of operatic theater. The two most famous examples of early verismo are Mascagni's *Cavalleria Rusticana* and Leoncavallo's *Pagliacci*, both about the murderous jealousies of poor people. Puccini directed verismo away from such sordid stories and more toward operatic realism, as opposed to Romantic operas about heroes and heroines. Puccinian verismo tries to present on stage the real lives of real people, as in *La Bohème*, *Gianni Schicchi*, and *Madama Butterfly*.

Vibrato A regular periodic oscillation of vocal tone above and below normal pitch level, but always within a half tone interval. Vibrato is a desirable and inevitable attribute of good vocal tone, adding warmth and life to a voice.

Wobble A vocal problem, and a synonym for tremolo. Singers with a wobble cannot control their voices; some wobbles occur on each note a singer produces, while other singers wobble only on certain notes, generally the high notes, which wobble out of control.

Zarzuela A Spanish form of operetta with spoken dialogue and musical numbers. Generally, the music in zarzuelas is not complex and the tunes are popular and rhythmic. The zarzuela has never been popular outside Spanish-speaking countries, although some are quite lovely. The famous zarzuela composers include Breton, Caballero, Moreno, Serrano, and Vives.

For Further Listening:
A Discography

Listed below, by composer, are recommended recordings of the operas in the standard repertory. When several attractive options exist, I have listed all of them. Most of these recordings are available in either record or cassette format, and many are also on compact disc.

Beethoven

Fidelio

Behrens, Ghazarian, Hofmann, Adam, Sotin.
Solti: Chicago Symphony Orchestra—London.

Bellini

Norma

Callas, Stignani, Filippeschi.
Serafin: La Scala—Seraphim.

Sutherland, Horne, Alexander.
Bonynge: London Symphony—London.

Berg

Lulu

Stratas, Minton, Schwarz, Riegel.
Boulez: Paris Opéra—DG.

Wozzeck

Lear, Wunderlich, Fischer-Dieskau.
Böhm: German Opera—DG.

Bizet

Carmen

Callas, Guiot, Gedda, Massard.
Prêtre: Paris Opéra—Angel.

Migenes-Johnson, Esham, Domingo, Raimondi.
Maazel: Orchestre National Radio de France—Erato.

Britten

Peter Grimes

Harper, Vickers, Summers.
Davis: Royal Opera—Philips.

Debussy

Pelléas et Mélisande

Von Stade, Denize, Stilwell, Van Dam.
Karajan: Berlin Philharmonic—Angel.

Donizetti

Don Pasquale

Freni, Winbergh, Nucci, Bruscantini.
Muti: Philadelphia Orchestra—Angel.

L'Elisir d'Amore (The Elixir of Love)

Popp, Dvorsky, Weikl, Nesterenko.
Walberg: Munich Radio Orchestra—RCA.

Lucia di Lammermoor

Callas, DiStefano, Gobbi.
Serafin: La Scala—Seraphim.

Sutherland, Pavarotti, Milnes, Ghiaurov.
Bonynge: Royal Opera—London.

Sills, Bergonzi, Cappuccilli, Díaz.
Schippers: London Symphony—Angel.

Gluck

Orfeo ed Euridice

Lorengar, Donath, Horne.
Solti: Royal Opera—London.

Rothenberger, Pütz, Bumbry.
Neumann: Leipzig Gewandhaus Orchestra—Angel.

Gounod

Faust

Sutherland, Corelli, Ghiaurov.
Bonynge: London Symphony—London.

Freni, Domingo, Allen, Ghiaurov.
Prêtre: National Philharmonic—London.

Leoncavallo

Pagliacci

Caballé, Domingo, Milnes.
Santi: London Symphony—RCA.

Mascagni

Cavalleria Rusticana

Scotto, Domingo. Elvira.
Levine: National Philharmonic—RCA.

De los Angeles, Corelli, Sereni.
Santini: Rome Opera—Angel.

Mozart

Così Fan Tutte

Schwarzkopf, Ludwig, Kraus.
Böhm: Vienna Philharmonic—Angel.

Caballé, Baker, Gedda, Ganzorolli.
Davis: Royal Opera—Philips.

Don Giovanni

Moser, Te Kanawa, Berganza, Riegel, Raimondi.
Maazel: Paris Opéra—CBS.

Nilsson, Arroyo, Schreier, Fischer-Dieskau, Talvela.
Böhm: Prague National Theater—DG.

Die Entführung aus dem Serail (The Abduction from the Seraglio)

Augér, Grist, Schreier, Moll.
Böhm: Dresden State Orchestra—DG.

Eda-Pierre, Burrows, Tear.
Davis: St. Martin's in the Field Orchestra—Philips.

Le Nozze di Figaro (The Marriage of Figaro)

Te Kanawa, Popp, Von Stade, Ramey, Allen.
Solti: London Philharmonic—London.

Norman, Freni, Minton, Ganzarolli.
Davis: BBC Symphony—Philips.

Die Zauberflöte (The Magic Flute)

Cotrubas, Donat, Tappy, Boesch, Talvela.
Levine: Vienna Philharmonic—RCA.

Lorengar, Deutekom, Prey, Burrows, Talvela, Fischer-Dieskau.
Solti: Vienna Philharmonic—London.

Moussorgsky

Boris Godunov

Vishnevskaya, Ghiaurov, Speiss, Talvela.
Karajan: Vienna Philharmonic—London.

Puccini

La Bohème

Freni, Pavarotti, Panerai.
Karajan: Berlin Philharmonic—London.

Caballé, Blegen, Domingo, Milnes, Raimondi.
Solti: London Philharmonic—RCA.

Madama Butterfly

Freni, Pavarotti, Kerns.
Karajan: Vienna Philharmonic—London.

Scotto, Domingo, Wixell.
Maazel: Philharmonia Orchestra—CBS.

Manon Lescaut

Caballé, Domingo, Sardinero.
Bartoletti: Philharmonia Orchestra—Angel.

Tosca

Callas, Bergonzi, Gobbi.
Prêtre: Paris Opéra—Angel.

Ricciarelli, Carreras, Raimondi.
Karajan: Berlin Philharmonic—DG.

Scotto, Domingo, Bruson.
Levine: Philharmonia Orchestra—Angel.

Turandot

Nilsson, Tebaldi, Bjoerling, Tozzi.
Leinsdorf: Rome Opera—RCA.

Sutherland, Caballé, Pavarotti, Ghiaurov.
Mehta: London Philharmonic—London.

Rossini

Il Barbiere di Siviglia (The Barber of Seville)

Sills, Barbieri, Gedda, Milnes, Raimondi.
Levine: London Symphony—Angel.

Horne, Nucci, Ramey, Dara.
Chailly: La Scala—CBS.

L'Italiana in Algeri

Battle, Horne, Palacio, Ramey.
Scimone: Solisti Veneti—RCA.

Strauss

Ariadne auf Naxos

L. Price, Gruberova, Troyanos, Kollo.
Solti: London Philharmonic—London.

Elektra

Nilsson, Collier, Resnik, Stolze.
Solti: Vienna Philharmonic—London.

Der Rosenkavalier

Schwarzkopf, Stich-Randall, Ludwig, Edelmann.
Karajan: Philharmonia Orchestra—Angel.

Crespin, Donath, Minton, Jungwirth.
Solti: Vienna Philharmonic—London.

Salome

Nilsson, Hoffman, Wächter, Stolze.
Solti: Vienna Philharmonic—London.

Behrens, Baltsa, Böhm, Ochman, Van Dam.
Karajan: Vienna Philharmonic—Angel.

Tchaikovsky

Eugene Onegin

Kubiak, Burrows, Weikl, Ghiaurov.
Solti: Royal Opera—London.

Verdi

Aïda

L. Price, Gorr, Vickers, Tozzi.
Solti: Rome Opera—London.

Caballé, Cossotto, Domingo, Cappuccilli.
Muti: New Philharmonia—Angel.

Don Carlo

Caballé, Verrett, Domingo, Raimondi, Milnes.
Giulini: Royal Opera—Angel.

Tebaldi, Bumbry, Bergonzi, Fischer-Dieskau.
Solti: Royal Opera—London.

Falstaff

Ricciarelli, Hendricks, Valentini, Bruson, Nucci.
Giulini: Los Angeles Philharmonic—DG.

Ligabue, Sciutti, Resnik, Fischer-Dieskau.
Bernstein: Vienna Philharmonic—Columbia.

La Forza del Destino

L. Price, Cossotto, Domingo, Milnes.
Levine: London Symphony—RCA.

Otello

Scotto, Domingo, Milnes.
Levine: National Philharmonic—RCA.

Freni, Vickers, Glossop.
Karajan: Berlin Philharmonic—Angel.

Rigoletto

Sutherland, Pavarotti, Milnes, Talvela.
Bonynge: London Symphony—London.

Sills, Kraus, Milnes.
Rudel: Philharmonia Orchestra—Angel.

La Traviata

Cotrubas, Domingo, Milnes.
Kleiber: Bavarian State Opera—DG.

Caballé, Stokes, Bergonzi, Milnes.
Prêtre: RCA Italiana Opera Orchestra—RCA.

Il Trovatore

L. Price, Cossotto, Domingo, Milnes.
Mehta: New Philharmonia—RCA.

Sutherland, Horne, Pavarotti, Wixwell.
Bonynge: National Philharmonic—London.

Wagner

Der Fliegende Holländer (The Flying Dutchman)

Martin, Kollo, Bailey, Talvela.
Solti: Chicago Symphony Orchestra—London.

Lohengrin

Grümmer, Ludwig, Thomas, Fischer-Dieskau.
Kempe: Vienna Philharmonic—Angel.

Tomowa-Sintow, Vejzovic, Kollo, Nimsgern.
Karajan: Berlin Philharmonic—Angel.

Die Meistersinger von Nürnberg

Donath, Kollo, Schreier, Adam, Evans.
Karajan: Dresden State Opera—Angel.

Bode, Hamari, Kollo, Bailey, Weikl.
Solti: Vienna Philharmonic—London.

Parsifal

Ludwig, Kollo, Fischer-Dieskau, Hotter.
Solti: Vienna Philharmonic—London.

Minton, Goldberg, Schöne, Haugland.
Jordan: Monte Carlo Opera—Erato.

The *Ring* Cycle: *Das Rheingold, Die Walküre, Siegfried, Götterdämmerung*

Nilsson, Flagstad, Crespin, Ludwig, Windgassen, London, Fischer-Dieskau, Hotter.
Solti: Vienna Philharmonic—London.

Crespin, Dernesch, Janowitz, Ludwig, Vickers, Thomas, Stewart, Talvela.
Karajan: Berlin Philharmonic—DG.

Jones, Altmeyer, Wenkel, Hofmann, Jung, McIntyre, Salminen.
Boulez: Bayreuth Festival—Philips.

Tannhäuser

Dernesch, Ludwig, Kollo, Braun, Sotin.
Solti: Vienna Philharmonic—London.

Silja, Bumbry, Windgassen, Wächter.
Sawallisch: Bayreuth Festival—Philips.

Tristan und Isolde

Nilsson, Ludwig, Windgassen, Wächter, Talvela.
Böhm: Bayreuth Festival—DG.

Dernesch, Ludwig, Vickers, Berry.
Karajan: Berlin Philharmonic—Angel.

M. Price, Fassbänder, Kollo, Fischer-Dieskau.
Kleiber: Dresden State Opera—DG.

For Further Viewing:

A Videography

Listed below, by composer, are recommended videotapes of some of the operas in the standard repertory. Most are available in both VHS and Beta formats.

Beethoven

Fidelio

Söderström, Ridder, Allman, directed by Peter Hall.
Haitink: Glyndebourne Festival Opera—Video Arts International.

Bizet

Carmen

Migenes-Johnson, Domingo, Raimondi.
Maazel: French National Opera—RCA Columbia/Corinth.

Britten

Peter Grimes

Harper, Vickers, Bailey.
Davis: Royal Opera—Thorn EMI/HBO Video.

Donizetti

Lucia di Lammermoor

Sutherland, Kraus, Elvira, Plishka.
Bonynge: Metropolitan Opera—Pioneer.

Mozart

Don Giovanni

Dean, Vakar, Luxon, directed by Peter Hall.
Haitink: Glyndebourne Festival Opera—Video Arts
International.

The Magic Flute

Hagegard, Kostlinger, Urilla, directed by Ingmar Bergman.
Ericsson: Swedish National Opera—Corinth Video.

Le Nozze di Figaro (The Marriage of Figaro)

Cotrubas, Te Kanawa, Von Stade, Luxon.
Pritchard: Glyndebourne Festival Opera—Video Arts
International.

Puccini

La Bohème

Stratas, Scotto, Carreras, Stilwell, directed by Franco Zeffirelli.
Levine: Metropolitan Opera—Paramount Home Video.

Madama Butterfly

Kabaivanska, Nazzareno, Antinori.
M. Arena: Arena di Verona—Thorn EMI/HBO Video.

Manon Lescaut

Te Kanawa, Domingo, Allen.
Sinopoli: Royal Opera—Thorn EMI/HBO Video.

Tosca

Behrens, Domingo, MacNeil, directed by Franco Zeffirelli.
Levine: Metropolitan Opera—Corinth Video.

Turandot

Marton, Ricciarelli, Carreras, directed by Harold Prince.
Maazel: Vienna State Opera—MGM/UA Home Video.

Strauss

Der Rosenkavalier

Schwarzkopf, Jurinac, Rothenberger, Edelmann.
Karajan: Salzburg Festival—Video Arts International.

Verdi

Aïda

Chiara, Cossotto, Martinucci.
Guadagno: Arena di Verona—Thorn EMI/HBO Video.

Don Carlo

Freni, Bumbry, Domingo, Quilico, Ghiaurov.
Levine: Metropolitan Opera—Paramount Home Video.

Falstaff

Ricciarelli, Hendricks, Bruson, Nucci.
Giulini: Royal Opera—Thorn EMI/HBO Video.

Otello

Te Kanawa, Atlantov.
Pesco: Arena di Verona—Pioneer.

La Traviata

Stratas, Domingo, MacNeil, directed by Franco Zeffirelli.
Levine: Metropolitan Opera—MCA Home Video.

Wagner

Parsifal

Minton, Goldberg, Schöne, Haugland, directed by Syberberg.
Jordan: Monte Carlo Opera—Corinth Video.

Tannhäuser

Marton, Troyanos, Cassilly, Weikl.
Levine: Metropolitan Opera—Bel Canto Video.

Index